Spotlight
on CAE

Francesca Mansfield and Carol Nuttall
Exam Booster with key

HEINLE
CENGAGE Learning

Australia • Brazil • Japan • Korea • Mexico • Singapore • Spain • United Kingdom • United States

Spotlight on CAE Exam Booster with key
Francesca Mansfield and Carol Nuttall

Publisher: Jason Mann

Commissioning Editor: John Waterman

Development Editor: Amanda Cole

Product Manager: Ruth McAleavey

Content Project Editor: Amy Smith

Manufacturing Buyer: Maeve Healy

Cover Designer: Lisa Sjukur

Text Designer: Sofia Ioannidou

Compositor: Sofia Ioannidou and Q2AMedia

Audio: Martin Williamson, Prolingua
Productions

ISBN 978-1-4240-6076-4

Heinle, Cengage Learning EMEA
Cheriton House
North Way
Andover
Hampshire
SP10 5BE
United Kingdom

Cengage Learning is a leading provider of customised learning solutions with office locations around the globe, including Singapore, the United Kingdom, Australia, Mexico, Brazil and Japan. Locate our local office at:
international.cengage.com/region

Cengage Learning products are represented in Canada by Nelson Education, Ltd.

Visit Heinle online at **elt.heinle.com**
Visit our corporate website at **cengage.com**

Printed in Singapore
1 2 3 4 5 6 7 8 9 10 – 12 11 10

Contents

	Vocabulary	Grammar	Use of English
Unit 1 **Beginnings**	• Origins and new experiences • Fixed phrases: *starting again* • Key word: *make*	• Past and present tenses	• Paper 3, part 5: key word transformations; similar meaning in transformed sentences
Unit 2 **A child's world**	• Childhood, education • 'Parts of the body' idioms • Phrasal verbs: *pick up* • Key word: *run*	• Passive forms	• Paper 3, part 1: words easily confused; multiple-choice cloze • Paper 3, part 5: key word transformations
Unit 3 **Are you game?**	• Endurance sports • Phrases with *up* and *down* • Phrases and phrasal verbs with *take*	• Modal auxiliaries (1)	• Paper 3, part 2: open cloze; grammatical and lexico-grammatical answers
Unit 4 **Eureka!**	• Science and discovery, future lifestyles, colourful language • Key word: *tell*	• The future	• Paper 3, part 3: prefixes; using stem words • Paper 3, part 5: key word transformations
Unit 5 **Safe and sound?**	• Crime and punishment, DNA Profiling • Verbs followed by particles • Phrasal verbs with *turn* • Key word: *law*	• Verbs followed by infinitive or *-ing*	• Paper 3, part 4: gapped sentences; finding the right word
Unit 6 **Hale and hearty**	• Healthy lifestyles, diet, nutrition, alternative medicine • Vocabulary and idioms • Key word: *life*	• Conditionals	• Paper 3, part 1: multiple-choice cloze; identifying collocations
Unit 7 **Wish you were there ...**	• Travel and tourism, virtual worlds, describing places • Phrases with *look* • Key word: *road*	• Inversion	• Paper 3, part 2: open cloze; contrast and negative ideas in the text
Unit 8 **Making our mark**	• Architecture, archaeology • Phrases with *bring* • Key word: *that*	• Relative pronouns; defining and non-defining relative clauses	• Paper 3, part 3: word building (noun groups); preparation

Reading	Listening	Speaking	Writing
• Paper 1, part 1: themed texts	• Paper 4, part 1: short extracts	• Paper 5, part 1: talking about new experiences	• Paper 2, part 2: writing a descriptive or narrative article
• Paper 1, part 2: gapped text	• Paper 4, part 2: sentence completion	• Paper 5, part 2: expressing opinions; comparing pictures	• Paper 2, part 2: a review
• Paper 1, part 3: longer texts; understanding attitude and tone	• Paper 4, part 3: understanding the speaker's attitude	• Paper 5, part 3: interactive	• Paper 2, parts 1 and 2: a formal letter; question types
• Paper 1, part 4: scanning texts for information	• Paper 4, part 4: getting the gist; multiple-matching tasks	• Paper 5, part 4: three-way task; follow-on questions	• Paper 2, part 1: an article; analysing and organising input material
• Paper 1, part 2: gapped texts; following a line of argument in a text	• Paper 4, part 2: sentence completion; distinguishing key information	• Paper 5, part 1: giving personal information; talking about yourself	• Paper 2, parts 1 and 2: planning a report
• Paper 1, part 1: understanding written texts (text analysis)	• Paper 4, part 3: multiple choice questions	• Paper 5, part 2: comparing pictures	• Paper 2, part 2: an essay; developing an argument
• Paper 1, part 4: multiple matching texts; interpreting the question	• Paper 4, part 4: multiple extracts; interpreting context to identify the speaker	• Paper 5, part 4: discussing possible future developments; following on from part 3	• Paper 2, parts 1 and 2: a proposal; supporting your ideas
• Paper 1, part 3: understanding opinion	• Paper 4, part 1: interpreting context; listening for context	• Paper 5, part 3: reaching a decision through negotiation	• Paper 2, part 2: a contribution to a longer piece

	Vocabulary	Grammar	Use of English
Unit 9 **Brushstrokes and blueprints**	• Forms of art and craft, feelings about art • Compound words • Key word: *pay*	• Changing sentence structure for emphasis or meaning	• Paper 3, part 5: key word transformations
Unit 10 **The good life**	• Family life, ethical living, community • Fixed phrases • Key word: *pull*	• Direct and reported speech	• Paper 3, part 4: gapped sentences; focusing on lexical contexts
Unit 11 **Making ends meet**	• TV game shows, credit card fraud, attitudes towards money • Idiomatic phrases with *out* and *money* • Key word: *money*	• Modal auxiliaries (2)	• Paper 3, part 1: multiple-choice cloze
Unit 12 **behind the silver screen**	• Describing film and technique, Hollywood • Modifying and intensifying adjectives with adverbs • Key word: *quite*	• Participle clauses	• Paper 3, part 2: open cloze
Unit 13 **Getting the message across**	• Sending messages, communicating ideas • Nouns followed by particles • Key word: *set*	• Text references; *it/there* as introductory pronouns	• Paper 3, part 4: gapped sentences • Paper 3, part 2: open cloze
Unit 14 **Gaia's legacy**	• The earth, history of the earth, Gaia theory, nature • Idioms from nature • Key word: *world*	• Unreal past	• Paper 3, part 3: word formation • Paper 3, part 5: key word transformations
Unit 15 **Our global village**	• Cultures, customs, taboos, people, civilisation • Phrasal verbs and phrases with *pass*	• Adverbial clauses	• Paper 3, part 2: open cloze text • Paper 3, part 4: gapped sentences
Unit 16 Endings ... and new beginnings	• Saying goodbye to a way of life, making changes • Word partners • Key word: *end*	• Making and intensifying comparisons	• Paper 3, part 1: multiple-choice cloze

Reading	Listening	Speaking	Writing
• Paper 1, part 1: understanding tone and implication in a text	• Paper 4, part 3: understanding stated opinion	• Paper 5, part 3: problem-solving	• Paper 2, part 2: competition entry
• Paper 1, part 2: gapped text: text structure, paragraph cohesion and coherence	• Paper 4, part 4: 'who says what'; identifying speakers	• Paper 5, part 2: organising a larger unit of discourse	• Paper 2, part 2: an information sheet
• Paper 1, part 3: interpreting literature; indirect meaning in literature	• Paper 4, part 2: sentence completion; listening for dates, statistics and/or figures	• Paper 5, part 4: disagreeing with someone else's opinion	• Paper 2, part 1: a report; being concise when writing a report
• Paper 1, part 4: gapped text; skimming and scanning	• Paper 4, part 1: understanding purpose and function	• Paper 5, parts 3 and 4: exchanging ideas	• Paper 2, part 2: a review; planning a review
• Paper 1, part 2: predicting information	• Paper 4, part 4: multiple matching; doing multiple tasks	• Paper 5, part 3: sustaining interaction	• Paper 2, part 2: contribution to a longer piece
• Paper 1, part 3: gist and detail; matching gist to detail	• Paper 4, part 2: sentence completion; focused listening	• Paper 5, part 3: evaluating (making choices)	• Paper 2, part 2: an essay (discussing issues that surround a topic); word length
• Paper 1, part 1: purpose and main idea	• Paper 4, part 3: multiple speakers • Paper 4, part 4	• Paper 5, part 1: talking about your country, culture, customs and background	• Paper 2, parts 1 and 2: an article or letter (personal experiences)
• Paper 1, part 4: multiple letter matching texts; looking for specific information	• Paper 4, part 1: three short extracts; recognising agreement and disagreement	• Paper 5, part 2: individual long turn; one minute of talking	• Paper 2, parts 1 and 2: a of reference

Overview of the exam

The Certificate in Advanced English examination, just like the First Certificate examination, consists of five papers, each worth an equal 40 marks of the maximum 200 marks. Grades A, B and C represent a pass grade. Grades D and E are a fail. It is not necessary to achieve a satisfactory grade in all five papers in order to receive a final passing grade.

PAPER 1 (1 HOUR 15 MINUTES)

Reading

- Four parts testing a range of reading skills
- You must answer all four parts
- There are 34 questions in total
- You receive two marks for each correct answer in parts 1, 2 and 3 and one mark for each correct answer in part 4.

Part 1: Multiple choice
You have to read three short themed texts from a range of sources. Each text is followed by two multiple choice questions with four options each.

Part 2: Gapped text
Six paragraphs have been removed from a longer text and placed in a jumbled order, together with an additional paragraph. You have to choose the missing paragraph for each gap.

Part 3: Multiple choice
A longer text followed by seven four-option multiple choice questions.

Part 4: Multiple matching
A text or several short texts is preceded by 15 multiple-matching questions.

SPOTLIGHT ON CAE

PAPER 1

See the following pages for Spotlights on Reading: 2, 10, 18, 26, 34, 42, 50, 58, 66, 74, 82, 90, 98

PAPER 2 (1 HOUR 30 MINUTES)

Writing

- Two parts
- You must answer both parts (a compulsory one in part 1, one from a choice of five in part 2)

Part 1: One compulsory question
You may be asked to write any of the following: an article, a letter, a proposal, a report. You must use the input material and write 180–220 words.

Part 2: One from a choice of writing tasks
You can choose one task from a choice of five questions (including the set text options). You may be asked to write any of the following: an article, a contribution to a longer piece, an essay, an information sheet, a letter, a proposal, a report, a review or a competition entry. You must write 220–260 words.

SPOTLIGHT ON CAE

PAPER 2

See the following pages for Spotlights on Writing: 8, 16, 24, 32, 40, 48, 56, 64, 72, 80, 88, 96, 104, 112, 120, 128

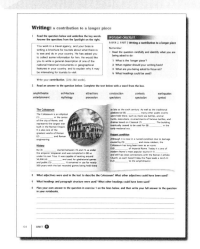

PAPER 3 (1 HOUR)

Use of English

- There are five parts with 50 questions in total
- Parts 1, 2 and 5 test both grammar and vocabulary. Parts 3 and 4 test vocabulary
- Parts 1, 2, and 3: each correct answer receives 1 mark. Part 4: each correct answer receives 2 marks. Part 5: each answer receives up to 2 marks.

Part 1: Multiple-choice cloze
A modified cloze test containing 12 gaps and followed by 12 four-option multiple choice items. You must choose the option that correctly fills the gap.

Part 2: Open cloze
A modified open cloze test containing 15 gaps. You must write one word to fill each gap.

Part 3: Word formation
You must read a text containing 10 gaps. Each gap corresponds to a word. The stems of the missing words are given beside the text.

Part 4: Gapped sentences
There are five questions, each of which contains three separate sentences. Each sentence contains one gap, which must be completed with one appropriate word.

Part 5: Key word transformations
There are eight separate questions, each with a lead-in sentence and a gapped second sentence to be completed in three to six words, including a given 'key word'.

SPOTLIGHT ON CAE

PAPER 3

See the following pages for Spotlights on Use of English: 7, 15, 23, 31, 39, 47, 55, 63, 71, 79, 119, 127

PAPER 4 (APPROXIMATELY 40 MINUTES)

Listening

- Four parts
- Each part contains a recorded text or texts and corresponding comprehension tasks
- Each part is heard twice
- There are 30 questions in total

Part 1: Multiple choice

Three short extracts, from exchanges between interacting speakers. There are two four-option multiple choice questions for each extract.

Part 2: Sentence completion

A monologue with a sentence completion task which has eight items. You must complete each sentence with a word that you hear in the recording.

Part 3: Multiple choice

A longer dialogue or conversation involving interacting speakers, with six multiple choice questions.

Part 4: Multiple matching

Five short themed monologues, with 10 multiple-matching questions. There are two tasks to complete.

SPOTLIGHT ON CAE

PAPER 4

See the following pages for Spotlights on Listening: 6, 14, 22, 30, 38, 54, 61, 69, 76, 85, 101, 110, 125

PAPER 5 (15 MINUTES)

Speaking

- Four parts
- There will be one interlocutor and one invigilator
- There will be two or three candidates per group
- You will be expected to respond to questions and to interact in conversational English

Part 1: Introductory questions

A conversation between the interlocutor and each candidate (spoken questions).

Part 2: Individual long turn

An individual 'long turn' for each candidate with a brief response from the second candidate (visual and written stimuli, with spoken instructions).

Part 3: Two way conversation

A two-way conversation between the candidates (visual and written stimuli, with spoken instructions).

Part 4: Extension of discussion topics

A discussion on topics related to part 3 (spoken questions).

SPOTLIGHT ON CAE

PAPER 5

See the following pages for Spotlights on Speaking: 8, 14, 30, 39, 46, 55, 71, 78, 93, 103, 110, 117, 125.

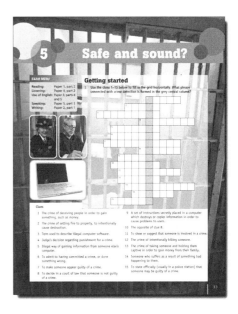

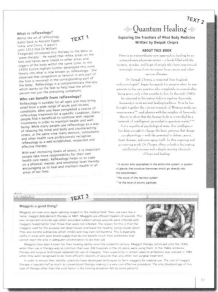

What are the differences between the old exam and the revised exam?

You're probably wondering what the differences between the old and revised exam are. There are still five papers, but overall time has been reduced in length by approximately one hour. It is now four hours and forty minutes. The new exam will also contain new and improved task types, and is designed to be more 'user-friendly'.

Revised Exam

① Paper 1: Reading [Four parts, 34 questions]
1 Themed texts (6 questions) **NEW**
2 Gapped text (6 questions)
3 Multiple choice (7 questions)
4 Multiple-matching (15 questions)

② Paper 2: Writing
1 Write one of the following: an article, a report, a proposal, a letter (compulsory task).
  Answer reduced to 180–220 words
2 Write one of the following: an article, a competition entry, a contribution to a longer piece, an essay, an information sheet, a letter, a proposal, a report, a review.
  Answer to be 220–260 words (1 task from a choice of 5)
  Possible set texts option. **NEW**

③ Paper 3: Use of English
1 Multiple-choice cloze (12 questions)
2 Open cloze (15 questions)
3 Word formation (10 questions)
4 Gapped sentences (5 questions) **NEW**
5 Key word transformations (8 questions) **NEW**

④ Paper 4: Listening
1 Short extracts (6 questions) **NEW**
2 Sentence completion (8 questions)
3 Multiple choice (6 questions)
4 Multiple matching (10 questions)

⑤ Paper 5: Speaking
1 Spoken questions between the interlocutor and each candidate (3 minutes)
2 Individual 'long turn' for each candidate and a brief response from the other candidate (1 minute + 30 seconds)
3 A two-way conversation between candidates with written and visual stimuli used in a decision making task (4 minutes) **NEW**
4 A discussion on topics related to the collaborative task (4 minutes)

Differences

Introduction of three texts in part 1, each with two four-option multiple choice questions.
A broader text range used (for example, fiction and reports are now introduced).

Candidate is given less material as a writing prompt.
Candidate's response is reduced from 250 words.
Tasks added: 'Contributions to longer pieces', 'essays' and set texts.

In part 4, the candidate now needs to complete a gap in a set of three sentences with the same word removed.
In part 5, the candidate needs to rewrite the first sentence into the second, using three to six words, including the 'key' word given.
The old section, error correction, has been removed.

Introduction of three extracts of interacting speakers in part 1, each with two three-option questions.
Candidates can now listen twice to all parts.

Candidate to candidate interaction removed from part 1
Written prompts with visuals now used in parts 2 and 3.

1 Beginnings

EXAM MENU

Reading: Paper 1, part 1
Listening: Paper 4, part 1
Use of English: Paper 3, part 5
Speaking: Paper 5, part 1
Writing: Paper 2, parts 1 and 2

Getting started

1 Complete the crossword using the clues provided and one of the words from the box below.

embark	generate	kick off	prompts	stimulate
establish	inaugurate	launch	provoke	trigger
found	initiate	produce		

Across

1 Officially make someone your leader with a special ceremony.

5 She _____ him whenever he forgets his lines in the play.

6 Pull this to make a loud noise – and start a sequence of events.

8 Blow the whistle – the game begins!

10 Make it, create it, and sell it.

11 Get it out on the water or out on the shelves.

12 Just give me a little to wake me up and get me going …

Down

1 Be the first to get something going …

2 Begin a journey, a new life, a career.

3 Do something to get a negative or violent reaction.

4 Set it up and make it work.

7 Start something that begins to grow by its own power.

9 Set up and begin a new organisation.

1

Reading: themed texts

1 Quickly scan the three texts that follow and decide which one contains:

   a technical information for a specific purpose
   b fictional writing and dialogue
   c factual information about a specific event

2 PAPER 1, PART 1 **You are going to read three extracts which are all concerned in some way with the beginning of something new. For questions 1–6, choose the answer (A, B, C or D) which you think fits best according to the text.**

SPOTLIGHT CHECKLIST

PAPER 1, PART 1 Themed texts
Tips

- Be aware of the thematic link between the texts as this will help you in moving from one text to the next.

- Read the text and the questions carefully.

- Look at the options and decide which one is the closest in answering the question.

- Underline the part of the text which answers the question.

- If possible, identify the part of the text which eliminates one or more of the distractor options.

Extract from a history book

The clock strikes twelve

The 20th century began with an argument. Britain could not make up its mind where the boundary between the two centuries lay. There were two schools of thought. The 'zeroists' were adamant that the new century started when 1899 gave way to 1900, but they were seen as a pedantic minority. Most people agreed that 1900 was the last year of the old century, and so Britons held their centennial celebrations on the eve of 1901. They could not know that their impatient descendants would take the opposite view and that the passing of the second millennium would be marked an incomplete 99 years hence.

Some people spent the last hours of the 19th century quietly at home. Others made their way to church or chapel, keeping the tradition of the night-watch service and listening in solemn silence for the first stroke of the midnight hour. In York, as the Minster bells struck, four revellers plunged into the icy waters of the River Ouse, determined to 'swim the old year out and start the new century clean'. Outside St Paul's Cathedral in London the excitement was more intense. 'The Scotch element was, as usual, well to the fore, and the singing of "Auld Lang Syne" could be heard all over the City,' reported the first 20th century edition of the *Daily Mail*.

1 According to the text, the 'zeroists'
   A celebrated the millennium a year early.
   B were impatient to celebrate the millennium.
   C believed the 19th century ended with 1899.
   D refused to celebrate with everyone else.

2 In the hours leading up to the beginning of the 20th century
   A most people stayed at home or went to church.
   B some people didn't speak until the clock struck midnight.
   C it was traditional to go swimming in a Yorkshire river.
   D everyone in Scotland was singing 'Auld Lang Syne'.

Extract from a novel

The beginning of an idea ...

'Mr Lyell is a genius,' said Darwin sniffily. 'He believes that the differences between two species of the same animal in two different regions cannot be superinduced during a length of time on account of the immutability of species.'

'It all depends on how one defines a species,' suggested FitzRoy. 'Every animal varies more or less, in outward form and appearance, from its fellows that habit different surroundings. But to fancy that every kind of mouse which differs externally from the mouse of another country is a distinct species is to me as difficult to believe as that every variety of the human race is a distinct species. A mouse is a mouse. A human is a human, be he an Englishman or a Fuegian. A fox is a fox, whether it be a Falklands fox or one of the type that Philos spends his days hunting to extinction in Shropshire. But a mouse cannot transmute into a cat. A fox cannot transmute into a penguin. A monkey cannot transmute into a human.'

'Philos is making a damned good job of extinguishing the race of Falklands foxes too, if you ask me,' said Sullivan. 'Expect to see it classified with the dodo soon.'

A chuckle ran round the room, and the hot breath of Darwin's laughter momentarily flared the glowing peat in the grate. 'I intend to make a special study of the tameness of the animal population before we leave', he said. 'To ascertain by experimentation how fast each species learns from danger – then, perhaps, to take specimens on board, and see if their offspring really can receive their parents' newly acquired knowledge at birth.'

3 According to FitzRoy
   A all animal species are a product of their location.
   B external variation alone can constitute a new species.
   C only animals that are closely related can diverge.
   D one species of animal cannot change into another.

4 Darwin hopes to show that
   A all the native animals are unnaturally tame and reckless.
   B some animals take longer to learn about danger than others.
   C acquired knowledge can be passed from parents to young.
   D the young of some animals can differ from their parents.

SEQA – Scottish Environment Agency.

Assistant Hydrologist

Salary from £16,300 (fixed term for 6 months) Ref. ES0024

This post is part of a small team responsible for the hydrometric networks in the Spey, Lossie and Banffshire Coastal catchments. You will spend most of your day in the field travelling to and from sites throughout the area, undertaking environmental sampling, monitoring and assessment. Accountable for the data generated from your survey sampling and analysis, you will also be responsible for assisting with the maintenance of field survey and data logging equipment.

With the ability to operate as part of a small team and also able to cope with lone working in the field, you must be resourceful, flexible and able to solve problems as they arise. Sound knowledge of hydrometry is preferred but not essential. Knowledge of Health and Safety procedures would be useful, as would knowledge of the appropriate legal procedures. Experience of fieldwork, particularly involving hydrological parameters, is desirable with experience in the operation and maintenance of mechanical or electronic instrumentation being an advantage.

Closing date 7th April 2010

To apply or for specific details on this post, or other opportunities within SEQA please visit www.seqa.org.uk/vacancies

Please quote the relevant post reference in any correspondence.

CVs will not be considered.

Successful applicants will be asked to provide a Basic Disclosure Scotland Certificate.

5 The position is seeking a person who will be mainly responsible for
   A co-ordinating the other members of the assessment team.
   B undertaking the transfer of data analysis from the field.
   C providing and analysing information from the environment.
   D looking after specialised equipment in the field

6 The person who applies for this post
   A must have a good knowledge of hydrometry.
   B will have to work alone most of the time.
   C will be tested on their knowledge of safety procedures.
   D ideally should know how to use the equipment.

3 **Underline the specific information in the text that provides the correct answers.**

Where possible, underline the parts of the text which eliminate the distractors in a different colour.

4 **Look back at the texts and find one expression with 'make' that means**

to decide or to agree *[text 1]* _____

to go somewhere *[text 1]* _____

to find out detailed information about something *[text 2]*

_____

Language development: fixed phrases – *starting again*

1 Complete the sentences below with a suitable phrase using the words in bold.

1 I realised that my plan was full of loopholes, so I decided to do it again from the beginning.
I realised that my plan was full of loopholes, so I decided to ...

_____ **scratch**

_____ **drawing**

_____ **square**

2 I decided to forget about my past mistakes and start a new lifestyle.
I decided to forget about my past mistakes and ...

_____ **fresh**

_____ **leaf**

_____ **slate**

2 Complete the sentences in A with the most appropriate clause in B.

A
1 'I stood on the table and shouted in order to
2 'Sometimes you just have to
3 'When she first set off on her solo voyage nobody knew if she would
4 'I explained it to you clearly so don't
5 'I'm fed up with my job. I'll need to find a new one.' 'That will
6 'I'd like a cheese sandwich please. No, in fact
7 'I don't want to do my homework today but dad will
8 'I don't know if the business will succeed, but I've decided to try and
9 'It's not much of a story but I expect it will
10 'I haven't been to the shops yet so you'll just have to

B
a make like you don't understand.'
b make that two.'
c make the evening papers.'
d make do with whatever's in the fridge.'
e make two of us then.'
f make myself heard.'
g make the most of what you have.'
h make me do it.'
i make it.'
j make a go of it.'

3 Replace the underlined part of each sentence with one of the phrasal verbs below. Make any grammatical changes necessary.

| make off | make out | make up |
| make off with | make something up to | make up for |

1 They jumped in the car and <u>headed</u> towards the port.

2 I'm sorry for the way I behaved. Let me <u>compensate</u> by taking you out to dinner.

3 There was too much background noise so I couldn't <u>hear</u> what they were saying.

4 Gerry didn't really go on the expedition – he <u>invented</u> that part of the story.

5 I trusted Jim so it came as a complete shock to me that <u>he left and took with him</u> the company funds.

6 Peter promised to work late all this week to <u>compensate</u> for the time he missed when he was ill.

Grammar: past and present tenses

1 Complete the sentences below with the correct form of the verb in brackets.

1 It was the most beautiful sunset I
_____ (have / ever / see).

2 I _____ (walk) for hours and my feet ached.

3 Jim _____ (listen) to the radio when I called him.

4 I _____ (never / be) abroad so I think I'll go to France next year.

5 Pete said he _____ (not / call) me yesterday because he was studying.

6 It _____ (take) eight minutes for the light from the sun to reach Earth.

7 'David _____ (go) into town. Do you want him to get anything?'

8 I _____ (sit) in front of this computer all day. It's time I took a break.

2 Underline the correct word or phrase in each sentence.

1 The children *ate / have eaten / have been eating* the biscuits already. I only bought them an hour ago!

2 While I *walked / was walking / have been walking* into town, I saw an accident.

3 Peter *works / has worked / has been working* on the project for a week now.

4 I *broke / was breaking / have broken* my leg in a skiing accident last May.

5 Julian *chopped / was chopping / has been chopping* the vegetables while I made the sauce.

6 I *didn't read / haven't read / haven't been reading* the book yet because I'm so busy.

7 Lillian *has / is having / has been having* her piano lesson at the moment.

8 What *did you do / were you doing / have you been doing*? You're covered in mud.

3 Complete the sentences that follow in your own words.

1 Late last night I _____ when _____.

2 What _____ this time next week?

3 Have you _____ any time recently?

4 I had already _____ when _____.

5 I'm _____ if you'd like to come too.

4 Read the text and complete the gaps with the correct form of the verb in brackets.

I **(1)** _____ (not / forget) the first time our team played in a knock-out football tournament. No one **(2)** _____ (expect) us to get as far as we did – all the way to the final – as we were generally considered to be the outsiders, but knowing we might be up against the long standing champions, we **(3)** _____ (train) every day for months.

On the day of the match, I **(4)** _____ (wake) to see that the sun **(5)** _____ (shine). I **(6)** _____ (put) on my football kit and **(7)** _____ (wait) eagerly for Dad to announce it was time to go. When we **(8)** _____ (arrive) at the football pitch I joined my team mates who **(9)** _____ (already / do) warm ups and there was a definite sense of excitement and tension in the air. Our coach said, 'Remember, you **(10)** _____ (train) for the past year for this moment. Give it all you've got!'

We **(11)** _____ (march) out onto the field, and after shaking hands with each other, the referee **(12)** _____ (toss) his coin and **(13)** _____ (blow) his whistle. The next 90 minutes **(14)** _____ (pass) in a blur, but I could hear kids from our school who **(15)** _____ (cheer) us on. The other team **(16)** _____ (put) pressure on us the whole time and there were some close shaves, until finally in the second half they managed to score. It **(17)** _____ (begin) to look bad for us; with only five minutes left of the game we were one goal down. Suddenly I **(18)** _____ (see) my chance! Thanks to a straight pass from a team mate I **(19)** _____ (kick) the ball straight into the net. The whistle blew. It **(20)** _____ (be) a draw, but then we went to penalties and beat them: five goals to four!

5

Listening: short extracts

1 🎧 1.1 PAPER 4, PART 1 You will hear three different extracts. For questions 1–6, choose the answer (A, B or C) which fits best according to what you hear. There are two questions for each extract.

Extract One

You hear two people talking about their earliest memories.

1 The man recounts
   A his first trip to an adventure park.
   B the day he lost a beloved toy.
   C the first time his parents took him out.

2 The man says that to begin with he felt
   A too small to join in with the older children.
   B frightened of playing in a strange place.
   C nervous because there were so many children.

Extract Two

You hear a radio programme about a pop star.

3 Kathy's first album was unusual in that
   A the songs had been written much earlier.
   B it seemed to be well thought out and refined.
   C it was unlike any other album around at the time.

4 Kathy felt that making an album
   A was the most important thing for her to do.
   B was not as important as fame and fortune.
   C would teach her how to enjoy what she did.

Extract Three

You hear a woman being interviewed about her new line of work.

5 The woman says that the South American pouch slings
   A have complicated straps and attachments.
   B are attractive, natural and easy to wear.
   C are not as popular as the metal framed slings.

6 One important advantage of her slings is that
   A newborn babies get a sense of security in them.
   B more than one child can be carried in them at a time.
   C they have been designed with the father's tastes in mind.

PAPER 4, PART 1 Short extracts

1 Read through the questions before you listen and think about what you are being asked to listen for.

2 Listen to the whole extract carefully once through before choosing an answer.

3 Do not assume too soon that you have heard the correct answer (because the two questions each have a different focus, information relevant to the answers could come from different parts of the recording).

4 Be wary of choosing an answer simply because it contains words and phrases heard on the recording.

5 Mark one answer to each question at the end of the first listening, even if you're not sure it is correct. The second listening can then be used to confirm this answer or not.

Use of English: key word transformations

1 PAPER 3, PART 5 **For questions 1–8, complete the second sentence so that it has a similar meaning to the first sentence, using the word given. Do not change the word given. You must use between three and six words, including the word given.**

1 Mum offered me another piece of pie, but I told her I was full.
HAD

I told Mum _____ when she offered me another piece.

2 John and Peter first met thirty years ago.
EACH

John and Peter _____ thirty years.

3 We haven't had a night out in ages.
SINCE

It's _____ had a night out.

4 They have been building their dream home for the past ten years.
UNDER

Their dream home _____ the past ten years.

5 We didn't like the holiday resort much but we decided to enjoy what we could.
MOST

We decided _____ the holiday resort even though we didn't like it much.

6 I didn't hear from Jane for another three years.
BEFORE

It _____ from Jane again.

7 Getting a place on the course was much harder than I thought it would be.
AS

It was _____ a place on the course as I thought it would be.

8 Greg has to work very hard to pay his bills.
ENDS

To _____ Greg has to work very hard.

PAPER 3, PART 5 Similar meaning in transformed sentences

Remember:

• The key word MUST be used in each answer.

• It may NOT be changed in any way.

• Your answer must NOT exceed six words.

• Contractions count as two words.

Tips

• Make a note of any new expressions which have parallel or synonymous meanings.

• Note also whether any phrasal verbs can substitute particular vocabulary or if tenses can be expressed with a particular expression.

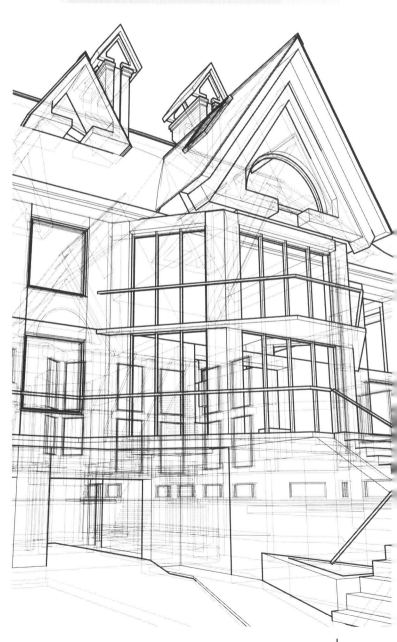

Speaking: spoken questions

1 Extra speaking practice. Ask other people to talk about their childhoods. Ask questions to help them give as many details as possible so they can talk for 2–3 minutes. Use some of the questions below to help you. Afterwards tell them about your childhood.

> *Did you have a happy childhood?*
> *What's your earliest memory?*
> *Do you remember your first day of school?*
> *Do you remember your first friend?*
> *If you have any younger brothers or sisters, can you remember when they were born?*
> *Do you remember the first time you got into trouble with your parents? Or a teacher?*

Writing: an article

1 **Look at the following question.**

You read the following announcement in a student magazine.

> A recent survey has shown us that good teachers do more than just teach – they also inspire and motivate. We would like you, the readers, to submit articles describing the best teacher you have ever had and explaining how they inspired and motivated you. We will publish the most interesting articles.

2 **Ask yourself the following questions:**

- What type of article am I being asked to write?
- Who is the target reader?
- Is description required?
- Is narrative required?
- Is a personal experience required?
- Does it need a title or headings?
- What register is required?
- Do I have enough experience or knowledge to answer the question?

3 **Plan and write the above article. Follow the steps below.**

1 **Brainstorm:** try to think of several ideas and choose the best one.

2 **Outline:** what will you say in each part of your composition.

   1 Opening / introduction: …

   2 Main part: …

   3 Ending / conclusion: …

3 **Select vocabulary:** you're being asked to describe a person. Think of colourful adjectives or interesting anecdotes that can 'paint a picture' of this person.

4 **Writing:** if you've planned your composition well it shouldn't take you so long to write. Make sure you allow enough time for both planning and writing both composition questions in the exam.

5 **Checking:** read what you've written. Look out for:

- grammatical errors (structures/tenses/syntax)
- inappropriate language/vocabulary
- spelling mistakes
- punctuation errors

2 A child's world

EXAM MENU

Reading: Paper 1, part 2
Listening: Paper 4, part 2
Speaking: Paper 5, part 2
Use of English: Paper 3, parts 1 and 5
Writing: Paper 2, part 2

Getting started

1 Use the clues below to find the words in the box which complete the grid. There are two extra words that you do not need to use.

1 Walk in a determined, purposeful manner

2 Run with a lot of energy and enthusiasm

3 Pull or lift something heavy with difficulty

4 Walk or stand in water

5 Climb with difficulty, using hands and feet

6 Fight with somebody or something by pushing them into difficult positions

7 Walk around an area without going in a fixed direction

8 Walk very quietly without putting your heels on the floor

bound	clamber	heave	march	paddle
stroll	tiptoe	wade	wander	wrestle

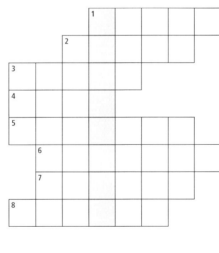

9

Reading: gapped text

1 **Read the extract below, ignoring the gaps, and answer the following questions.**

   a How many people are mentioned?
   b How many people speak?
   c Who is on the train?

2 a Underline the parts of the text which show you Joseph Hooper's thoughts.
   b When the writer refers to 'Hooper', are they talking about the father or the son?
   c What does Edmund Hooper seem to be preoccupied with?

3 **PAPER 1, PART 2 You are going to read an extract from a book. Six paragraphs have been removed from the extract. Choose from the paragraphs A–G (on page 11) the one that fits each gap (1–6). There is one extra paragraph which you do not need to use.**

PAPER 1, PART 2 Gapped text

Tips

- Do not focus on each gap separately, but examine the text as a whole.

- Check the option you choose fits both the text before the gap, and what follows it.

- If more than one option seems possible, decide which one seems more logical in the context of the text as a whole.

- Notice discourse markers – time words or phrases, cause and effect, contrast and concession etc.

- Consider how many people are mentioned. Full names are usually used to introduce a person into a text, and thereafter, first name, or surname only may be used, or simply a pronoun.

- Notice repetition of a point made earlier, and the use of verb tenses when reading a text about the development of events.

Father and son

On the train from London, Joseph Hooper said, 'I hope you are friendly with young Charles Kingshaw, now. I have not seen you about the place together very much.'

Hooper looked up from *The Scourge of the Marsh Monster*.

'I can't help it if he locks himself up, can I?'

'In his room?'

'Somewhere. In some room or other. *I* don't know.'

'That sounds to me a very strange way of going on. What is this all in aid of, what does he do?'

Hooper shrugged.

1 [...]

'But then, I daresay he is a little shy. You will have to be understanding about that, Edmund, there must always be a little give and take in this sort of friendship. That is a lesson I hope that you will learn in life very quickly. He has no father, when all is said and done.'

Hooper looked up briefly, raising his eyebrows.

2 [...]

But I came through, he said to himself now, I daresay that I am normal enough, that there is nothing so much wrong with me, in spite of it all. I shall not allow myself to feel guilty about it. Edmund will be like any other healthy boy, I am not to blame.

He watched the darkening countryside and then, after a time, returned to his magazine, more settled in his mind. He felt exonerated.

3 [...]

He thought, tomorrow I shall find out about Kingshaw, just by waiting and going into every room in the house, one after the next, very quietly. For he was irritated by the feeling that the other boy had somehow slipped through his fingers, had taken a little of the initiative. He had been here almost three weeks.

4 [...]

Over the business of the stuffed crow, Hooper had felt a grudging respect, though he had withdrawn it later, in fury, when Kingshaw had derided him the next morning. And now, he had started taking himself off to some other part of the house, a room that Hooper did not know had become Kingshaw's fortress.

5 [...]

Though he remembered that he had rarely been allowed beyond the garden. They had said, the girls will follow, there will be an accident. But it was not because of that. He had been summoned by his father to go and sit in the Red Room, to watch the moths in the poison bottle, to smell the smell of old books and stuffed weasels and watch the sunshine lying across the garden, beyond the high windows.

6 [...]

'You should get out into the fresh air and the sunshine, not mew yourselves up inside the house. It seems to me a very unhealthy way of going on. I shall insist upon your going off into the garden tomorrow, the moment you have eaten breakfast.'

A Looking up now, suddenly, he saw what it was about his own son that reminded him so vividly of himself. He was very pale. The village boys of Derne had always gone about half-naked, their bodies brown as Indians, through the summers, but Joseph Hooper had rarely gone out, and never been allowed to strip off his shirt, and so he had been very pale. Now, his own son was pale.

B Mr Hooper coughed, turned his face away, and shifted a little in his seat. There is no telling, he thought, perhaps he does remember something of his mother, after all. We cannot fathom the minds of young children. He was discomforted by his own lack of insight. He tried to find some clue, in his son's facial expression, as to what might be going on in his mind, but there was only a blank. He could recall nothing of himself at the same age except that he had loathed his own father.

C He made plans for a long time, almost a week. Everything was worked out, except the time. He had to find the right day. But, to begin with, it was harder than he had anticipated to get the things together. He was a methodical planner, but he was feeling his way.

D Slowly, remorselessly, the huge feet carried the hulking beast forward. The stench of the marshes hung about it and the mud on its scaly hide was mud formed at the dawn of history. The blood and death it now sought were …
'I suppose that I must speak to his mother.'
The train crossed over some points.

E Joseph Hooper was saying, 'You had better both go off on some expedition or other, this weather is too good to last. I cannot remember being at a loose end here, in the summer holidays when I was your age.'

F It was unexpected, Kingshaw was not that sort of a boy. Hooper could see quite clearly that the experience of being tormented and disliked and repelled was new to him. For a while, in the beginning, he had flinched in surprise, retreated, wondering how to cope. But he was quick, his defences had gone up now.

G Edmund Hooper stared down at his own finger, as it lay across the comic, at the crinkled skin and the dry, ragged line of nail. He imagined what his hands would be like in a flat, solid block of flesh, without the divisions of fingers. Fingers were queer. But it was amazing to realise what things he would not be able to do. Underneath his hand were the gruesome drawings of the Marsh Monster.

Language development:

'parts of the body' idioms

1 PAPER 3, PART 5 **For questions 1–8, complete the second sentence so that it has a similar meaning to the first sentence, using the word given. Do not change the word given. You must use between three and six words, including the word given.**

1 'What's up with Jane? She doesn't look very happy.'
   MOUTH

   'Jane looks rather _____.
   Is anything up?'

2 I'd expected Nick to be nervous about going on stage, but he wasn't bothered at all.
   BAT

   Much to my surprise, Nick _____
   about going on stage.

3 I have no idea why, but Katie just totally ignored me in the supermarket!
   SHOULDER

   I wonder why Katie _____
   in the supermarket?

4 Sally was so nervous during her presentation that she dropped her notes on the floor!
   FINGERS

   Sally _____
   during her presentation, and dropped her notes on the floor!

5 Paul never stops talking in class! It's so annoying!
   NECK

   Paul _____!
   He never stops talking in class!

6 The subject of politics has always caused friction between Harry and his father.
   EYE

   Harry and his father _____
   over politics.

7 Peter's come up with a brilliant idea for a theatre group.
   BRAINWAVE

   Peter's just _____
   about setting up a theatre group.

8 I don't feel Tim's got enough experience yet to deal with such an important client.
   EARS

   I think Tim's still _____
   to deal with such an important client.

2 **Complete the following sentences with phrases from the box below. There are two extra phrases.**

picked holes in	pick up the pieces
pick your brains	picky
pick you up	picked it up
picked up on	take your pick
picked her way	pick-me-up

1 'Sue, can I borrow one of your books?' 'Sure, _____.'

2 'Brian, can I _____ for a moment? I need some advice on this report I'm writing.'

3 'You've got a dose of gastric flu, Mrs Brown. You probably _____ on your business trip last week.'

4 Heidi _____ through the pile of toys lying scattered all over the bedroom floor to where her son sat.

5 'There's no point in taking two cars tonight, Jim. So, I'll _____ from the office at 5.30. OK?'

6 It's taken Paul a while to _____ after his wife left him, but he's coping a lot better since he sold the house.

7 My boss really _____ my report this morning, and after I'd worked so hard on it!

8 At the meeting, Tina _____ what George had said about the problem of security at the festival.

Key word: *run*

3 **Circle the correct word in *italics* to complete the following sentences.**

1 Alice wanted to become politically active, so she ran for *cover / office*.

2 David realised he was running a *fever / risk* by going to see Helen, but he had to talk to her.

3 'Could you run a(n) *errand / story* on the fire in the next issue?'

4 'Your proposal runs *counter / parallel* to company policy, and so I cannot support it.'

5 'Do you expect me to keep the *car / engine* running while you talk on the phone for ten minutes?'

Grammar: passive forms

1 For the following sentences, choose the passive form which best reflects their meaning.

1 It is a good idea to teach children the value of saving money.
   a Children will be taught the value of saving money.
   b Children should be taught the value of saving money.

2 People sometimes exaggerate the dangers of boys playing with toy guns.
   a The dangers of boys playing with toy guns can be exaggerated.
   b The dangers of boys playing with toy guns should be exaggerated.

3 People are certain to question the ethics of building a factory so near to the school.
   a The ethics of building a factory so near to the school will be questioned.
   b The ethics of building a factory so near to the school should be questioned.

4 It is possible that people will criticise the new teaching policy.
   a The new teaching policy will be criticised.
   b The new teaching policy may be criticised.

5 People sometimes doubt the value of teaching boys Domestic Science.
   a Doubts may be raised about the value of teaching boys Domestic Science.
   b Doubts can be raised about the value of teaching boys Domestic Science.

2 Rewrite the following sentences using two different passive forms.

1 People think nine-year-old James Edwards is very talented.

   It is thought that ... _____

   Nine-year-old James Edwards is thought to be ... _____

2 There have been rumours that Mrs Reed is leaving the school.

   a It ... _____

   b Mrs Reed ... _____

3 People believed the new sports programme had benefited the school.

   a It ... _____

   b The school ... _____

4 People have suggested that graphic novels could encourage children to read.

   a It ... _____

   b Suggestions ... _____

5 People often assume that an only child will be selfish.

   a It ... _____

   b Assumptions ... _____

3 Complete the following sentences.

1 Sarah had _____ stolen yesterday.

2 Paul _____ mended by the plumber this morning.

3 Ann went to that new hairdresser to _____ done for the wedding.

4 We _____ smashed by a brick last night.

5 Timmy got _____ trapped in the door, and had to be taken to hospital!

Listening: sentence completion

PAPER 4, PART 2 Sentence completion

1 Read the introductory rubric and the gapped sentences carefully, to get an idea of what you are going to hear.

2 Try to predict the kind of information and form of word you will need to fill each gap, e.g. statistics, a noun, a name or title etc.

3 Usually, no more than three words are required for each gap.

4 Use specific words from the listening text, but check you have written them in the correct form – that is, singular or plural – to fit the task sentence.

1 ⌕ 2.1 **PAPER 4, PART 2 You will hear a representative from the National Association for Teaching English giving a talk on the use of graphic novels in the classroom. For questions 1–8, complete the sentences.**

According to the speaker, one of the reasons that children today are not interested in reading is that books are not as [1] as video games.

The speaker suggests that presenting students with [2] in comic format may help them develop their language and communicative skills.

The comic book version of Shakespeare's *Romeo and Juliet* is set in [3].

Purists may disagree with teaching children an abridged version of a Shakespeare play, because it will lose some of the [4].

Presenting Shakespeare as a graphic novel can be seen as a [5] towards children appreciating Shakespeare in its original form.

Macbeth and *Henry V* are being produced as graphic novels with [6] versions of text.

The publisher's idea is to make Shakespeare accessible to students of [7].

The speaker doubts whether this idea is [8], but likes the idea of using the graphic novel in the classroom.

Speaking: expressing opinions

> What do the children gain from playing with these toys? How might the children be feeling?

1 The pictures show children playing with different toys. Compare two of the pictures, and say what children gain from playing with these toys, and how they might be feeling. Use some of the phrases below to help you.

They seem to be really enjoying themselves ...
He/she is obviously absorbed in what they are doing ...
They are really excited/frustrated/deep in concentration ...
I think the benefits of playing in this way are many ...
I'm reluctant to say this toy has no value, but its value is rather limited ...
I think this needs to be carefully monitored by parents ...

PAPER 5, PART 2 Comparing pictures

Remember:

• You'll be shown a set of three pictures, but will be asked to comment on two of them.

• Listen carefully to what the examiner asks you to do.

• The examiner's prompt question is written above the set of pictures, so use it to help you focus.

• When your partner is speaking about their pictures, listen carefully. You'll be asked to comment on what they said.

Tips

• Practise comparing pictures in class, and expressing opinions about them.

• Build up a record of useful words and phrases for comparing pictures and expressing opinions.

Use of English: words
easily confused

PAPER 3, PART 1 Multiple-choice cloze

Remember:

- Read the title and text through carefully, before you answer any questions, to get a clear idea of the subject.

- For each question, consider the options carefully before choosing your answer.

- Some of the options may appear to be suitable, but only one will be both contextually and grammatically correct.

- Once you have completed the task, read it through, with the completed gaps, to make sure it makes sense.

Tips

- Build up your knowledge of collocations, phrasal verbs, and prepositional phrases.

- Keep a record of words which are easily confused, and be aware of the differences between them.

1 **Choose the correct word in italics to complete the sentences below.**

1 Her *perception / conception* of an office was one in which large windows let in plenty of natural light.

2 James put on his football boots *unwitting / unconscious* of the fact that the match had been cancelled.

3 She was *inlaid / imbued* with wonder at the beauty of the ornate engagement ring.

4 Whenever they think there is something wrong with their child, a parent should trust their *senses / instincts*.

5 Sally has developed a new *method / means* for getting children to express their feelings.

6 'I'm *entitling / entrusting* you with this information in the hope that you will use it wisely.'

7 The *findings / reports* show a 20% increase in the number of under-age drinkers in Britain.

8 She has little *motive / incentive* to do well in school, as her parents show no interest in her progress.

2 **PAPER 3, PART 1 For questions 1–12, read the text below and decide which answer (A, B, C or D) best fits each gap.**

Goodbye to Action Man?

After forty years of devoted service to the British toy industry, Action Man has officially been (1) _____ from duty. He is to be 'left on the (2) _____', literally.

This much-loved toy has a fascinating history, which began in 1966, when he first hit the British market, and altered the playtime habits of boys across the nation forever! (3) _____ by his American counterpart, GI Joe, who had taken the American toy market (4) _____ two years previously, British toy company *Palitoy* sought permission from *Hasbro*, the makers of GI Joe, to market and sell the toy in the UK. However, it soon became clear that the name was not suitable for the British market. The name 'Action Man' was (5) _____ by *Palitoy's* production manager, Les Cooke, and it stuck. Action Man was (6) _____ articulated movable joints and impressive military outfits, and *Palitoy* marketed him as a 'fighting figure' rather than a doll for boys. His impact was instant and dramatic, taking his manufacturers by surprise.

Action Man had his (7) _____ during the 1970s and early 80s, with imaginative new outfits and accessories being developed constantly. His creators never rested in their endeavour to ensure that their product maintained its appeal. Even his appearance (8) _____ several changes. For example, his painted hair was replaced by 'fuzzy' flock hair, he grew a beard made of the same material, and developments in plastic (9) _____ Action Man was soon equipped with 'gripping' hands, enabling him to actually hold onto his increasingly sophisticated accessories. Gradually, he moved away from being a military, fighting figure to become more a man of adventure, his uniforms giving (10) _____ to spacesuits, deep sea diving suits and the khaki of an intrepid explorer.

(11) _____ of us who were boys during that period do not remember with affection the hours of creative fun afforded us by this toy, so it is with regret that we say goodbye. But all may not be lost! *Hasbro* has brought out several Anniversary figures to celebrate Action Man's fortieth birthday, and these are bound to appeal to collectors, as they (12) _____ the style of the original 1960s figure. Enthusiasts need not despair, either, as there is a Collector's Club they may join, where they can continue to indulge their abiding interest in this toy icon.

1	A expelled	B discarded	C fired	D discharged
2	A street	B table	C shelf	D road
3	A Inspired	B Influenced	C Installed	D Inlaid
4	A like lightning	B by storm	C to heart	D head on
5	A thought	B derived	C coined	D contrived
6	A supplied	B given	C provided	D equipped
7	A prime	B heyday	C heights	D success
8	A undertook	B entailed	C underwent	D followed
9	A meant that	B involved	C led to	D allowed for
10	A away	B way	C up	D in
11	A Several	B Many	C Most	D Few
12	A reflect	B depict	C reveal	D convey

Remember:

- Read the question carefully, and make sure you understand what is required. Underline the key points to help you focus.

- Think of the style, structures and vocabulary you will need, and make sure you feel confident about answering the particular question.

- After you have written your answer, check that your style and content are relevant to the question.

Tips

- Read reviews of various kinds – film, holidays, television programmes, consumer goods etc, to get a clear idea of the style.

- Practise describing items and explaining how they work.

- Keep a record of useful words and phrases for making recommendations.

Writing: a review

1 Read the following question, and underline three key points that your review must include.

> A well-known market research consultancy is conducting an online survey of mobile phones. They have asked visitors to their website to send in reviews of a mobile phone, describing the services it provides, and stating whether all the added services are really useful. You have decided to write a review, and conclude by saying who you would recommend your choice of mobile phone to and why.

2 Look at the following introductory paragraphs, and decide which one is the most suitable for this task. Why are the others unsuitable for this question?

> The purpose of this report is to examine different types of mobile phone, the value of the services they provide, and to make recommendations regarding the suitability of each one.

> People buy mobile phones for numerous reasons. Not only is it useful, it has also become a fashion accessory, a status symbol. Your mobile phone says something about the kind of person you are. Phones of various shapes, sizes, and colours abound, but one model worth considering when making your choice is the Nokia 980i.

> I've had the latest model of the Sony Ericsson mobile phone for the last three months, and I think it's great! It's got a huge number of gadgets, and I can take photos and even video my friends, if I want to. I like it for the reasons that I mention below.

3 Writing a suitable conclusion is just as important as the introduction. Look at the following conclusion to the task in exercise 1. What is wrong with it?

> For these reasons I like this particular model of mobile phone. I carry it with me wherever I go, and wouldn't be without it!

4 Think of suitable structures and descriptive vocabulary you could use in your answer to this question. Use some of the words and phrases below to help you. Space has been provided for you to add to the list.

revolutionary design	status symbol	complex
streamline or slimline shape	accessory	sophisticated
bulky or awkward	gadgets or extras	plain or patterned
_____	_____	_____

5 Plan and write your review. Make sure you include the key points mentioned in the question, and include a suitable introduction and conclusion.

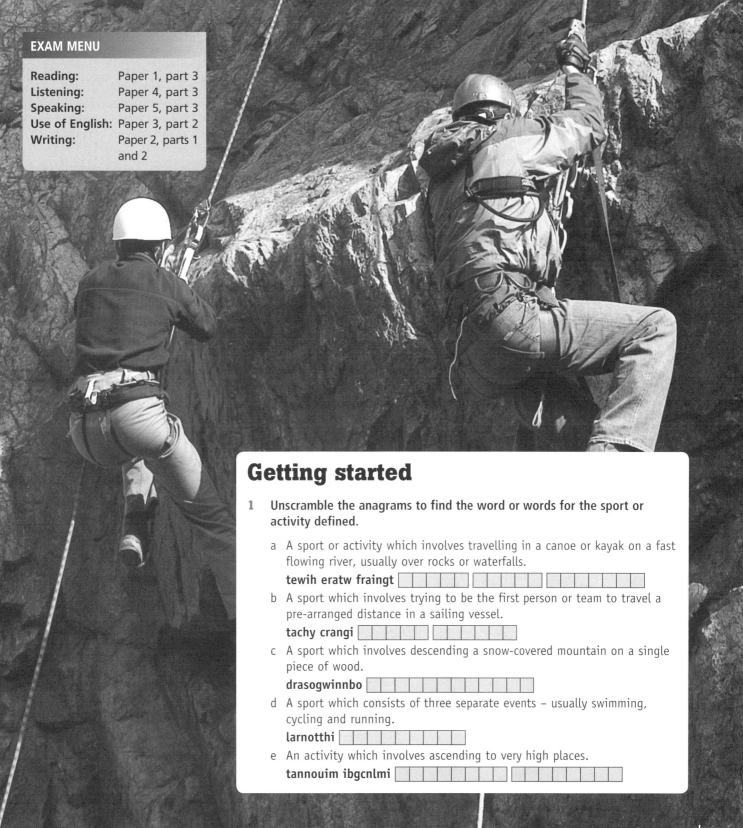

3   Are you game?

EXAM MENU

Reading: Paper 1, part 3
Listening: Paper 4, part 3
Speaking: Paper 5, part 3
Use of English: Paper 3, part 2
Writing: Paper 2, parts 1
                 and 2

Getting started

1   Unscramble the anagrams to find the word or words for the sport or activity defined.

    a   A sport or activity which involves travelling in a canoe or kayak on a fast flowing river, usually over rocks or waterfalls.
       tewih eratw fraingt

    b   A sport which involves trying to be the first person or team to travel a pre-arranged distance in a sailing vessel.
       tachy crangi

    c   A sport which involves descending a snow-covered mountain on a single piece of wood.
       drasogwinnbo

    d   A sport which consists of three separate events – usually swimming, cycling and running.
       larnotthi

    e   An activity which involves ascending to very high places.
       tannouim ibgcnlmi

Reading: longer texts

SPOTLIGHT EXAM GUIDANCE

PAPER 1, PART 3 Understanding attitude and tone

In this part of the Reading Paper, there's an emphasis on a longer text, and questions may test your understanding of detail, opinion, purpose, main idea, implication, tone and attitude.

1 Try to distinguish between apparently similar viewpoints, outcomes or reasons.

2 Try to also deduce meaning from context and interpret the text for inference and style. (The final question may depend on interpretation of the text as a whole, such as the writer's purpose, attitude, or opinion.)

Practise:

• reading relatively long and complex texts;

• reading each question very carefully, as well as the four possible answers (the questions can be answered correctly only by close reference to the text);

• reading texts in which opinion, attitudes and feelings are expressed.

1 PAPER 1, PART 3 **You are going to read a magazine article. For questions 1–6, choose the answer (A, B, C or D) which you think fits best according to the text.**

CYCLE TODDLING: An Adventure in

by Stuart Wickes and Kirstie Pelling

My mother sat in silence, stunned by Stuart's guided tour of websites of adventurous families. A global cast of parents and grandparents who refuse to put adventure on the back burner until their kids grow up. Families biking around the world for charity, sailing the globe in search of their roots, learning about our fragile environment, seeing the world through children's eyes. From every continent, in every different family combination, we found people on boats, bikes and hikes, demonstrating that adventure doesn't have to die when a new life is created. As one South African couple put it on their website, 'This is your one and only chance to explore the world with your children as they are now.'

'See, the only limitation is the parents' imagination,' said Stuart in a rendition of Nadine and Bernard's song, accompanied by this new chorus of families. My mother's voice refused to join the chorus. 'Interesting, but unnecessary. There's plenty of time to see the world when they grow up. Why can't you be like everyone else?'

'What and sit at home like couch potatoes, watching TV and eating junk? Sorry Mum, I'm getting back on my bike.'

Our five hundred mile, four kingdom tour taught us what cycle toddling was really about. No more whistling through villages and grinding up high passes to meet obsessive daily mileage targets. Instead we struck up a rhythm of two hour trundles, interspersed with play, swimming, and picnics. In the mornings, a single ray of light was enough to spring Cameron from his slumber and launch the day. Bounce, bounce and moments later there were two of them tearing through the tent. 'Wakey, wakey, we're on our holidays.' Our starts were earlier, our days longer and everything more unpredictable than ever before.

'Mikey gone!' yelled Matthew.

'Gone where?' asked Stuart, alarmed at the thought of losing the only toy we let him bring.

'On road. I dopped him!' he wailed. We turned around and retraced our path.

'Is lost for ever.' Matthew sobbed, mourning his one eyed green friend from *Monsters Inc.*

'No … wait, there it is!' cried Stuart as he rounded a bend, hurrying towards six inches of plastic monster abandoned on the road. Then, around the bend skidded an immaculate white BMW, Britney Spears pumping. We moved nervously into the hedge.

'Whoops I did it again' screeched Britney as the wheels crunched over Mikey, scattering monster body parts.

'Oh no, there's Mikey's eye,' Stuart said quietly, lifting a hapless green eyelid from the top of the buggy, wondering whether Matthew witnessed the accident.

'And his hand,' exclaimed Matthew joyously. 'And a leg. Daddy, look there's one of Mikey's legs, in the hedge.' We salvaged the eye, eye lid, two legs and an arm and ceremoniously hid the shattered torso in the hedge.

Mikey's apparent death gave us a glimpse into Matthew's world, where this tragic accident transformed Mikey from one toy into five, which were more flexible and fun to play with. The limb collection toured the four kingdoms with us, a lesson to us in how to adapt to life on the road.

Our extended tour was a resounding success. Life was simple, uncluttered, and filled with unexpected joys. And everybody loved it.

Parenting

'Mum,' I began awkwardly a few weeks ago. 'We're going travelling again.' 'Is it Florida or Paris dear?' she asked.

'Neither … it's New Zealand, six months cycling end to end. It's going to be amazing mum. Two islands, two bikes, two trailers, two toddlers and two thousand miles.'

'Two thousand nappies more like.'

My mother wasn't the only one to raise objections. While friends and family were impressed by our bravery, they were horrified at what it would entail. 'No nursery, no babysitters, no bath time, no peace, no escape, no TV. A 24/7 babywatch in unknown and hazardous environments? Rather you than me.' And that was before we mentioned the real practicalities; pulling 50kg of trailer, toddler, and baggage. And of course the obligatory nappies.

'There's no ozone layer you know,' my mother informed us, 'And it's not exactly flat. And how will you protect yourself against the Orcs? Look, is there nothing I can say to put you off?'

'No, Mum,' I replied with conviction, 'Nothing at all.'

'Well, we'll see about that. There's plenty of time.'

The challenge of dealing with my mother's phone-in of potential disasters is as great as anything we may have to face on the road. Meanwhile we rush to toilet train both children to avoid the nappy carrying Armageddon she predicted. Amidst the voices of doubt and disapproval, I still sometimes wonder if we are mad; but know we aren't mad alone. We have now made contact with many of the families we showed my mother on the web. And we can feel our own voice getting stronger and more confident with their encouragement, advice, and support.

Our family adventures began with the inspiration offered by Bernard and Nadine, now back in New Zealand. They're busy figuring out how to overcome their latest setback; teenage children who don't want to travel … We hope to compare notes on the challenges and joys of adventurous parenting, and get a few tips for the forthcoming teenage years.

And now we know there are so many families out there adventuring, we're already developing ideas for a future trip, a world tour, to meet some of these families, talk with them about their experiences and spread the word about the possibilities for independent family adventure. As Bernard and Nadine said, 'The only limit is the parents' imagination.' We intend to let ours run riot.

1 The writer's mother seemed amazed that
  A Stuart knew so much about adventure travel on the Internet.
  B so many people go on adventure travels with small children.
  C adventure tends to become more important after children are born.
  D there are a number of different ways to see the world with children.

2 According to the writer, adventure travel with children is
  A something you can only do when they are young.
  B limited by the imaginative capabilities of the parents.
  C essential for their education and intellectual development.
  D much better for their health than a sedentary lifestyle.

3 The writer soon discovered that cycling with small children
  A meant they had to miss some interesting locations.
  B inspired them to reach a more ambitious target each day.
  C necessitated a change in rhythm and routine.
  D allowed them to sleep better than before.

4 The writer recounts the toy incident because it
  A shows one may have to cope with unexpected events.
  B highlights the dangers of travelling by bicycle.
  C demonstrates the caring nature of both parents.
  D reveals Mathew's resilient nature while travelling.

5 When the writer announced their plans for touring New Zealand with children
  A she received encouragement from some of her friends.
  B some family members were shocked by the idea.
  C she realised she hadn't considered the practical difficulties.
  D her mother presented arguments in an attempt to dissuade her.

6 When contemplating the upcoming New Zealand tour the writer expresses
  A worry that her mother will continue to interfere in their travelling plans.
  B dismay at the need to prepare her children psychologically for the trip.
  C uncertainty about whether or not they will be able to pull it off.
  D comfort in the knowledge that they are not the only ones to attempt this.

7 In talking about the future, the writer and her husband
  A admit planning a reunion party with their friends/mentors.
  B express fear that their teenage children will rebel against them.
  C hope to meet other families and share their experiences.
  D say they have already finalised their plans to travel the world.

Language development:
phrases with *up* and *down*

1   Complete the gaps in the sentences with *up* or *down*.

   a   Mr Reynolds reminded us that our break was over and it was time we got _____ to some work.

   b   Michael asked me what was _____ because he said I was looking a bit gloomy.

   c   Lyra explained that she'd been feeling a bit _____ since she'd changed school.

   d   Maureen asked me what I was _____ to because I'd been in my bedroom for so long.

   e   Shaun didn't think the musical was _____ to much and suggested we went for a meal instead.

   f   I said it was _____ to Gill to decide what we had for dinner because I didn't really mind.

   g   I thought I had made a profit, but after calculating all the production costs I realised I was in fact _____ by €20.

   h   Gordon's happy – they finally announced he's _____ for promotion.

Phrasal verbs with *take*

2   **Replace the underlined part of each sentence with a phrasal verb [verb + particle] formed with *take*.**

   a   Unfortunately Brian resembles his father far more than me! _____

   b   Dad asked me if I would like to assume responsibility for the family business when he retired. _____

   c   Claudia felt awful about what she'd said and asked if she could retract her last comment. _____

   d   Pauline didn't hesitate and said she was happy to accept the burden of their invalid mother. _____

   e   'It seems I was wrong about you, Lesley. I had assumed you were a person I could trust!' _____

   f   As a child he used to disassemble anything electronic. Trouble was he could never put it together again. _____

   g   Sally and Susie liked each other immediately and were firm friends thereafter. _____

   h   Luke has just started to play tennis. I doubt he'll keep it up for long though. _____

Phrases with *take*

3   **Complete the following sentences using an expression formed with *take* from the box below.**

   take it from me
   take it with a pinch of salt
   take it or leave it
   take the bull by the horns
   take it out of you
   take the wind out of somebody's sails
   take it lying down
   take your hat off to

   a   When the management announced that 300 workers would be out of a job, the Union immediately retorted that they were not going to **take** their threats _____.

   b   I tried to bargain for more pay, but my boss told me I could **take** _____.

   c   I had been timid most of my life, so when the chance to finally prove myself arose, I decided to **take** _____ and go for it!

   d   I don't know how Samantha managed to cope as a single parent of three kids under five and run a business. I really **take** my _____!

   e   After working for over a year on that script, the reviewers' feedback was so negative that it just **took** _____.

   f   Gloria regaled us with tales of her exploits in far off countries, but I told the kids to **take** everything she said _____.

   g   A long walk in that heat could really **take** _____.

   h   You can **take** _____ that you won't get anywhere in this world without hard work.

4   **PAPER 3, PART 3 Complete the sentences below with one word.**

   •   'Oi mate! What's your _____?' the policeman yelled at the shadowy figure across the street.

   •   Billy nearly gave the _____ away by saying he had to go somewhere tonight.

   •   'Hey Millie, I'm going to enter into the national cycling competition. Are you _____?'

Grammar: modal auxiliaries (1)

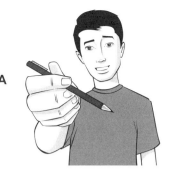

A

B

C

D

1 **Match the captions below to the cartoons on the right.**

1 'That must be Jim. He promised to call around 7.'

2 'It can't be snowing – it's the middle of April!'

3 'That might be for me. I ordered some books.'

4 'That could be mine but I'm not entirely sure.'

2 **Match the modal auxiliary phrases in A with the most suitable sentence in B.**

A

1 It might help if you put your glasses on.

2 It might be a blackbird on that roof.

3 It can't be lunchtime already.

4 It must be time for her nap.

5 It could be an 's' or a 'c'.

6 It might have been a dolphin you saw.

7 It could have been worse.

8 It must have been dreadful.

9 It can't have been John you saw in town.

10 It couldn't have been anything serious.

B

a I've only just had breakfast.

b That's why she's getting crotchety.

c You feel better now don't you?

d I'm glad I wasn't there when it happened.

e You know you can't read in this light.

f Pass the binoculars please!

g He's gone to Portugal for the summer.

h Hand me my reading glasses if you will.

i Did it have a dorsal fin on its back?

j You might have been out of a job altogether.

3 **Which of the sentences in exercise 2A above …**

a indicates a suggestion? ☐

b shows speculation about the present? ☐

c refers to a present or future certainty? ☐

d refers to a past possibility? ☐

e refers to a past certainty? ☐

4 **Which of the sentences in each pair below is correct?**

1a I might be exhausted, but I can still finish the project.

b I might have been exhausted, but I can still finish the project.

2a I must have been mad, but I'm still going to invite my in-laws for Christmas.

b I must be mad, but I'm still going to invite my in-laws for Christmas.

Listening: understanding the speaker's attitude

1 **Put the words below into the right category to show what they might reflect.**

annoyed	exuberant	confident	frustrated
cynical	hesitant	definite	irked
delighted	secure	doubtful	thrilled
elated	unambiguous	exasperated	unconvinced

certainty	uncertainty

positive feelings	negative feelings

2 🎧 **3.1 Listen to the following sentences and choose the correct answer in each case according to the speaker's attitude.**

Sentence 1 What emotion is the speaker expressing?

A excitement   B fear

C depression   D boredom

Sentence 2 The speaker expresses a feeling of …

A fury   B trepidation

C annoyance   D nervousness

Sentence 3 How did the speaker feel about her lodger's request to lend him more money?

A insecure   B cynical

C foolish   D impatient

3 🎧 **3.2 Now listen to the speakers again and answer the following questions.**

1 Gillian says that jumping out of an aeroplane

A was a very exciting experience for her.

B is something she'd be afraid to do again.

C should only be attempted by younger people.

D is something she doesn't think her daughter can do.

2 In recounting what happened to him, Peter says that

A he can't remember anything about the incident.

B he was annoyed that he couldn't find the man who helped him.

C he thinks the police aren't doing their job properly.

D he thinks Glasgow is more dangerous than it used to be.

3 In describing the incident Angela says that

A the young man came from a good home.

B her lodger couldn't keep up with his payments.

C she had offered to lend her lodger some money.

D she began to suspect her lodger of deceit.

Speaking: interactive

1   PAPER 5, PART 3 **Read the interlocutor's instructions below and write a dialogue in your notebook to answer the questions within the time limit. Write the dialogue for both Student A and Student B.**

[Interlocutor] Now, I'd like you to talk about something together for about three minutes. [five minutes for groups of three].

I'd like you to imagine you are planning an adventure trip with a friend where you would learn how to do one extreme sport with a qualified instructor. Here are some of the activities that you have been offered.

→ Speaking Reference 3, page 169

First, talk to each other about how dangerous these sports may be.

Then decide which two you would most like to attempt.

Use of English: open cloze

SPOTLIGHT CHECKLIST

PAPER 3, PART 2 Grammatical and lexico-grammatical answers

Remember:

- For this part of the exam you will be required to draw on your knowledge of the structure of the language and understanding of the text in order to fill the gaps.

- The focus of the gapped words is either grammatical, such as articles, auxiliaries, prepositions, pronouns, verb tenses and forms; or lexico-grammatical, such as phrasal verbs, linkers and words within fixed phrases.

- Any preparation task which promotes grammatical accuracy is useful, especially those which focus on verb forms and the use of auxiliary and modal verbs, pronouns, prepositions, conjunctions, modifiers and determiners.

Tips

- There may be more than one permissible answer for a question. However, you should only give one answer for each question.

- Some gaps can be filled by referring just to the immediate phrase or sentence, but others will require understanding of the paragraph or whole text.

- Spelling, as in all parts of the Use of English Paper, must be correct.

1   PAPER 3, PART 2 **For questions 1–15, read the text below and think of the word which best fits each gap. Use only one word in each gap.**

FEAR FACTOR

Fear Factor is an American stunt reality show, first aired in 2001, that was adapted from the original Dutch show entitled *Now or Neverland*. The show pits contestants (1) _____ each other to complete a series of stunts better and/or quicker (2) _____ all the other contestants (3) _____ a grand cash prize. The contestants were generally three men and three women, all playing for themselves, or four teams of two people, each with a pre-existing relationship (4) _____ one another, all playing for a shared prize of the (5) _____ amount.

The first stunt is designed to physically test (6) _____ of the contestants, for example by asking them to jump off one building to another. The two men and two women – or the three teams – to best complete the stunt (7) _____ whichever restrictions (such as the fastest, or furthest distance, or number of flags collected in under a certain time) would move on to the second stunt. The rest would (8) _____ eliminated. The second stunt is meant to challenge the contestants mentally, and usually involves ingesting a revolting animal, such as a cockroach. It (9) _____ also involve getting close to an animal (10) _____ many people would find scary. In later episodes, a common (but not always used) rule was that no one would be eliminated (11) _____ the second stunt; (12) _____, the contestant or team performing the best would (13) _____ a prize, such as a car or a prize package similar in value. The third and (14) _____ stunt often involves doing an extreme type stunt, (15) _____ as flipping a car or escaping from a sinking aircraft fuselage. The player who wins this round wins the prize, usually US$50,000.

Writing: a formal letter

A **LETTER** is written in response to the situation outlined in the question, which should be consistently appropriate for the specified target reader. You may be asked to write formal or informal letters.

SPOTLIGHT CHECKLIST

PAPER 2, PARTS 1 and 2 Question types

Remember:

- Read the instructions carefully and identify the key words so that you know what you have to do.

- Use the input material appropriately in your answer.

- The focus is on content, effective organisation of the input material, appropriacy of the piece of writing to the intended audience, and accuracy.

- You need to adopt an appropriate style, layout, register and tone so that the effect on the target reader is positive.

- Pay attention to organisation and cohesion, as well as accuracy of language. Evidence of a range of language is also required, which means building on key words from the input rather than lifting whole segments.

- Part 1 also offers you the opportunity to expand on the information given and enables you to demonstrate your range of language.

1 PAPER 2, PART 1 **Look at the question below.**

You have recently seen the following advertisement for a research scientist to join a scientific cruise in the Antarctic. Read the advertisement below, and the notes you have made, then write your letter of application, and say why you think you would be the most suitable person to go on the cruise.

Are you looking for something completely different to do between November and March? Do you have a science degree? Do you like adventure, exploration, and discovery? Can you cope with extreme conditions? If so, we may be looking for you. We are a team of highly motivated research scientists organising an expedition to Antarctica next year to find out more about how climate change is affecting the delicate ecosystems at the South Pole. Write to us now if you think this is for you.

Yes!

I've been mountain climbing in Tibet!

Main interests are environment and ecology!

Environmental Biology

Ever since I was a kid!

2 Before you begin remember to ask the following questions.

1 Who am I writing to?
2 What tone or register should I use?
3 What two things do I need to do?
4 What points should I include?
5 What shall I say in each paragraph?

3 Write your answer in 180–220 words in an appropriate style. You should use your own words as far as possible.

4 Eureka!

EXAM MENU

Reading:	Paper 1, part 4
Listening:	Paper 4, part 4
Speaking:	Paper 5, part 4
Use of English:	Paper 3, parts 3 and 5
Writing:	Paper 2, part 1

Getting started

1 Group the words below into the appropriate category (A–E). Some words fit into more than one category.

A Prehistory and palaeontology
B Modern science and technology
C Future exploration and discovery
D Science of the mind and psychology
E Space and astronomy

androids	artificial intelligence (AI)	artificial life	black hole
cells	cortex	Cretaceous	dark matter
DNA	$E=MC^2$	erosion	evolution
extraterrestrial	forensic	fossils	genetics
geology	grey matter	laboratory	microchip
Jurassic	tyrannosaurus rex	nanotechnology	neurology
robotic implants	supernova	sci-fi (science fiction)	virtual reality

2 Which words above mean the following …?

a The study of fossils in order to learn about the history of life on earth. _____
b A robot that looks like a human. _____
c The science of working with microscopic things. _____
d A being from another planet. _____
e The substance which determines the characteristics of a living being. _____
f The scientific study of the human mind and the reasons for people's behaviour. _____
g The outer layer of the brain. _____
h Material that cannot be seen, but is believed to form a large part of the universe. _____
i Technology which is involved in making machines work in a similar way to how the human mind works. _____
j Another name for our brain, or intelligence. _____

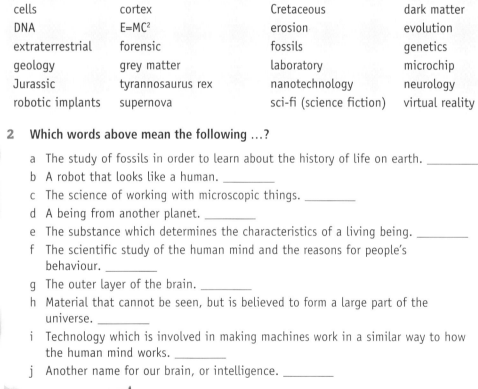

Reading: scanning texts

PAPER 1, PART 4 Scanning texts for information

Tips

- Read the questions carefully, to make sure that you understand any detail or opinion expressed.

- Scan the text to locate the section which expresses the ideas in the particular question.

- Disregard parts of the text which may seem to reflect similar ideas but do not express the whole of the question.

Practise:

- scanning texts for specific information, such as dates and times, rather than reading the whole of the text;

- reading a wide range of articles and reviews in which different people discuss work, books, films etc.

1   PAPER 1, PART 4 **You are going to read an article on the science of persuasion. For questions 1–15, choose from the sections (A–D). The sections may be chosen more than once.**

In which section are the following suggested?

- the means of communication affects how easily someone can be persuaded.   1 _____
- a positive, confident attitude helps you to be more convincing.   2 _____
- people can be more easily persuaded when they're tired.   3 _____
- women respond more positively to personal contact.   4 _____
- how you say something is more important than the words you use.   5 _____
- certain tactics fail once people understand what you're trying to do.   6 _____
- making people feel bad about themselves is not an effective means of persuasion.   7 _____
- you should avoid confrontation after a hard day's work.   8 _____
- communication by email can be more effective between highly competitive men.   9 _____
- people who are angry about an injustice can be manipulated.   10 _____
- asking your target to perform a mental task before you approach your main subject can be effective. 11 _____
- you should instil a sense of urgency in your target's mind.   12 _____
- men and women are essentially different in the way they communicate with members of their own sex. 13 _____
- you should convince people there's a solution to their problem.   14 _____
- self-control plays a major role in how susceptible someone is to persuasion.   15 _____

The Science of Persuasion

Psychologists have long been fascinated by persuasion – why some people are more persuasive than others and why some strategies work where others fail. We bring together some recent insights into the science of persuasion.

Reporting by Dan Jones and Alison Motluk

A Hunger is a powerful thing, but how many times have you reached for a quick snack, only to regret it when it's lying heavily in your stomach? Just as your standards for food quality can slip when your stomach is empty, so you should avoid engaging in argument or doing battle with sales people when your mental batteries are running low. Conversely, if you're trying to be persuasive, strike when your target is running low on mental energy.

Edward Burkley of Oklahoma State University in Stillwater studied the impact of cognitive exhaustion on the resistance levels of 78 students. The plan was to try to convince them to accept one month's summer holiday instead of three. Half the students came to the study fresh. But the other half first had to complete a self-control task in which they wrote down all thoughts that came into their heads while suppressing any thoughts about a white bear.

This task, Burkley argued, would use up some of their reserves of self-control. He found that the students who had performed the white bear task were less resistant to the idea of giving up two months of holiday.

B In this fast-paced world, we seldom have time for face-to-face meetings. Rosanna Guadagno of the University of Alabama and Robert Cialdini of Arizona State University have been comparing the persuasive power of online communication with face-to-face meetings.

In a study published in 2002, Guadagno and Cialdini had a group of students discuss the introduction of new exams. The group was split into same-sex couples. Unbeknown to the subjects, each pair included an accomplice of the experimenters whose role was to provide arguments in favour of the idea. Half the discussions took place in an online chatroom, the other half sat face-to-face.

While overall men rated the proposals similarly whether they participated in the electronic or face-to-face sessions, women in face-to-face sessions rated them more highly than those who only took part online. Guadagno and Cialdini suggest this is because groups of women tend to form communal bonds and reach agreement. Electronic communication disrupts the exchange of social cues women use to establish a communal bond and is therefore less conducive to persuasion.

On the other hand groups of men typically try to establish their competence and independence, which can lead to competitive encounters. When two men who have not met before debate a point, online interaction is about as persuasive as face-to-face. But if they have met and had a competitive exchange, subsequent face-to-face meetings are less productive, whereas online exchanges fare far better. So while online communication can prevent women 'connecting', it can help men suppress competitive urges that hamper persuasion.

C It was midnight when the knock came at the door. It was 'Paul', a 'neighbour', who'd 'just moved in'. He spoke non-stop, without pause or hesitation, detailing a problem with a truck that had run out of gas and his need for $20, which he would, of course, return first thing in the morning. Later, Kurt often looked back and wondered just how it was he got taken in so easily. 'Paul' was a master of his craft: Kurt later learnt that four other people on the street had also been taken in by the con.

Maybe we shouldn't be so surprised when things like this happen. Persuasion, it turns out, may have as much to do with how you say something as what you're saying. And the less time you're allowed to think about the content, the more the style of delivery matters. At least, those are the findings of two marketing professors who decided to tease style and substance apart.

John Sparks at the University of Dayton in Ohio and Charles Areni at the University of Sydney, Australia, asked 118 undergraduates to read a transcript of a testimonial about a scanner. In one version, the speaker used hesitations like 'I mean' and 'ummm'; in the other, he used none. They also gave half the students enough time to read it thoroughly, while the others got just 20 seconds, to see how limiting a person's understanding of the substance would alter the persuasiveness of the style.

The researchers found that in both versions style was important. When hesitant language was used, people

were less easily convinced that this was a scanner worth buying – even when it was a better scanner at a lower price. Style was especially important, the researchers found, when time was limited. 'If you can't pay attention to what the speaker is saying,' Sparks says, 'you pay attention to how they say it.'

D Angering people may seem like an odd way to go about persuading them, but according to Monique Mitchell Turner, a communications professor at the University of Maryland, College Park, it is seriously underrated as a tool of persuasion.

Much study has gone into how emotions aid persuasion. The best known and most studied is fear. It serves well in campaigns that try to steer you clear of certain activities, like smoking. But fear doesn't always work, says Turner, and over time, people become more resistant to scare tactics. The same applies to guilt. It can be effective (think of maternal guilt), but not once people clue into the fact that they're being manipulated. Worse, it has to be carefully calibrated: too much and people resist. 'We don't want people telling us we're bad people,' says Turner.

Anger is different. For one thing, it's focused on someone else's misdeeds, not your own. Also, it's a very utilitarian emotion, she says, usually in response to a perceived injustice. 'Anger makes people feel empowered,' Turner says. There has been a long debate, she says, about whether anger can be constructively harnessed. In studying groups that employ anger as a tactic – most notably animal rights groups such as *People for the Ethical Treatment of Animals*, as well as environment organisations and even political campaigns – she has found that, given the right conditions, it can.

First, people have to be convinced that the issue is relevant to them, that it affects them or their children or their community. At that point, says Turner, you need to hammer home what's wrong with the world as it is. Once you have got people roiled up, you can offer them a way to remedy the situation.

Language development:
vocabulary in context

1 Look back at the text on pages 26–27 and find words and phrases which mean the following.

a person you are trying to persuade _____

b connected with the process of knowing and understanding _____

c trying to stop, block out _____

d assistant in doing something secretively _____

e connected with sharing, being part of a group _____

f helpful in leading towards (a goal) _____

g obstruct _____

h trick in which someone pretends to be something he/she is not _____

i description of something and how it works _____

j balanced _____

Key word: *tell*

2 Complete the following sentences with a suitable phrase with *tell*.

1 Lynette remained calm throughout most of her training, but as the day of the race drew near, the pressure _____.

2 'These two cars are so alike, it's impossible to _____!'

3 'Come on, what have you done? I promise I won't _____ you.'

4 'So, what happened?' 'Well, I'm not absolutely certain, but _____, George asked her to marry him and Fiona turned him down!'

5 'Now, I know you said this would happen, so don't say " _____ "'!

6 It looks as though i-pods and MP3s will render CDs obsolete, but _____.

7 'Does Alice like Jane?' 'You _____ with Alice; one minute she likes you, the next, she doesn't want to know you.'

8 'I wouldn't trust Alex, if I were you. She's a bit of a _____, and is bound to talk to Mum.'

3 The phrases below are all parts of 'colour idioms'. Decide which colour (*red, blue, green* or *black*) completes each one, and then place them in the appropriate colour spot at the bottom of this page.

a She appeared out of the _____.

b I've spent too much money and I'm in the _____.

c He's got _____ fingers; he's good with plants.

d When people throw their litter into my garden, I really see _____!

e You can talk until you're _____ in the face, but I won't change my mind.

f There's a _____ mark against you, after you were cruel to that dog.

g The girls were caught _____ handed trying to steal the exam papers.

h I'm sick of all the _____ tape involved in trying to get a visa to visit that country!

i There's a lot of _____ humour in that comedy series, and so it doesn't appeal to everyone's tastes.

j You're so lucky to be going to the Maldives! I'm _____ with envy!'

k I've been feeling so _____ ever since Oliver left me. I miss him so much!

l Stop moaning and be happy with what you've got! Remember, the grass looks _____ on the other side!

m My husband doesn't very often surprise me, but once in a _____ moon, he'll do something really special!

n Ian's on Mr Smith's _____ list for losing all those files this morning!

o The police thought they had found important evidence, but it turned out to be a _____ herring!

p The news of Harry's failure came like a bolt from the _____, and shocked us all.

4 Now colour each spot, to help you visually recall these phrases.

red
_____
_____
_____
_____
_____

blue
_____
_____
_____
_____
_____

black
_____
_____
_____

green
_____
_____

Grammar: the future

1 Decide which sentence in each of the following pairs is the most appropriate in the context given.

1 Tim, I need to talk to you!
   a *What are you doing this afternoon?*
   b *What will you do this afternoon?*

2 When you arrive in Paris,
   a *Georges will wait for you.*
   b *Georges will be waiting for you.*

3 I've got five minutes' break now, so …
   a *I think I'll phone Paul.*
   b *I'm phoning Paul.*

4 Annie, are you free on Saturday?
   a *We'll have a party!*
   b *We're having a party!*

5 Oh, no! My pen's run out of ink!
   a *What am I doing now?*
   b *What am I going to do now?*

6 By this time next week,
   a *I'll go to a beach in Rhodes.*
   b *I'll be lying on a beach in Rhodes.*

7 Boys, stop doing that, or
   a *I'll get angry!*
   b *I'm getting angry!*

2 Circle the most appropriate word or phrase in italics.

a Wait here, as he'll be back *in ten minutes / after ten minutes*.
b Right! I'm off. See you *in three weeks' time / three weeks later*!
c You can't move in on Friday. The decorators won't have finished *until then / by then*!
d Don't hesitate to contact me *as soon as / at the time* the baby is born.
e Well, Dave is going to call me to confirm, so we won't do anything *until then / by then*.

3 PAPER 3, PART 5 For questions 1–8, complete the second sentence so that it has a similar meaning to the first sentence, using the word given. Do not change the word given. You must use between three and six words, including the word given.

1 'What do you intend to do about your appalling school grades, Matt?'
   GOING

   'Your grades are appalling, Matt! What _____ them?'

2 Peter will definitely pass his driving test.
   BOUND

   Peter _____ his driving test.

3 The future of the sport is looking uncertain.
   HOLD

   No one knows _____ for the sport.

4 We're celebrating the company's tenth anniversary next month.
   BUSINESS

   Next month, the company _____ for ten years.

5 'I'll see you outside the cinema at eight o'clock tonight.'
   WAITING

   I _____ the cinema at eight o'clock tonight.'

6 Scientists have almost discovered how to make objects invisible.
   POINT

   Scientists _____ how to make objects invisible.

7 'Dave's available to help us move house next weekend.'
   COMING

   'Dave _____ with the move next weekend.'

8 'Be careful! The building's about to collapse!'
   TO

   'Look out! The building _____ collapse!'

Listening: getting the gist

PAPER 4, PART 4 Multiple-matching tasks

Remember:

- In this part of the Listening Paper, you need to complete two multiple-matching tasks, each with a different focus.

- You'll hear five different speakers, but they talk about a linked theme.

Tips

- To answer well, you need to display different aspects of gist understanding.

- Choose your own strategy for tackling these tasks. You will only hear the monologues twice. You can attempt one task on each listening, or both simultaneously. You must complete both tasks, however, by the end of the second listening.

1 ⌐ 4.1 PAPER 4, PART 4 Listen to five different people talking about the connection between science fiction and science. While you listen, you must complete both tasks.

Task One

For questions **1–5**, choose the person who is speaking from the list **A–H**.

A a writer

B a science teacher

C a student

D a film critic

E a research scientist

F a marketing executive

G a doctor

H a sociologist

Speaker 1	1
Speaker 2	2
Speaker 3	3
Speaker 4	4
Speaker 5	5

Task Two

For questions **6–10**, choose what each speaker is expressing from the list **A–H**.

A Science fiction sometimes overlooks the potential negative implications of future technological developments.

B Diverse scientific ideas are given expression in science fiction.

C Science fiction films sometimes reflect current scientific research.

D Fiction has no place in scientific development.

E Scientific progress would have been slower without the aid of fiction.

F Interest in the one can generate interest in the other.

G The fiction allows scientific creativity to flow without restraint.

H Science fiction lacks realism.

Speaker 1	6
Speaker 2	7
Speaker 3	8
Speaker 4	9
Speaker 5	10

Speaking: three-way task

1 Refresh your memory by looking at the part 3 Speaking Paper task which appears in Unit 3 (page 22).

Create an alternative question to follow that task, which will be addressed to both candidates for discussion.

_____

_____

_____

_____

_____

2 Form an answer to your question. Think about ways of expanding it.

3 Answer the following question, and think of questions you could ask your partner to include them in the discussion.

> An increasing number of people are warning of the dangers of using mobile phones. Are we likely to get rid of them and, if so, what will be the consequences?

PAPER 5, PART 4 Follow-on questions

After you have completed part 3, you will be asked a follow-on question, related in some way to what you've been talking about. It is useful to be able to:

1 Predict the kind of question you might be asked.

2 Think of things to say.

3 Make use of points raised in part 3.

Use of English: prefixes

SPOTLIGHT CHECKLIST

PAPER 3, PART 3 Using stem words

Remember:

- You need to be able to effectively use prefixes, suffixes, compounds and any other alterations necessary to form words from stem words.

- You should focus on the context in order to decide which type of word (noun, verb, adjective or adverb) is required in each gap.

- You need to demonstrate understanding of the text as a whole in order to recognise when a negative idea is being expressed.

Tips

- Check the context for negative ideas. You may need to use a negative prefix.

- Check that the word you've formed fits into the context of the text as a whole.

- Check your spelling! A misspelt word will lose you marks.

1 Scan the text below, and identify any gaps which will need negative prefixes.

2 PAPER 3, PART 3 **For questions 1–10, read the text below. Use the word given in capitals at the end of some of the lines to form a word that fits in the gap in the same line.**

Dirt is Good for You!

It would be wrong to call dairy farming a dirty job. But workers on dairy farms do have to deal with vast quantities of manure. In fact, they (1) _____ end up breathing in a lot of dust consisting largely of dried manure, along with all the bacteria that grew in it. That sounds (2) _____, and in some ways it is, but it does have one benefit: dairy farmers are as much as five times less likely to develop lung cancer.

As strange as it sounds, (3) _____ are starting to uncover some (4) _____ links between our exposure to dirt and germs, and our risk of cancer later in life. Children who attend day care in their first few months are much less likely to develop leukaemia than those who stay at home, for instance, while some tuberculosis vaccines reduce the risk of skin cancer. Such (5) _____ point towards a curious possibility: one way to avoid dying of cancer may be a hefty dose of germs.

The notion that (6) _____ dirty has benefits may ring a bell. Researchers have been debating the 'hygiene hypothesis' for years, but it is (7) _____ discussed as an explanation for the rising incidence of allergies and asthma in developed countries, not cancer. The idea is that our immune systems evolved to conduct a (8) _____ war on pathogens, parasites, and other microbes, but modern lifestyles mean we face fewer threats. This throws our immune systems out of kilter, making them prone to (9) _____ to certain stimuli like pollen or peanuts.

Now some researchers are starting to wonder whether the higher incidence of certain cancers in affluent populations – including breast cancer, lymphoma, and melanoma – might also have something to do with sanitised, infection-free living. If they're right, the (10) _____ are huge.

1	INEVITABLE
2	HEALTH
3	EPIDEMIOLOGY
4	EXPECT
5	FIND
6	LIVE
7	TYPICAL
8	CEASE
9	REACT
10	IMPLY

Writing: an article

1 Read through the following question, and underline the key parts of the input material you would need to include in an answer.

PAPER 2, PART 1

> A consumer magazine has asked readers to send in articles about how they see the future for high street shops. Read the extract below and comments from members of the public, and write an article for the magazine, referring to the points raised and describing your own view of the future of shopping.

In a survey conducted last month, many people suggested that the days of the high street store are numbered. Below are some comments made to our reporter. Read them, and send us your views in an article entitled, 'Is high street shopping a thing of the past?

'It's so much easier to order my books online!'

'You can find things reasonably priced, and you save time.'

'Shopping is one of my favourite activities, and I love to browse.'

'Online shopping means avoiding parking fees, and crowds.'

'Going shopping gives me the chance to meet up with friends.'

PAPER 2, PART 1 Analysing and organising input material

Remember:

- In part 1 of the Writing Paper, the question may contain input material of up to 150 words.

Tips

- Analyse the material and organise the points you need to form your answer.

- Make a plan which addresses all the points required by the question.

- Underline the key parts of the question and input material, and use these to make your plan.

- Arrange the points into paragraphs, using language to link your ideas effectively.

2 Using the points you've underlined and the outline below, prepare a plan for an article in answer to the question.

Outline plan for an article:
'Is high street shopping a thing of the past?'

Paragraph 1:

Paragraph 2:

Paragraph 3:

Paragraph 4:

3 Write your article, in 180–220 words, in an appropriate style.

Safe and sound?

EXAM MENU

Reading: Paper 1, part 2
Listening: Paper 4, part 2
Use of English: Paper 3, parts 4 and 5
Speaking: Paper 5, part 1
Writing: Paper 2, part 1

Getting started

1 Use the clues 1–15 below to fill in the grid horizontally. What phrase connected with crime detection is formed in the grey central column?

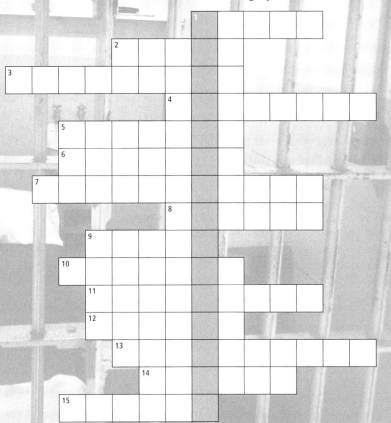

Clues

1 The crime of deceiving people in order to gain something, such as money.

2 The crime of setting fire to property, to intentionally cause destruction.

3 Term used to describe illegal computer software.

4 Judge's decision regarding punishment for a crime.

5 Illegal way of gaining information from someone else's computer.

6 To admit to having committed a crime, or done something wrong.

7 To make someone appear guilty of a crime.

8 To decide in a court of law that someone is not guilty of a crime.

9 A set of instructions secretly placed in a computer which destroys or copies information in order to cause problems to users.

10 The opposite of clue 8.

11 To show or suggest that someone is involved in a crime.

12 The crime of intentionally killing someone.

13 The crime of taking someone and holding them captive in order to gain money from their family.

14 Someone who suffers as a result of something bad happening to them.

15 To state officially (usually in a police station) that someone may be guilty of a crime.

Reading: gapped texts

1 **PAPER 1, PART 2** You are going to read an article from a newspaper on page 35. Six paragraphs have been removed from the extract. Choose from the paragraphs A–G the one which fits each gap 1–6. There is one extra paragraph which you do not need to use.

newspaper on page 35

A

'They've not much to look forward to,' Platt admits, 'and so something like today's event really does give them a focus. In many ways, it's not so much a luxury as a lifesaver. When the Meerkatz last played, we had no reports that evening of any prisoner self-harming. These kinds of things make them feel better about themselves, it lifts their spirits. That's very encouraging to us.'

B

Back in the hall, it's almost five o'clock now. A side door opens, and the national treasure finally emerges. The crowd immediately start shouting: 'WHO ARE YOU? WHO ARE YOU?' but it's good-natured and fun, and after a flurry of 'sorrys', Bragg accompanies the Meerkatz and all seven finalists in a shambolic version of 'Route 66', twirling the arsonist round and round with an outstretched arm. So whipped up in the atmosphere does he become that, as the band segues into 'Johnny B Goode', he removes his jacket and, uncharacteristically, indulges in the kind of overly elbowed dance familiar to all drunken uncles of a certain age. 'I'm playing with the Pogues in Manchester tomorrow night,' he tells the cheering, jeering crowd at one point. 'I can't see it getting any wilder than this, can you?'

C

'In the past,' Platt tells me, 'we've found art therapy to be highly beneficial for inmates. A lot of the women we have here suffer from mental health disorders, or from drug problems, and a great many of them self harm. For all sorts of reasons, then, these are very damaged women, and while we can offer no magic cure, we have found that by engaging their creative side we can often help them, if you like, "escape" their surroundings. Because nobody controls your thoughts, do they?'

D

'I never ask the prisoners I meet why they are inside,' he responds tartly. 'When I'm with them, I'm dealing with them strictly as individuals. What they did to get themselves in here in the first place is none of my business. I don't want to judge them on that, not least because they've been judged on it already – they're banged up, aren't they? And anyway, these instruments aren't presents, they're a challenge, a challenge for them to try to make something of themselves. My hope is that they will see this as an opportunity to take that first step on the path back to society.'

PAPER 1, PART 2 Following a line of argument in a text

Remember:

- Read through the whole text before attempting the task, to get an idea of the development of the text.

- Read through all of the options before choosing an answer.

- One opinion may be followed by an opposing point of view, so look out for this.

E

'It's all very well practising the song in my cell, like,' she tells me afterwards, scratching at the self-inflicted scars that line her arms like irregular train tracks, 'but on stage, with all the lights, the microphone and the crowd – well, that's another story.'

F

The singer-songwriter Billy Bragg was supposed to be here an hour ago in his role as figurehead of the Jail Guitar Doors initiative, bringing with him £1600 worth of donated musical instruments, but he is currently stuck in traffic on a motorway far, far away. By the time he does finally turn up, huffing and puffing and full of apology, many of the congregated prisoners here will very likely have already made bail. But few right now are lamenting his tardiness. As the Meerkatz reach the climax of the Band Aid Christmas perennial, seven young women congregate on the side of the stage, each of them glammed up for their moment in the spotlight, and anxious for the microphone.

G

The Guy's Marsh project went well, so much so that when Bragg was later invited to the NME Awards he decided to use the event to give the campaign some necessary oxygen. Taking the stage, he told the assembled wealthy rock stars of his plans to raise sufficient funds to get acoustic guitars into every prison in the country, and that he would be willing to accept any and all donations. 'People were very kind, very generous indeed,' he says.

BEHIND BARS: Bragg to bring sound of music to prisons

As part of a unique initiative, Billy Bragg (with a little help from Mick Jones and others) wants to get musical instruments into all of Britain's prisons. But to the Bard of Barking, these aren't gifts: they're potential lifesavers.

Nick Duerden reports

On a makeshift stage that, on any other day, is merely storage space within a cavernous gym hall, a band called the Meerkatz are halfway through a spirited rendition of 'Do They Know It's Christmas?' The singer is a healthcare worker by day here at Styal women's prison in Wilmslow, near Manchester. If the crowd seems more appreciative than one would expect of an audience at three o'clock on a freezing winter's afternoon, it's because it is made up exclusively of inmates who would otherwise be doing, according to prisoner Adele, 'boring stuff like learning how to read and write'.

1 [...]

When Bragg last visited a prison, as part of his year-long trek around Her Majesty's establishments proffering musical gifts as incentives for self-betterment, it was to Pentonville in late November. There, in a small room far from the din and clang of the cells, a group of no more than a dozen inmates turned up to show appreciation. In Styal, however, it's more like 175, and they've taken over the darkened gym for an afternoon of raucous celebration. The Head of Interventions here, Annick Platt, thought it would be a good idea to make a day of it, and ran an X Factor-like competition offering inmates a chance to appear on stage alongside today's visiting national treasure, irrespective of the fact that many of the entrants had little idea precisely who the national treasure was. 'Billy who?' asks Adele. Perhaps tellingly, Adele is just 24.

2 [...]

It is only through art, she continues, that many are able to express themselves at all. Those too shy or too awkward to talk of their pain and suffering with social workers can instead articulate it in painting or poetry, examples of which adorn the walls throughout the complex. After today, they'll also be able to express themselves in song.

3 [...]

Which is why the atmosphere on stage right now is close to fever pitch. True, none of the seven women who won last week's contest is ever likely to impress Simon Cowell with their vocal prowess, but few could fault their enthusiasm. This line-up of excitable, giggling twenty-somethings includes an arsonist and a repeat drug offender. One by one, they come to the centre of the stage and accompany the band on a selection of current hits and old favourites. One of the less serious offenders, twenty-one-year-old Alicia, a heavyset girl with a head full of tight curls and a voice of considerable volume, lets loose on an almighty rendition of Lulu's 'Shout' until stage fright descends, and she runs off, furious with herself.

4 [...]

Alicia, who has never heard of Billy Bragg either but is grateful for his 'support', was raised in a succession of care homes across the north-east of England, and says that anger is her most voluble emotion: 'That's when I'm most likely to sing, when I'm angry. It's how I unstress myself.'

5 [...]

Jail Guitar Doors, Bragg will later explain to me over a meal in a deserted Indian restaurant, is an independent initiative aiming to supply musical equipment to inmates of Her Majesty's prisons nationwide via donations. Taking its name from the B-side of The Clash's 1978 single 'Clash City Rockers', Jail Guitar Doors came into being in the early part of last year after the singer received a letter from Malcolm Dudley, a prison rehabilitation officer at Guy's Marsh in Dorset, asking for help in getting musical instruments into prison on the conviction that they could do good, and perhaps even affect long-term change. Bragg had already undertaken a similar initiative in a hospice, helping dying women articulate their terror of leaving behind family members through music.

6 [...]

'It's not easy getting things like guitars into prisons,' he points out, 'because there's the fear that they could be used as weapons – although they never yet have, to my knowledge. I've spent much of the past twelve months giving the same spiel over and over again to each new governor, and slowly but surely the message is getting out there, and people are becoming increasingly receptive. With good reason, too.' He gives an example. Of those prisoners at Guy's Marsh who actively participated in music sessions before they were paroled, only 10 to 15 per cent have since re-offended. The national average is 61 per cent. 'So there's your proof,' he says. 'It works.'

Language development: verbs followed by particles

1 Choose the best answer to complete the following sentences.

1 'Please _____ from standing on your seats.'
  a deter   b refrain
  c resist   d avoid

2 The evidence _____ Kelvin in the crime.
  a implicated   b involved
  c incriminated   d incorporated

3 Helen _____ Paul of cheating on her, but decided to get proof before saying anything.
  a suspected   b accused
  c blamed   d charged

4 It is believed that the fire resulted _____ a leaking gas pipe.
  a in   b from
  c of   d as

5 Annie finished college last year and now works _____ advertising.
  a on   b in
  c for   d at

6 Kelly blamed her mother-in-law _____ the breakup of her marriage.
  a on   b for
  c of   d in

7 Mai has been working _____ an IT consultant for five years now.
  a in   b of
  c by   d as

8 Ian _____ to having embezzled the company's pension fund.
  a denied   b rejected
  c admitted   d refused

9 Penny was convicted _____ drinking and driving, and had her licence taken away for 12 months.
  a of   b at
  c on   d to

10 Daniel found it hard to _____ with all the paperwork after his boss resigned.
  a get   b attend
  c achieve   d deal

Phrasal verbs with *turn*

2 Decide whether the following definitions are true or false.

1 To *turn in* means to go to bed.   T / F

2 If you *turn to* someone, you attack them.   T / F

3 To *turn* someone *down* means to refuse an offer. T / F

4 If you *turn* someone *in*, you deliver a suspect to the police.   T / F

5 To *turn over* a profit means to lose it.   T / F

6 To *turn* someone *out* is to tell someone to leave the premises.   T / F

7 If you *turn up*, your voice becomes louder.   T / F

8 If you *turn* someone *off*, you kill them.   T / F

Key word: *law*

3 Complete the sentences below with one of the verbs or phrasal verbs in the box.

break	enforce	lay down	obey

1 It is the responsibility of the police to _____ the law.

2 The reformed criminal tried hard to _____ the law, by getting a regular job.

3 If you _____ the law for the first time, you may not be sent to prison.

4 Some parents try to _____ the law with their teenage children, which can cause problems.

4 Match the captions to the correct picture (a–c). There is one extra caption you do not need to use.

1 *'What you're doing is against the law.'*

2 *'Some people believe they are above the law.'*

3 *'You should always remain within the law.'*

4 *'The law of attraction overcomes all obstacles ...'*

Grammar: verbs followed by infinitive or *-ing*

1 Read the article below, and choose the correct form (infinitive with *to* or *-ing*) of the verbs in the box to fill each gap.

board	chase	continue	defend	do	drop	find	kill
head	knock	race	ram	see	steal	tie	

Pirates beware!

A family of four displayed amazing courage yesterday when a band of armed pirates attacked their sailing vessel off the coast of Montevideo in Uruguay.

Mr George Lewis (54), his wife, Joyce and their two sons, Nick (14) and Mark (11), were heading north towards Porto Alegre when they saw a dirty-looking fishing boat (1) _____ towards them. As it drew near, one of the men on board fired shots at the yacht, and ordered Mr Lewis (2) _____ his sails. Mr Lewis refused (3) _____ so, and instead decided (4) _____ the fishing boat.

As the pirates attempted (5) _____ the yacht, Mr Lewis steered into them, managing (6) _____ one of them into the water. However, this only angered the others, who started shooting at him. Afraid that one of the boys would get hurt, Mr Lewis gave up and the men boarded the boat. The eldest one, obviously the leader, instructed the others (7) _____ Mr Lewis up and went below to where the boys and Mrs Lewis were hiding. Nick bravely tried (8) _____ his mother and brother, but the man hit him across the face and threatened (9) _____ them all unless they cooperated.

He hadn't reckoned on Jack. The little dog, enraged by the man's violent outburst, attacked him and bit him in the leg. 'I remember (10) _____ him throw himself in between Nick and the man,' recalled Mark. 'He was amazing. Then we heard this shot, and poor Jack yelped and fell to the ground. They just left him there, but Nick picked him up and laid him in the corner of the cabin.'

The men searched the yacht for money, but they failed (11) _____ very much. Frustrated, they went on (12) _____ the navigation equipment instead, before finally abandoning their efforts and leaving the yacht. 'I lay on the cabin floor terrified that I would find George dead, so you can imagine the relief when I heard his voice calling me to come and untie him!' recalled Mrs Lewis. 'He contemplated (13) _____ after them, but I wasn't having it. We'd been in enough danger for one day, and the police could deal with it better than us, anyway.'

Their first concern was Jack. The brave Yorkshire terrier had been shot in the leg, but fortunately, wasn't badly wounded. Mr Lewis patched him up and the family decided (14) _____ back to Montevideo, where they reported the incident to the police and the British authorities.

Although shaken by their ordeal, they intend (15) _____ their journey until they reach their final destination, Rio de Janeiro.

'We're not going to let a bunch of bullies stop us!' says Mr Lewis, adamantly.

Listening: sentence completion

1   Match the following words connected with prison with their definitions.

A	B
1 probation	a someone serving a prison sentence
2 prison officer	b a person who is responsible for guarding the prisoners
3 parole	c a crime
4 probation officer	d system of deciding whether prison is necessary for a convicted criminal
5 inmate	e a person who is responsible for watching prisoners' progress and advising them
6 offence	f permission for someone to leave prison, provided he behaves well

2   ∩ 5.1 PAPER 4, PART 2 **You will hear a probation officer giving a talk about her work. For questions 1–8, complete the sentences.**

According to the speaker, the probation officer is responsible for assessing (1) _____ an inmate presents to society.

In the prison where she works, the speaker can seek professional advice via a (2) _____.

One of her concerns is the increasing pressure on (3) _____ with regard to paperwork.

The speaker stresses the importance of having (4) _____ with an inmate.

In her opinion, treating each person with (5) _____ is the key to success.

She feels that the profession has received a lot of (6) _____ recently.

According to the speaker, the number of people who re-offend while under supervision is relatively (7) _____.

She advises prospective trainees to be prepared for (8) _____ during their working day.

Use of English: gapped sentences

SPOTLIGHT EXAM GUIDANCE

PAPER 3, PART 4 Finding the right word

In this part of the Use of English Paper, you need to remember that the gapped word is common to all three sentences. Also, remember to:

1 Check the word you choose fits all three sentences, and that you've spelt the word correctly.

2 Check (if the missing word is a noun) whether you need the plural or singular form.

3 Check (if the missing word is a verb) which form is being used – it should be the same in each sentence (i.e. past tense/participle).

1 **PAPER 3, PART 4 For questions 1–5, think of one word only which can be used appropriately in all three sentences.**

1 'So, you can play the piano. Can you play any other _____?' asked John.

The nurse laid out the surgical _____ that would be needed for the operation.

'We were sailing along when suddenly the wind _____ started to go wild.'

2 'You are required by _____ to have a licence for your dog in this country.'

The new teacher decided to lay down the _____ in her first lesson, so the students thought she was really strict.

'You may be a big film star, Brad, but you're not above the _____.'

3 'I could just make out the _____ of a man's face through the darkness.'

Investigators are trying to create a _____ of the murderer's character.

'Since he embarrassed himself at his sister's party, David's been keeping a low _____.'

4 Billy Bragg is filled with the _____ that he can make a difference within British prisons.

He said he was looking forward to the wedding, but his voice lacked _____.

The judge said that although Jane's crime was not serious, this would be her fourth _____ in 12 months, and so the punishment would have to be severe.

5 Oliver was sitting in the coffee shop when suddenly, the man at the next table _____ on him with a knife.

The two men had had too much to drink, and when they started fighting, the landlord _____ them out of the pub.

Matt _____ the page of the magazine, and was amazed to find a photograph of his wife under the headline, 'Woman caught shoplifting'!

Speaking: giving personal information

1 ⌕ 5.2 Listen to a candidate answering the following question: *'What do you like about the town you live in?'* List any useful phrases he uses to talk about:

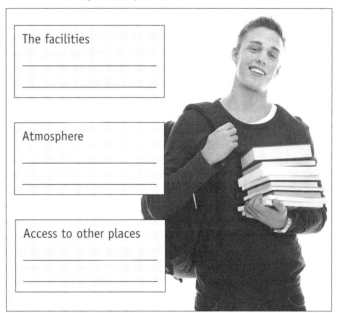

The facilities
_____
_____

Atmosphere
_____
_____

Access to other places
_____
_____

2 Now practise answering the same question about your own town.

SPOTLIGHT CHECKLIST

PAPER 5, PART 1 Talking about yourself

Remember:
• In part 1 of the Speaking Paper, the interlocutor will ask you questions about yourself. You may be asked about your family, work/studies, leisure interests, travel experiences and daily life.

• You need to be able to interact with the interlocutor in a natural manner.

Tips
• Avoid rehearsing speeches, as this is usually obvious, and often inappropriate to specific questions.

Writing: a report

1   A student made the following notes in preparation for answering the question below. Read the question, and the notes below. What is wrong with them?

Possible risks of using mobile phones – electromagnetic radiation affects brain, causes headaches, loss of concentration, increased risk of cancer and Alzheimer's.

→ UK government scientist's report – no evidence found that mobile phones harm health.

→ Scientists suggest children at greater risk – brains not fully developed, more sensitive to radiowaves.

→ 75 per cent of students in school have a mobile phone

→ Teachers should tell them to switch off phones in the classroom.

PAPER 2, PART 1

> The Parents and Teachers Association at the school where you work has expressed concern about the number of children using mobile phones in the school. The principal has sent you an email asking you to write a report on the use of phones by students, the potential dangers they pose, and to make recommendations for improving the situation.
>
> Read the extract, and the comments you have made on it.

Ken,

As you know, several PTA members feel that students are using mobile phones too widely in the school. Could you look into this, and write a report on the number of students using phones, any risks involved in doing so, and what you think could be done about the situation?

Thanks,
Bill

students are told to switch off phones while in school

approximately 75 per cent

dangers unknown, but possible brain damage. Increased risk of disease from long term exposure

Write your **report.**

2   Using the points in the Spotlight checklist above, prepare your own plan in answer to the question.

6 Hale and hearty

EXAM MENU

Reading: Paper 1, part 1
Listening: Paper 4, part 3
Speaking: Paper 5, part 2
Use of English: Paper 3, part 1
Writing: Paper 2, part 2

Getting started

1 Unscramble the anagrams below to find the alternative health therapies.

a *cnurcpeuatu*	**b** tarohaeryapm
c *bearshilm*	**d** *phoomyheat*
e xeroglyleof	**f** emdttianoi

2 Complete the definitions below by writing in the name of each branch of healing or medicine from the list above.

1 _____: the practice of using herbs to treat illness.

2 _____: the treatment of a person's illness or pain by sticking fine needles into their body in specific places.

3 _____: a type of treatment which involves massaging the body with the fragrent essential oils of selected plants, or inhaling their scent.

4 _____: a way of treating sick people that involves prescribing them very small amounts of a substance that produces similar symptoms to the ones they are experiencing.

5 _____: the practice of massaging particular areas of the body, in particular the feet, in order to heal particular organs in the body.

6 _____: the act of remaining in a silent and calm state for a period of time so that you are better able to deal with the problems of everyday life.

3 ◯ 6.1 Listen to three people talking about some alternative health treatments. Match each speaker to one of the treatments listed above.

Speaker 1 _____

Speaker 2 _____

Speaker 3 _____

Reading: understanding written texts (text analysis)

SPOTLIGHT CHECKLIST

PAPER 1, PART 1 Understanding written texts

Tips:

- Try to familiarise yourself with a wide range of sources, registers, topics and lexical fields.

- Practice reading a text quickly for a first overall impression, followed by close reading of the text in order to prevent any misunderstanding.

- Refer to the text when answering a question – don't just choose an answer which sounds plausible or reflects your own ideas.

- Avoid just matching words in the text with words in the question or option.

1   You are going to read three short texts connected to medicine and healing. Scan the texts quickly on page 43 to find out what aspects of healing they deal with.

Text 1 _____

Text 2 _____

Text 3 _____

2   For questions 1–6 choose the answer (A, B, C or D) which you think fits best according to the text.

Text 1:

1 Reflexology works by
  A helping to relieve acute pain and cure chronic illnesses.
  B teaching patients to cope with physical, mental and emotional stress.
  C reducing symptoms that cannot be identified by conventional techniques.
  D releasing tension in the foot that corresponds to blockages in the body.

2 Modern reflexology
  A was developed in the twentieth century.
  B was discovered in ancient times.
  C is not considered effective by modern doctors.
  D can eradicate serious medical problems.

Text 2:

3 Deepak Chopra's main influence for writing this book appears to be
  A the remission of disease in terminally ill patients.
  B a form of ancient Indian healing therapy.
  C Western medicine and scientific discovery.
  D the power of human beings to cure disease.

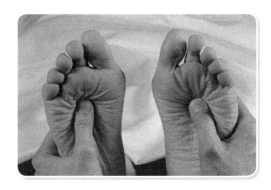

4 The theory behind 'quantum healing' says that
  A we need to re-programme our psychological intelligence.
  B our bodies are intelligent enough to heal themselves.
  C a combination of western and eastern medicine can cure cancer.
  D intellectual thought is the magic behind recovery.

Text 3:

5 Maggots have long been used to clean wounds because
  A they can easily be found on battlefields.
  B they prevent infected tissues from growing.
  C they have antibiotic properties.
  D they increase blood supply to all tissues.

6 Maggots made a comeback when
  A modern medical practices could no longer keep up.
  B they proved to be the best cleaners of infected tissue.
  C they became more effective wound cleaners than surgery.
  D it was realised they were twice as cheap as medications.

3   Look at the reading texts on page 43 and find a word which means the following.

Text 1

1 _____: [adj] a type of therapy that is different from, but can be used with conventional medicine.

2 _____: [n] another word for a doctor or specialist who gives you advice about something medical.

Text 2

3 _____: [adj] something that is not very serious but affects only the surface of the body.

4 _____: [n] the necessary abilities or qualities to do something successfully.

Text 3

5 _____: [v, past tense] full of (something in large numbers, usually unpleasant or unwanted).

6 _____: [phrase] a quality that causes someone to feel disgust.

Reflexology
What is it?

Reflexology helps people of all ages by bringing relief from a wide range of acute and chronic conditions. Reflexology is a complementary therapy that works on the feet to help heal the whole person, rather than simply address symptoms. It works on the basis that reflex areas on the feet and hands are linked to other areas and organs of the body within the same zone. If the feet are placed together, the reflex points on the soles represent a very accurate map of the body.

Benefits

Reflexology is particularly helpful in cases of acute back pain, when body massage has been deemed inadvisable. Reflexology also relieves stress, and is a wonderful way to relax the mind and body. An increasing number of doctors, consultants and other health care professionals recognise and respect reflexology as a well established and effective therapy, and even refer patients to a registered reflexologist for treatment.

History

Reflexology is an ancient method of stimulating the body's own healing forces through foot and hand massage that was used in Ancient Egypt, India and China. The therapy was only introduced to the West at the beginning of the twentieth century, but it was later developed in the 1930s into what is now known as reflexology.

⊰ Quantum Healing ⊱
Exploring the Frontiers of Mind Body Medicine
Written by Deepak Chopra

ABOUT THIS BOOK

Here is an extraordinary new approach to healing by an extraordinary physician-writer – a book filled with the mystery, wonder, and hope of people who have experienced seemingly miraculous recoveries from cancer and other serious illnesses.

Dr Deepak Chopra, a respected New England endocrinologist*, began his search for answers when he saw patients in his own practice who completely recovered after being given only a few months to live. In the mid-1980s he returned to his native India to explore Ayurveda, humanity's most ancient healing tradition. Now he has brought together the current research of Western medicine, neuroscience**, and physics with the insights of Ayurvedic theory to show that the human body is controlled by a 'network of intelligence' grounded in quantum reality***.

Not a superficial psychological state, this intelligence lies deep enough to change the basic patterns that design our physiology – with the potential to defeat cancer, heart disease, and even aging itself. In this inspiring and pioneering work, Dr Chopra offers us both a fascinating intellectual journey and a deeply moving chronicle of hope and healing.

A doctor who specialises in the endocrine system or system of glands that produce hormones which go directly into the bloodstream.

**the study of the nervous system*

***at the level of atomic particles*

Maggots a good thing?

Maggots are now once again gaining respect in the medical field. Their use even has a name, maggot debridement therapy or MDT. Maggots are efficient healers of wounds. This was recognised centuries ago when wounded soldiers whose wounds were infested with maggots healed better than those that were not infested. The reason for this is that the maggots used for this purpose eat dead tissues and leave the healthy, living tissues alone. They also excrete substances which inhibit and may even kill bacteria. This is especially useful in areas with poor blood supply that do not benefit much from antibiotics that cannot reach the area in adequate concentration to do their job.

Maggots have been known for their healing ability since the sixteenth century. Maggot therapy continued until the 1930s when their use in therapy was so common that over 300 hospitals in the US alone were using them. In the 1940s antibiotic therapy and surgical techniques replaced the use of maggots. Their superiority in certain cases to antibiotics was realised in 1989 when they were recognised to be more efficient cleaners of wounds than any other non-surgical treatment.

In order to ensure their sterility, scientists have developed techniques to farm maggots for medical use. The cost of maggot therapy is typically half as much as conventional therapy making it a very cost effective procedure. The only disadvantage of this type of therapy other than the yuck factor is the tickling sensation felt by some patients.

Language development:
vocabulary and idioms

1 Choose the most appropriate response in each of the following situations. Correct the wrong expression or say why it is used incorrectly.

1
> Miriam's been promoted but she's had to take a pay cut too.

  a 'I know – her job has been selling like hotcakes.'

  b 'Well she can't expect to have her cake and eat it!'

2
> Cherie says she is going to give all her savings to charity.

  a 'Anyone who can afford the salt of the earth would do that.'

  b 'I would take that with a large pinch of salt if I were you.'

3
> Have you noticed that Karen keeps inviting her boss round for dinner?

  a 'She obviously knows which way her bread is buttered!'

  b 'That's because butter wouldn't melt on her toast.'

4
> Julian wanted to know if I could lend him some money, but he took out a bank loan last month.

  a 'It smells a bit fishy if you ask me.'

  b 'He probably spilled his beans everywhere.'

5
> I have agreed to take on another project, in addition to managing the last one.

  a 'Well you can't break eggs without making an omelette!'

  b 'I think you've bitten off more than you can chew.'

6
> Jonathon works so hard at his job his family hardly ever sees him.

  a 'That's because he has to bring home the dough in order to make the bacon.'

  b 'If you ask me he's got his finger in the pie – he's next up for promotion.'

Key word: *life*

2 Complete the text that follows with one of the phrases from the box below.

a lifetime's ambition	lay down their lives
a matter of life and death	lifelong friends
a new lease of life	life-jackets
fact of life	life-threatening illness
have the time of their lives	the life and soul of the party

Arnold and Graham were (1) _____
and they were incredibly close – in fact they were so close that I am sure they would have been willing to (2) _____ for each other. Unfortunately, one day doctors diagnosed Arnold with a (3) _____, which they said was due to old age, an inevitable (4) _____. Graham quickly pointed out that there was still time for them to do the things they had always wanted and (5) _____. Arnold had always been (6) _____ and so he suggested they go on a world cruise together, (7) _____ for him. At first their other friends tried to talk them out of it, but when they explained that it was (8) _____, everyone wished them well. To keep them happy, Arnold and Graham promised they would wear their (9) _____ the whole time! The funny thing was that when they came back from the cruise, the doctors announced that Arnold's illness had totally disappeared. It seems that doing the thing he had always wanted to do had given him (10) _____.

Grammar: conditionals

1 Rewrite the following sentences, using the words in brackets.

1 If you went to America, which state would you most like to visit? (were to)

_____

2 If you see Garry in town, can you tell him Jane is looking for him? (should)

_____

3 If you eat all your green vegetables, I'll let you have some dessert. (as long as)

_____

4 If you find a brown wallet anywhere with money in it, it belongs to me. (happen)

_____

5 If Julian had not intervened, Pete and I would probably have had an argument. (but for)

_____

6 If you had been invited to the party, would you have gone? (had)

_____

7 You wouldn't have enjoyed the performance even though you were late. (even if)

_____

2 Complete the gaps in the sentences with a suitable conditional phrase, using the word in brackets.

1 If he _____ (remember) to fill up the car with petrol, he _____ (run out).

2 If he _____ (have) his mobile phone with him, he _____ (be able to) call someone.

3 If he _____ (walk) 10 kilometres, he _____ (be) exhausted.

4 If he _____ (not / drive) out of town, he _____ (get) some petrol easily.

5 If he _____ (take) the train, he _____ (be) there by now.

6 Unless someone _____ (come) by, he _____ (have) a long walk ahead.

7 If he _____ (be) low on petrol, why _____ (he / not) fill up?

8 If a car _____ (run out) of petrol it _____ (stop).

Listening: multiple choice questions

1 🎧 **6.2 PAPER 4, PART 3** You'll hear part of a radio interview in which the medical writer and historian Gordon Bennett is talking about his most recent book. For questions 1–6, choose the answer (A, B, C or D) which fits best according to what you hear.

1 Dr Bennett says that the earliest form of medicine
   A is older than civilisation.
   B began in prehistoric times.
   C is unknown to us.
   D was based on the consumption of plants.

2 As far back as 9000 years ago, the people of ancient India had developed
   A the science of the living.
   B a form of dentistry.
   C cosmetic surgery.
   D a system of learning through study.

3 The first known doctors in ancient Egypt
   A performed surgical operations.
   B were more likely to have been women.
   C kept medical records at least 5000 years ago.
   D acquired knowledge from the Babylonians.

4 Avicenna was
   A the first trained Persian doctor.
   B Persia's most famous philosopher.
   C the most famous Persian in Europe.
   D the writer of an important medical book.

5 Dr Bennett believes
   A that Chinese medicine deserves a chapter of its own.
   B that Chinese medicine is very old and should be modernised.
   C that the use of needles in medicine is dangerous.
   D that acupuncture needs to be taken more seriously in the West.

6 Hippocrates
   A invented new words for illnesses.
   B classified illnesses into categories and stages.
   C did not believe that food affected one's health.
   D discovered many of our modern medicines.

Speaking: comparing pictures

What different aspects of medicine do these pictures show? How might these people feel about what they do?

PAPER 5, PART 2 Comparing pictures

Tips

• Listen carefully to the interlocutor's questions and instructions.

• Refer to the written prompts on the visuals page to remind yourself of what you have to do in the tasks.

• Try to relate the visuals to the tasks rather than simply describe them.

• Speculate about what might be happening or how people might be feeling.

Practise:

• by collecting pictures from newspapers and magazines and comparing them;

• by grouping pictures into sets and imagining what you might be asked to talk about in a part 2 exam task.

1

2   3

1   ∩ 6.3 Listen to a student comparing two pictures. Tick the expressions she uses.

  • These pictures both show ... ☐
  • What they both have in common is ... ☐
  • While this picture shows ... the other ... ☐
  • The main similarity/difference between the two pictures is that ... ☐
  • They must be feeling ... ☐
  • If I were him/them, I would ... ☐
  • The message they are trying to get across is ... ☐

2   Imagine you are student B being asked to comment on the pictures above. Answer the following question. Try to speak for about 30 seconds. Which of the pictures shows the most effective form of treatment in your opinion?

3   Practise comparing two of the pictures on page 170 and say how exercise affects different people. Make sure you speak for one full minute.

Use of English: multiple-choice cloze

PAPER 3, PART 1 Identifying collocations

Remember:
- In this part of the Use of English Paper, the question types may test phrasal level gaps, such as collocations and set phrases or meaning at sentence level or beyond, with some processing of the text required.

Tips
- Try to develop an efficient personal system for recording the new vocabulary.

- Record information about complementation and collocations of words learnt.

- When studying vocabulary in preparation for the paper, pay attention to collocation, the shades of meaning differentiating sets of similar words, and complementation (such as whether words are followed by a certain preposition, or by a gerund or an infinitive).

1   PAPER 3, PART 1 **For questions 1–12, read the text below and decide which answer (A, B, C or D) best fits each gap.**

Echinacea

Perhaps the most popular medicinal herb being used today, Echinacea has had hundreds of journal articles written about it during the last century. Echinacea is an attractive perennial flower, native to North America, with pretty white, pink or purple daisy-like flowers, which grows up to five feet tall. To the Native American Indians, it was a (1) _____ flower and was (2) _____ used by them for innumerable medicinal purposes. In fact at least 14 different tribes used echinacea for colds, infections, inflammations, sore throats, coughs, tonsillitis and even snakebite.

Echinacea has long been used for its anti-viral, anti-bacterial, and anti-microbial (3) _____, but more than ever the efficaciousness of echinacea in stimulating the body's immune system is being (4) _____. Experiments have shown that polysaccharides within the plant can increase the response of white blood cells to (5) _____ an attack on invading organisms by up to 40 per cent. Echinacea also causes an increase in the number of immune cells and (6) _____ their response. Many users of echinacea have claimed that, by (7) _____ doses of the plant at the first symptoms of a cold or flu, the symptoms disappear within 24 hours.

It has also been shown that echinacea is able to inhibit the (8) _____ of an enzyme which is secreted by invading bacteria so that they can (9) _____ themselves to healthy cells and destroy them. By suppressing the enzyme, echinacea helps the cells (10) _____ up a more effective defence. And not only is the plant useful in helping us to (11) _____ the common cold virus – echinacea has been seen to have an activating effect on macrophages, which (12) _____ out and destroy cancer cells, and helps to produce interferon, which inhibits the growth of tumour cells.

1	A worshipped	B specialist	C holy	D sacred
2	A usually	B widely	C mostly	D generally
3	A assets	B properties	C resources	D features
4	A valued	B absorbed	C claimed	D recognised
5	A launch	B establish	C set	D give
6	A speeds up	B brings along	C calls down	D gives off
7	A having	B taking	C getting	D obtaining
8	A responses	B deeds	C actions	D conduct
9	A grip	B glue	C stick	D attach
10	A put	B make	C give	D send
11	A win	B defeat	C conquer	D triumph
12	A find	B seek	C bring	D take

Writing: an essay

PAPER 2, PART 2 Developing an argument

An essay needs to present an argument and give reasons that support it. You'll be expected to give opinions. Effective planning and paragraphing is important in essay writing, as is the correct use of appropriate linking words and phrases. It's essential that you address the points in the question and not just write about an issue which is loosely connected to the topic.

- Feel free to agree or disagree with the statement in the task, or discuss both sides.

- Write appropriate opening and concluding paragraphs.

- Don't try to reproduce a task that you have done in class on the same topic as this is unlikely to address the specific points in the task set.

1   Decide whether you agree or disagree with the Paper 2, part 2 statement on the left below or whether you agree with both sides.

2   Plan your essay to show the development of this argument using some or all of the discussion points.

3   Write your essay (220–260 words).

PAPER 2, PART 2

Prevention is better than cure.

Your class has just held a discussion about health and disease. Your teacher has asked you to write an essay on the above topic, saying whether or not you agree with this statement, and explaining your views. The class discussion has thrown up the following points:

Write your **essay**.

<u>Reasons for the statement</u>

- If you never get ill you don't need treatment.
- A strong immune system is the best defence against any illness.
- Most medicines, or 'cures' destroy the body's ability to heal itself.

<u>Reasons against the statement</u>

- Our immune system cannot protect us from every disease or infection.
- Some diseases are very serious, or fatal, and can only be combated by medical treatment.
- If we can cure the disease, we won't need to worry about what may have caused it.

EXAM MENU

Reading:	Paper 1, part 4
Listening:	Paper 4, part 4
Use of English:	Paper 3, part 2
Speaking:	Paper 5, part 4
Writing:	Paper 2, part 1

Getting started

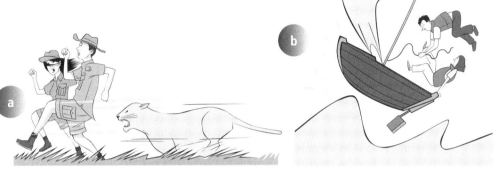

1 Complete the sentences below with a word from the box. More than one answer is possible in some sentences.

cruise	excursion	flight	journey	package holiday
ride	safari	travel	trip	voyage

1 'Matthew, you're back! How was your business _____ to Dusseldorf?'

2 'Anna and David have just been on _____ in Kenya, where they encountered lions!'

3 The group _____ to Meteora leaves daily at 8 o'clock in the morning.

4 'How about coming for a _____ on my motorbike?'

5 'For their anniversary last year, Mum and Dad went on a _____ around the Greek islands.'

6 'I like to have everything arranged for me, so I always go on a _____.'

7 'The _____ from Ostend to Harwich was rather frightening, because the sea was so rough!'

8 'Attention, please! This is the last call for passengers boarding _____ BA452 to Mars.'

9 'Time _____ has always appealed to me; do you think we'll ever be able to do it?'

10 'Ah, I'm exhausted! The bus _____ home today seemed to take forever!'

2 Now match four of the sentences from exercise 1 with the cartoons on this page.

Reading: multiple matching texts

SPOTLIGHT CHECKLIST

PAPER 1, PART 4 Interpreting the question
Remember:

In this part of the Reading Paper, you need to look for information in the text which is relevant to the question, and disregard information which is not relevant.

1 Read the questions carefully, to make sure you understand what kind of information they are asking you for.

2 Pay careful attention to the wording of questions which ask you to look for an opinion or attitude expressed, as these are sometimes misleading.

Practise:

• reading texts to find one specific piece of information, especially ones in which more than one opinion is expressed.

1 PAPER 1, PART 4 **You are going to read part of a tourist brochure offering different kinds of adventure family holidays. For questions 1–15, choose from the holidays (A–D). The holidays may be chosen more than once.**

Which adventure holiday(s) …?

• includes accommodation in unique surroundings	1 _____	
• would you choose if you like observing wildlife	2 _____	3 _____
• offers more luxurious accommodation than the others	4 _____	
• allows visitors time to adapt to the change of environment	5 _____	
• offers you the chance to observe an amazing natural phenomenon	6 _____	
• allows you to sleep 'like the natives'	7 _____	
• require you to travel using unusual modes of transport	8 _____	9 _____
• is centred mainly around watersports	10 _____	
• may enable you to meet some native inhabitants	11 _____	12 _____
• would you choose if you don't want to travel around much	13 _____	
• offer activities which are dependent on external conditions	14 _____	15 _____

A

Amazon Adventure – a family holiday in Brazil

South America is nothing if not a culture shock, and after arriving in Rio we gradually 'acclimatise' with a range of excursions, from the fabled Maracana stadium to the famous Sugar Loaf mountain, reached by cable car. Continuing on to Iguaçu Falls, we explore the Brazilian side of the falls where we will also stop to admire the impressive Itaipu Hydroelectric Plant. The following day there is the option to visit the Argentinean side where you can travel by train, on rafts, by speedboat right up to the thundering cascades and finally by army truck through the jungle where we also hope to visit one of the local tribes and learn about their way of life. We will also visit the TAMAR turtle project that is based here and 'mother nature' permitting, we have the opportunity to take an optional whale watching excursion.

B

Croatian Active Adventure – a family holiday in Croatia

Our home away from home is a family-run pension, a comfortable base where we can relax by the pool after our day's activities and enjoy traditional Dalmatian home-cooked food in the evenings. After experiencing the thrill of white-water rafting down the Cetina River there's time to relax by the pool or take an optional trip following the Cetina Gorge to its natural end in the medieval pirate town of Omis. Next we head back to the Cetina River for a thrilling day of canyoning down water-polished chutes, abseiling down the Gubavica waterfall and bathing in natural basins. Finally, a short drive away from our pension lies Brela, from where we take sea kayaks out to explore coastal caves and swim in the crystal clear waters of the Marskara coastline – the perfect way to end our week.

C

Arctic Ice Adventure – a family holiday in Sweden

A thrilling five-day break in the frozen forests and lakes of Swedish Lapland, with a chance to enjoy a host of winter activities. Try your hand at dog and reindeer sledding, snowmobiling, snowshoeing, and ice fishing and stay overnight in the famous Icehotel. And, weather permitting, there's a very good chance of enjoying one of nature's greatest spectacles: the Northern Lights. Based in the northern outpost of Kiruna, our adventure starts with a dogsled safari. With teams of huskies attached to each sled (plus a skilled local doing the driving!) we 'mush off' into the wilderness. There's also the option of snowmobiling cross-country and over frozen lakes towards Kebnekaise, Sweden's highest peak.

D

Gobi Adventure – a family holiday in Mongolia

Our camp of traditional felt tents known as *gers*, is located in a strikingly beautiful and remote setting in the upper Tuul valley. There's an alpine feel to this area of meadowlands, larch and pine forest which is the southernmost reach of the Siberian Taiga and home to endangered moose and brown bear, plus over 250 species of bird. Inflatable rafts are loaded onto yak carts and we trek upstream before a gentle afternoon's rafting on the Tuul river.

A drive across the vast emptiness of the steppe takes us to our second ger camp on the edge of the Gobi desert, where we'll take a short trek into the sands for an overnight camp experience. Two-humped Bactrian camels are the perfect steed for the desert; and they'll accompany one of our treks to give us the chance of a ride. Wolves, gazelles, ibex and the giant Argali sheep (the largest in the world) inhabit the region. Traditionally a nation of Nomads, many Mongolians still roam the vast open spaces with their flocks and we hope to visit some nomadic families and learn about their lifestyle. These friendly people are proud of their heritage as descendants of warrior leader Ghengis Khan.

Language development:
describing places

1 Choose the best answer to complete the sentences.

1 The sight of the Niagara Falls is positively _____.
   A threatening   B grand
   C breathtaking   D appealing

2 At night, a fog often descends over the river, creating a(n) _____ atmosphere.
   A magical   B eerie
   C attractive   D sober

3 The structure and size of the London Eye is
   _____.
   A industrious   B shoddy
   C awe-inspiring   D dusty

4 The guesthouse had a warm, _____ atmosphere, with floral furnishings and a welcoming fire blazing in the parlour.
   A cosy   B crumbling
   C magical   D grand

2 Complete the following sentences with one of the phrases in the box below. Make any grammatical changes necessary.

by the looks of it	look him in the eye
get a look-in	look the other way
like the look of it	much to look at
look ahead	overlook

1 The weather was getting worse, and she didn't _____, so she went home.

2 'Phil might not have been _____, but I thought he was a really nice guy.'

3 My Dad got on so well with my new boyfriend that they spent all day talking about cars, and I didn't _____!

4 Paula had seen the boy steal the CD and couldn't _____, so shouted, 'Stop thief!'

5 Sarah _____ and said coldly, 'You're a liar!'

6 'As this is the first time you've played truant, Tibbs, I'll _____ it, but don't do it again!' said the headmaster.

7 In any business, it's important to _____ and anticipate changes in the market.

8 Heather and John are together all the time and, _____, there'll be wedding bells soon.

Key word: *road*

3 Make a suitable compound word or phrase using *road* and one of the words in the box to match the definitions below.

block	hog	house	map	rage
show	side	sign	test	works

a restaurant or bar on a main road outside a city or town
   _____

b angry, violent behaviour of car drivers
   _____

c practice of checking that a car is safe to drive
   _____

d the edge of the road
   _____

e someone who drives carelessly without thinking of anyone's safety
   _____

f a guide showing the road network of a particular country
   _____

g repairs that are being carried out on a road
   _____

h point on the road where police are stopping traffic
   _____

i a board next to the road which gives information to drivers
   _____

j group of people who travel round the country, entertaining
   _____

Grammar: inversion

1 Circle the most suitable words in italics in the following sentences.

a Sal assured them that *never would the rope / the rope would never* break.

b At no time *she was aware / was she aware* that he was having an affair.

c Hardly had one group of visitors left *than / when* another arrived.

d Under no circumstances *should you leave / you should leave* the house!

e Not until *he had left / had he left* did she realise how much she loved him.

f Rarely *have we seen / we have seen* strawberries out so early in this area!

g Only Daniel and George *failed / did they fail* their driving test that day.

h No sooner *they had arrived / had they arrived* than Ben went down with the flu.

i On no condition *I am to be / am I to be* disturbed, Miss Sims!

j Only after Laura *had finished / had she finished* did she realise her mistake.

2 Make the following sentences more emphatic by inverting the underlined words. Use the word at the end of each sentence to help you.

1 The details of the scandal <u>were only made known</u> to the public <u>later</u>. WERE

_____

2 She left <u>as soon as we</u> arrived. SOONER

_____

3 <u>The concert had barely started</u> when there was an explosion. BARELY

_____

4 <u>You seldom see</u> cormorants in this part of the country any more. DO

_____

5 <u>You mustn't</u> contact him <u>on any account</u>! NO

_____

6 <u>I have never seen</u> such poor acting! HAVE

_____

7 <u>Gina had scarcely walked</u> into the classroom when her bag split open. HAD

_____

8 <u>He's a musician and also</u> an accomplished artist. ONLY

_____

3 For questions 1–5, complete the second sentence so that it has a similar meaning to the first sentence, using the word given. Do not change the word given. You must use between three and six words, including the word given.

1 No sooner had the fireman come out than the building collapsed.

JUST

The fireman _____ the building collapsed.

2 You won't be allowed into the country until they have checked your passport.

WILL

Not until they _____ be allowed into the country.

3 Shortly after the plane took off, one of its engines failed.

WHEN

Hardly _____ one of its engines failed.

4 Tom never apologised for his rudeness to the teacher.

APOLOGISE

At no _____ for being rude to the teacher.

5 It was only when the bus driver stopped that he realised a passenger was missing.

DID

Only when _____ realise that a passenger was missing.

PLEASE DON'T FEED THE DRIVER

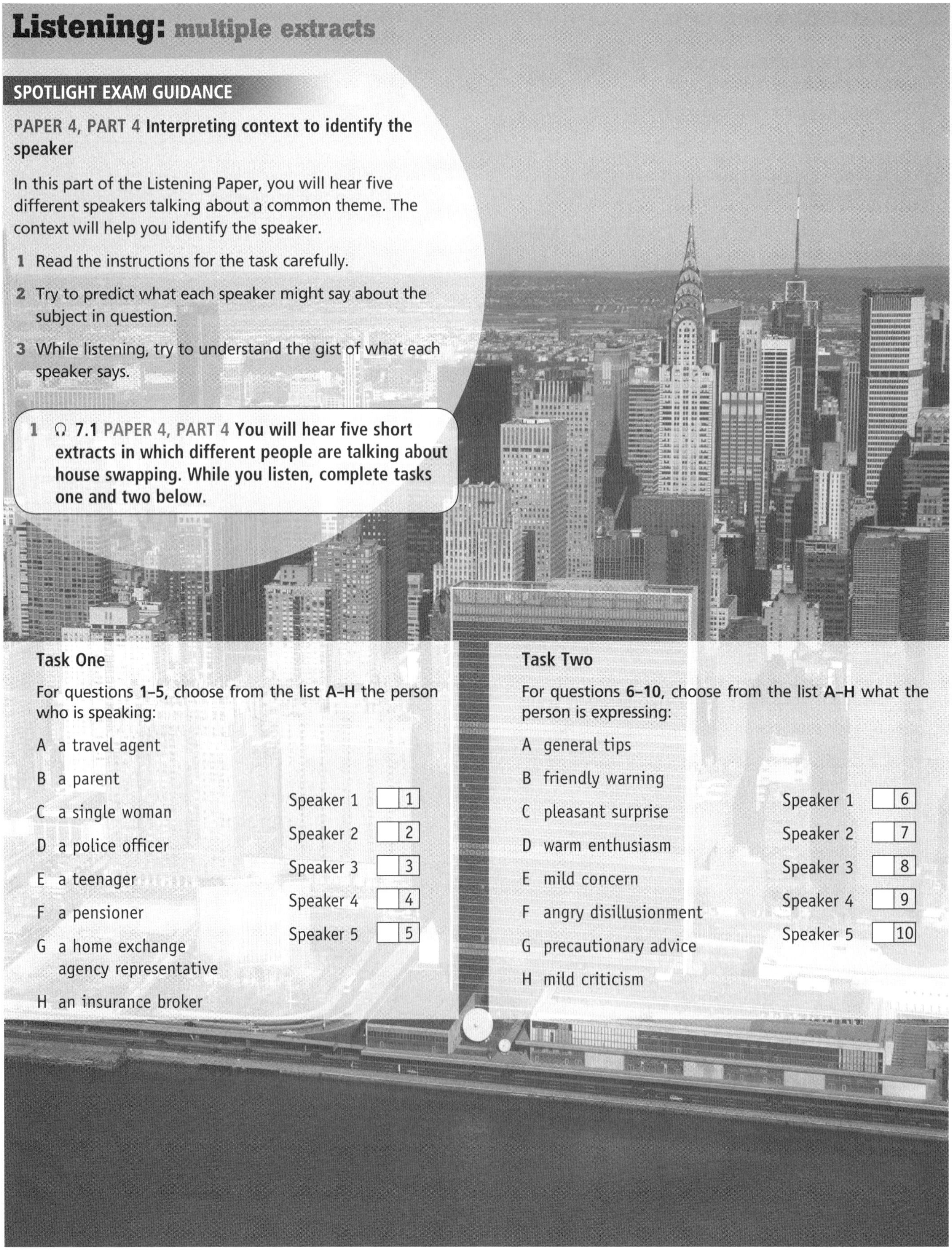

Listening: multiple extracts

PAPER 4, PART 4 Interpreting context to identify the speaker

In this part of the Listening Paper, you will hear five different speakers talking about a common theme. The context will help you identify the speaker.

1 Read the instructions for the task carefully.

2 Try to predict what each speaker might say about the subject in question.

3 While listening, try to understand the gist of what each speaker says.

---

1 ⌂ 7.1 PAPER 4, PART 4 You will hear five short extracts in which different people are talking about house swapping. While you listen, complete tasks one and two below.

Task One

For questions **1–5**, choose from the list **A–H** the person who is speaking:

A a travel agent

B a parent

C a single woman

D a police officer

E a teenager

F a pensioner

G a home exchange agency representative

H an insurance broker

Speaker 1	1
Speaker 2	2
Speaker 3	3
Speaker 4	4
Speaker 5	5

Task Two

For questions **6–10**, choose from the list **A–H** what the person is expressing:

A general tips

B friendly warning

C pleasant surprise

D warm enthusiasm

E mild concern

F angry disillusionment

G precautionary advice

H mild criticism

Speaker 1	6
Speaker 2	7
Speaker 3	8
Speaker 4	9
Speaker 5	10

Use of English: open cloze

1   PAPER 3, PART 2 **For questions 1–15, read the text below and think of the word which best fits each gap. Use only one word in each gap.**

Catch Me a Colobus* by Gerald Durrell

For some considerable time I had been endeavouring to persuade the BBC to film an animal-collecting trip, but they had been very myopic about the whole thing. I tried to convince them that the fascination of the trip lay (1) _____ only in catching the animals but in keeping them as well, and then bringing them back by sea. I felt (2) _____ would all make excellent film material. (3) _____, they dithered about it for a year or so, before (4) _____ saying yes. I was delighted, as I thought it (5) _____ be excellent for the Trust. First of all, the publicity would be considerable; secondly, the Trust would be (6) _____ some nice animals for its collection; and, thirdly, though hitherto I (7) _____ had to find the money for all my expeditions myself, the BBC would at least be assisting me with financing this (8) _____. The Trust at that time, (9) _____ doing very well, could not afford to start indulging in collecting trips.

We first thought of going to Guyana, (10) _____ the political unrest there at the time made it seem a (11) _____ unwise spot to choose. I had once been caught in a revolution and had been forced to (12) _____ half my animals go, and I didn't want (13) _____ to happen in the middle of filming a series for the BBC. After some thought I decided on Sierra Leone. It was a part of West Africa that I had (14) _____ visited, it contained some particularly rare creatures (15) _____ the Trust could do with, and also I happened to love West Africa and its inhabitants very much indeed.

*Note: A Colobus is a species of monkey; Gerald Durrell founded the Jersey Wildlife Preservation Trust, and dedicated his life to studying and preserving rare species of wild animals.

SPOTLIGHT CHECKLIST

PAPER 3, PART 2 Contrast and negative ideas in the text

Remember:

- The text may contain contrasting ideas, or opposing views. It is possible that some of the gaps will require a negative word, or a linking word which signifies contrast.

- It is important to get an understanding of the text as a whole, in order to recognise where contrasting ideas occur.

Tips

- Read through the whole text carefully, to get an idea of its content and the writer's attitude.

- Notice where contrasting ideas are mentioned, or where a sentence contains antithesis.

- When you complete the task, check that your completed text makes sense.

Speaking: discussing possible future developments

SPOTLIGHT CHECKLIST

PAPER 5, PART 4 Following on from part 3

Tips

- Pay close attention to what is said during part 3, and try to think of possible follow-on questions.

- Learn useful phrases for expressing opinions, and responding to other people's ideas.

Practise:

- using modal auxiliaries for making predictions and speculating about the future, because follow-on questions often ask for your ideas about how something will develop in the future.

1   ∩ 7.2 **Listen to two candidates discussing how the following have affected tourism, and make notes.**

- package tour operators

  _____

- the Internet

  _____

2   **Following on from what they say, form an answer to the following question. Think of ways to ask a partner for their response to your ideas.**

How do you think technology will affect the future of travel?

55

Writing: a proposal

SPOTLIGHT CHECKLIST

PAPER 2, PART 1 and 2 Supporting your ideas
Remember:

- A proposal is written for a superior, or a peer group, and is a formal piece of writing.

- You'll be expected to make suggestions and support these, in order to persuade the target reader to adopt your ideas.

- Your ideas should be organised under headings, so make use of the task instructions to help you decide on these.

Practise:

- using language to make suggestions.

- finding at least two examples to support your ideas.

- using persuasive language to make your suggestions convincing.

PROPOSAL TO UPDATE WEBSITE

1 Colourful homepage:

   _____
   _____
   _____

2 Three main holiday categories:

   _____
   _____
   _____

3 Special Features and Last Minute Offers section:

   _____
   _____
   _____

1 Read the question below, and underline the key points you will need in order to answer it.

PAPER 2, PART 1

> You work for a tourist agency specialising in offering adventure holidays. The manager has sent you the email below.
>
> Read the email, on which you have made some notes. Then, using the information carefully, write a proposal, suggesting the best ways to update the company website.

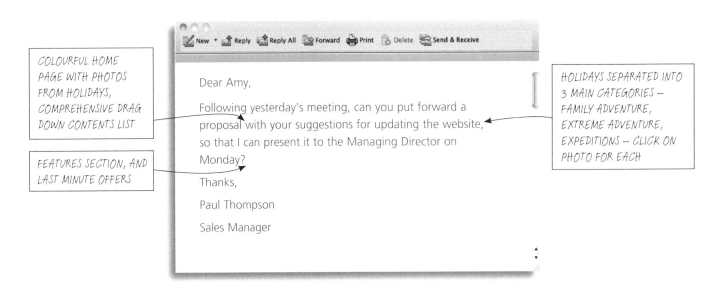

COLOURFUL HOME PAGE WITH PHOTOS FROM HOLIDAYS, COMPREHENSIVE DRAG DOWN CONTENTS LIST

FEATURES SECTION, AND LAST MINUTE OFFERS

HOLIDAYS SEPARATED INTO 3 MAIN CATEGORIES – FAMILY ADVENTURE, EXTREME ADVENTURE, EXPEDITIONS – CLICK ON PHOTO FOR EACH

New ▾ Reply Reply All Forward Print Delete Send & Receive

Dear Amy,

Following yesterday's meeting, can you put forward a proposal with your suggestions for updating the website, so that I can present it to the Managing Director on Monday?

Thanks,

Paul Thompson

Sales Manager

2 You have made the outline plan at the top right hand corner of this page in answer to the question above. Read it, then note down two reasons or examples to support each suggestion.

3 Using the points you made in exercise 2, write your answer to the task in exercise 1. Use the Spotlight above on the left to help you focus your ideas. Remember to write between 180–220 words.

8 Making our mark

EXAM MENU

Reading:	Paper 1, part 3
Listening:	Paper 4, part 1
Speaking:	Paper 5, part 3
Use of English:	Paper 3, part 3
Writing:	Paper 2, part 2

Getting started

1   Look at the extracts from some historical books below. Write the name of each monument from the list below. One name is not used.

Stonehenge	The Burj Dubai
The Eiffel Tower	The Great Sphinx of Giza
The Parthenon	The Statue of Liberty

1   _____ is a large half-human, half-lion statue in Egypt, on the Giza Plateau at the west bank of the Nile River, near modern-day Cairo.

2   One of the most famous prehistoric sites in the world, _____ is composed of earthworks surrounding a circular setting of large standing stones.

3   _____ is a temple of the Greek goddess Athena built in the fifth century BC on the Acropolis of Athens.

4   _____ is the tallest structure in Paris and one of the most recognised structures in the world.

5   _____ is of a female figure standing upright, dressed in a robe and a seven point spiked rays representing a nimbus (halo), holding a stone tablet close to her body in her left hand and a flaming torch high in her right hand.

2   Match the remainder of each description to the sentences on the left.

A   6,719,200 people visited the tower in 2006 and more than 200,000,000 since its construction. This makes it the most visited paid monument in the world per year. Including the 24 m (79 ft) antenna, the structure is 324 m (1063 ft) high (since 2000), which is equivalent to about 81 levels in a conventional building.

B   It is the most important surviving building of Classical Greece, generally considered to be the culmination of the development of the Doric order. Its decorative sculptures are considered one of the high points of Greek art. It is regarded as an enduring symbol of ancient Greece and of Athenian democracy, and is one of the world's greatest cultural monuments.

C   It is one of the largest single-stone statues on Earth, and is commonly believed to have been built by ancient Egyptians in the third millennium BC. It is the earliest known monumental sculpture.

D   The statue was presented in 1886 to the United States by France as a gesture of friendship and commemorates the centennial of the United States Declaration of Independence.

E   Archaeologists believe them to have been erected around 2200 BC and the surrounding circular earth bank and ditch, which constitute the earliest phase of the monument, have been dated to about 3100 BC. Various theories about its function include astrological calendar, burial ground, religious sacrifice, temple of worship etc.

Reading: understanding opinion

1 **PAPER 1, PART 3 You are going to read an article about an ancient historical site. For questions 1–7, choose the answer (A, B, C or D) which you think fits best according to the text.**

1 Why does the writer tell us about the time he carved initials into a tree?
   A To prove that he loved his girlfriend.
   B To tell us about the damage we can do to the landscape.
   C To illustrate our need to preserve the present into the future.
   D To show that nothing lasts forever.

2 The writer mentions the area around Oxford to illustrate that it
   A has featured in too many books and films.
   B lends itself to the creation of hill carvings.
   C is covered in chalk and grass.
   D is covered in carvings of horses.

3 The horse of Uffington differs in that
   A it's not as well known as many of Britain's monuments.
   B nobody knows why it was originally built.
   C it wasn't carved into the chalk like the others.
   D it's the only horse that does not face to the left.

4 The White Horse of Uffington
   A is the largest carved chalk figure in Britain.
   B may well have inspired similar designs.

   C was first mentioned 3000 years ago.
   D is a few centuries older than originally thought.

5 The true function of the white horse is thought to be
   A a religious symbol.
   B a monument to a victory in battle.
   C a decorative design.
   D a mystery.

6 The writer believes
   A the carving looks more like a horse than a dragon.
   B the horse was originally meant to be a dragon.
   C the carving has changed shape over the years.
   D the original design is restored every seven years.

7 The writer believes that
   A the horse may have been built to attract extra terrestrials.
   B there's no logical reason to assume the carving was intended for aliens.
   C the whole horse can be seen well from several places.
   D it's unclear how the original designers used perspective.

Uffington White Horse: ancient hillside chalk art

When I was a teenager, I once carved my initials and those of my girlfriend into a tree, something I thought of at the time as being a permanent statement of our eternal devotion to each other. When we broke up a year later, I felt obliged to return to the tree, put an X through our initials, and add the words 'Null and Void'. The next time I went to find the tree, a number of years after that, it was gone. My guess is that the tree was so ashamed at having been defaced with self-contradictory graffiti that it simply fell over in an act of suicidal protest.

The urge to leave one's mark on the landscape – whether in a tree, a newly poured sidewalk, or the wall of a cave – goes way, way back. One rather unusual form of ancient markings is found in the picturesque, pastoral setting of rural England. About a 30-minute drive from the city of Oxford is a large area covered with the rolling green hills and herds of grazing sheep that have found their way into countless works of literature and film. Beneath the veneer of grass and soil, some of these hills are made of chalk. And over the millennia, the landscape has become dotted with at least fifty large images made by carving through the top layers of earth to expose the chalk beneath. Of these, about a dozen are pictures of horses, and of the horse carvings, the oldest and best known is the Uffington White Horse.

A Horse of a Different Colour

Although less famous than, say, Stonehenge, the Uffington White Horse ranks right up there among ancient and inexplicable English monuments. It is a highly stylised outline of a horse – recognisable, but not as well-defined as the other, more solid horse images. The carving is about 374 feet (113m) long, with the lines forming it ranging in width from about five to ten feet (two to three metres). This particular carving doesn't actually go all the way through the crust to the chalk beneath; instead, a relatively shallow trench was dug and filled in with chalk to make it almost flush with the surface.

The Uffington White Horse has the distinction of being the largest of Britain's horse carvings (measured from head to tail). It's also one of only four such horses facing to the right, though no one knows for sure the significance of the horse's direction, if any. And it's the oldest horse carving, meaning it may have served as a prototype for the others.

This Old Horse

Scientists have determined that the carving is about 3,000 years old (give or take a few centuries), and though it is mentioned in literature dating back to the eleventh century, its original purpose – along with the identity of its creators – is uncertain. Conjecture ranges from a tribal emblem, the equivalent of a modern flag, to a commemorative symbol of King Alfred's triumphs over the Danes. Or perhaps it was a Celtic symbol of the goddess Epona, whose job it was to protect horses. It may have been a territory marker, or simply (perish the thought) a giant piece of abstract art. Although it has been referred to as a 'horse' for at least 1,000 years, there are some who believe that it was intended to represent a dragon. If so, then dragons must have been much more horse-shaped in those days. In any case, the carving has been well tended over the centuries. Every seven years, weeds are removed and the outline smoothed to maintain its original size and shape.

One of the most interesting things about the Uffington White Horse is that the only place to get a good view of the whole thing is from the sky above. There are a few spots several miles away that provide a fair view of most of the outline, but the local topography is such that there is just no vantage point from which you can get a good view of the whole horse. This has, predictably, led some people to speculate that it was created as a signal to UFOs, although what exactly it would signify is a bit unclear ('Horses for sale – next exit'?). Be that as it may, this peculiarity of perspective must have made it a challenge to carve, and it makes the horse's original purpose all the more mysterious.

Language development:
phrases with *bring*

1 Rewrite the underlined part of the following sentences using an expression with *bring*.

1 Seeing my children laughing on the beach <u>made me realise</u> just how lucky I was.

2 Losing his job in the same week that his wife left him really <u>caused him to collapse</u>.

3 A little colourful descriptive language can really <u>make your characters more realistic</u>.

4 Going to Disneyland <u>reminded me of</u> the time my parents took me to my first fair.

5 No matter how much prize money they were offering, nothing could <u>make me eat</u> those bugs!

6 Cynthia <u>has given birth to triplets</u>!

2 Some of the following sentences contain mistakes. Find the mistakes and correct them.

1 The revolution managed to bring about the government.

2 Gillian and Mark have decided to bring forward the date of the wedding to March.

3 They are hoping that the sale of the Christmas cards will bring by enough money for the children's charity.

4 I don't know how Angela manages to bring out running a business and raising three kids single-handedly.

5 A week at the seaside has managed to bring in the best in Rupert.

Key word: *that*

3 How many times has the word *that* has been used in the text on page 59? Underline them and decide how many times *that* has been used.

a as a relative pronoun (instead of *who* or *which*) _____

b to introduce reported speech, a thought, or an idea _____

c as a reference device (to refer back to something previously mentioned) _____

d to refer to something the speaker is physically distant from or not involved in _____

e after adjectives, or adjective phrases using '*so ...*' or '*such ...*' _____

4 How many times can *that* be omitted from the text?

_____

Grammar: relative pronouns/ defining and non-defining relative clauses

1 Some of the sentences below contain mistakes. Decide which sentences are incorrect and correct them.

1 John arrived at the office at ten past nine by that time the meeting was over.

2 That's the woman who's cat scratched me.

3 To whom were you speaking just now Miss Jones?

4 Sally and Brenda, neither of them had been to France before, had a great time.

5 Isn't that the man which you were telling me about?

6 The play had almost finished by the time William turned up.

7 Would you like to come and see the house which I was born?

8 Sean and Mark, both of whom I went to school with, are in a rock band.

2 Decide whether the following rules apply to defining (D) or non-defining (ND) relative clauses.

1 The clause must be separated from the main clause by commas.

2 You cannot use *that*.

3 The word *that* can be omitted altogether.

4 The clause gives extra optional information about the subject.

5 The clause gives essential information about the subject.

3 Complete the sentences with one suitable word.

1 Portugal scored a goal in the ninetieth minute, at which _____ the referee blew the whistle.

2 You said you can't speak any German, in which _____, there's not much point asking you what this says.

3 We didn't get to bed until 5.30 am, by which _____ the sun was already coming up.

4 Lucinda got the measles, as a _____ of which she wasn't allowed to take part in the race.

5 Rex and Timmy, _____ of whom had ever seen the sea before, ran straight in, tails wagging.

6 Carl and Boris, _____ of whom could speak a little Russian, offered to translate the text for me.

7 The paintings, some of _____ needed to be restored, were in surprisingly good condition.

8 The refugees, all of _____ were tired and hungry, needed immediate care.

Listening: interpreting context

1 ⌂ **8.1 Listen to one sentence from each of three short listening extracts and match them to the following contexts.**

    a someone explaining why he built a large wall.

    b someone talking about elephants painting.

    c someone talking about his work as a pavement artist.

2 ⌂ **8.2 PAPER 4, PART 1 Now listen to the whole extracts. For questions 1–6, choose the answer (A, B, or C) which fits best according to what you hear. There are two questions for each extract.**

PAPER 4, PART 1 Listening for context

In this part of the Listening Paper, you need to read the questions carefully and identify keywords.

1 Try to interpret the context of what you will hear from the questions and what you hear while you are listening.

2 Mark the option you feel is most likely to be correct on your first listening, and then check your answer on the second listening.

Extract One

You hear part of a radio interview in which a man named James talks about his work.

Now look at questions 1 and 2.

1 What does the interviewer find hard to understand about what James does?

    A That James doesn't mind working in the rain.

    B That James doesn't mind working on something that doesn't last.

    C That James likes to work on something that no one else will ever see.

2 Why does James compare his work to someone cooking a meal?

    A Because it takes the same amount of time to do what he does.

    B Because his work has less practical value than eating a good meal.

    C To emphasise that it is the process that counts and should be acknowledged.

Extract Two

You hear part of a conversation between two people discussing an elephant called Emma.

Now look at questions 3 and 4.

3 Why does the man seem impressed with Emma's painting?

    A Because she is an elephant.

    B Because she is only two.

    C Because he can tell what it is.

4 What do we learn about Emma's painting now?

    A She likes to paint things in the enclosure.

    B She likes to paint colourful splotches.

    C She seems to vary her subject matter often.

Extract Three

You hear part of a conversation between two people discussing a wall.

Now look at questions 5 and 6.

5 What does the woman find hard to understand?

    A Why the man would design such an ugly house.

    B Why the man doesn't want anyone to come near his house.

    C Why the man would hide his house behind a high wall.

6 What do we learn about the man?

    A He doesn't like other people to see into his private space.

    B He thinks his house is as big as a castle.

    C He likes ugly things.

Speaking: reaching a decision through negotiation

| Why might these monuments or markings have been created? |

1 PAPER 5, PART 3 **Look at the pictures showing different mysterious monuments or markings. The examiner has asked you and your partner to talk to each other about why you think the monuments or images in each picture may have been created and to discuss why they are so mysterious. Remember your knowledge is not being tested. Consider what you would say.**

2 **Read the conversation below and fill in the dialogue with your own words. (You can refer back to the Getting Started section for more information.)**

Student: Well there is certainly a lot of mystery surrounding all of these places. Don't you think so?

You: _____

_____

Student: No, I don't know much about them either. I think I've heard that the pyramids were built as a tomb for a pharaoh by the ancient Egyptians, but I don't really know much about it, or why the Sphinx was built.

You: _____

_____

Student: You're probably right. What about this one – the picture shows a group of standing stones? It's called Stonehenge and I think it is in England. Do you know anything about it?

You: _____

_____

Student: That's really interesting, but it could have been built for so many reasons. It's not surprising it's a mystery though.

You: _____

_____

Student: Yes, so much of what was made in the ancient past is a mystery to us now ... like these Nazca lines. I have no idea what they are. Perhaps they were just some kind of ancient artwork.

You: _____

_____

Student: You could have a point there. Personally I think that we will never really know why any of these things were built, or who built them, but it is this that makes them so fascinating to us now.

You: _____

_____

Use of English: word building (noun groups)

SPOTLIGHT CHECKLIST

PAPER 3, PART 3 **Preparation**

Remember:

- Note down the derivatives of all new vocabulary.

- In the case of nouns, note if there is more than one noun form.

- Read the text carefully and note which part of speech is required.

1 PAPER 3, PART 3 **For questions 1–10, read the text below. Use the word given in capitals at the end of some of the lines to form a noun that fits in the gap in the same line.**

Termite mounds

The termites of sub-Saharan Africa have something very important to teach us about the way we build our homes. The remarkable, seemingly random piles of mud which they build are renowned for their ability to regulate and control the internal environments of their homes, to the extent that the system can respond to changes outside as effectively as those found within our own bodies. They are able to do this by forming (1) _____ systems which heat and cool their structures. No other (2) _____ on earth is known to engineer the environment to this level.

1 VENTILATE
2 ORGAN

With literally millions of (3) _____ in a single mound, located in a nest buried approximately a metre beneath the ground, termites face a formidable challenge maintaining temperature control whilst protecting the (4) _____ from the (5) _____ of the outside environment where they would surely perish. These termites have become so specialised in their method of (6) _____ that they must construct their habitats with the same due (7) _____ as we would in placing a human being on another planet.

3 INHABIT
4 COLONISE
5 HARSH
6 SURVIVE
7 DILIGENT

Where we struggle to derive enough energy to thrive with our current technologies, termites have evolved (8) _____ methods relying solely on the (9) _____ of renewable energy sources. To us, it is currently inconceivable that renewable energy resources alone can supply enough power for our race. So how successful is their race? Current (10) _____ suggests there to be some 500 kilograms of termites for every human alive, which shows they must be doing something right.

8 CONSTRUCT
9 UTILISE
10 ESTIMATE

Writing: a contribution to a longer piece

1 Read the question below and underline the key words. Answer the questions from the Spotlight on the right.

> You work in a travel agency, and your boss is writing a brochure for tourists about what there is to see and do in your country. He has asked you to collect some information for him. He would like you to write a general description of one of the national historical monuments or geographical features in your country, and to explain why it may be interesting for tourists to visit.

SPOTLIGHT CHECKLIST

PAPER 2, PART 2 Writing a contribution to a longer piece

Remember:

- Read the question carefully and identify what you are being asked to do:

  1 What is the 'longer piece'?

  2 What register should your writing have?

  3 What are you being asked to focus on?

  4 What headings could be used?

2 Read an answer to the question below. Complete the text below with a word from the box.

| amphitheatre | architecture | attractions | construction | contests | earthquakes |
| entertainment | mythology | procession | spectators | spectacles | symbol |

The Colosseum

The Colosseum is an elliptical (1) _____ in the centre of the city of Rome, and represents the largest ever built in the Roman Empire. It is also one of the greatest works of Roman (2) _____ and Roman engineering.

History

Its (3) _____ started between 70 and 72 AD under the emperor Vespasian and was completed in 80 AD under his son Titus. It was capable of seating around 50,000 (4) _____, and used for gladiatorial games and public (5) _____. It remained in use for nearly 500 years with the last recorded games being held there as late as the sixth century. As well as the traditional gladiatorial (6) _____, many other public events were held there, such as mock sea battles, animal hunts, executions, re-enactments of famous battles, and dramas based on Classical (7) _____. The building eventually ceased to be used for (8) _____ in the early medieval era.

Present condition

Although it is now in a ruined condition due to damage caused by (9) _____ and stone-robbers, the Colosseum has long been seen as an iconic (10) _____ of Imperial Rome. Today it is one of modern Rome's most popular tourist (11) _____ and still has close connections with the Roman Catholic Church, as each Good Friday the Pope leads a torch-lit (12) _____ to the amphitheatre.

3 What adjectives were used in the text to describe the Colosseum? What other adjectives could have been used?

4 What headings and paragraph structure were used? What other headings could have been used?

5 Plan your own answer to the task in exercise 1 on the lines below, and then write your full answer to the question in your notebooks (220–260 words).

_____

_____

_____

_____

_____

9 Brushstrokes and blueprints

EXAM MENU

Reading: Paper 1, part 1
Listening: Paper 4, part 3
Use of English: Paper 3, part 5
Speaking: Paper 5, part 3
Writing: Paper 2, part 2

Getting started

1 Which of the following types of art are the pictures examples of …? Two types of art are not used.

a Graphic art

b Caricature

c Abstract art

d Watercolour

e Oil painting

f Graffiti

g Screen printing

h Sketching

2 How important is good design in the following public places? Place them in order of importance, 1–6:

hotel

public library

school

shop

town centre

train station

Reading: understanding tone and implication in a text

PAPER 1, PART 1 Understanding tone and implication

Remember:
- Read the question very carefully, especially when it is in the form of an incomplete sentence. Make sure that the whole sentence matches what is written in the text, not just the wording in the option.

Practise:
- recognising writers' attitude within a text;
- differentiating between fact and opinion;
- paraphrasing the main ideas in a text.

1 PAPER 1, PART 1 **You are going to read three extracts which are all concerned in some way with art or design. For questions 1–6, choose the answer (A, B, C or D) which you think fits best according to the text.**

TEXT 1

A Map with a Purpose

The London Underground Map is exactly what you would most want it to be. It is a map simply showing how the different Underground railways link up with other underground-lines. If you have ever been to London you will appreciate how comforting it can be to be able to plan a journey using a simple map and then to actually find the map helps you to achieve that. Providing you are on the right 'coloured' line and are heading in the right (there are after all only two) direction on any given line, seeing the expected names of the stations appear as the train enters the station calms you into feeling a part of the city – without needing to know of the complexities of the street and buildings above.

The use we have for the map now is much the same as when it was created except that Beck's design included only eight lines whereas now there are fourteen – clearly we have a more complicated network to navigate than in the 1930s. It is of course much the same in many other large and sprawling cities with their own 'underground systems' but this map was the first to take a sideways step at the task of laying out a simple map unrelated to the topography that lay above it – a step that has been copied by railway companies, airlines and shipping lines across the world. A visit to any of the websites belonging to the major airlines may reveal maps with a very similar structure to that of the underground network.

1 The writer implies that the beauty of the London Underground Map lies in its

A intricacy.

B functionality.

C originality.

D complexity.

2 According to the writer, Beck's design is special because it

A has endured the passage of time.

B revolutionised transport map design.

C can be adapted to a more complicated network.

D bears little relation to the topography of the area.

NOW SHOWING ...
Exhibition of film posters

'Now Showing' is essentially an art experiment, devised to see how a selection of today's illustrators and designers would respond to a brief asking them to create their own poster for a cult or obscure film from the past.

The idea was born out of my love for trashy film posters, which I guess stems from my obsession with anything vintage and also from an appreciation of screenprinted work. There is something really refreshing about film posters that predate the 1980s. They felt more like works of art, pieces crying out to be encased within a frame. And in many old film posters it's easy to see styles and approaches that have been revisited or adopted by illustrators working today.

From the 80s onwards, the humble poster played a smaller part in the overall film promotion process as TV commercials and trailers came to the fore. Hence the tagline for the exhibition: The lost 'art' of the film poster. The lost 'art' refers to the actual illustrative process involved in the poster, not the quality. I certainly wouldn't be as bold or presumptuous as to say that modern, photography-based posters aren't any good, but there is a certain charm and character that the illustrative film poster offered. This project was a light-hearted way of indulging that nostalgia, and feeding it with current illustrative and graphic styles.

Power of the Image

Why is this rebirth of the serious graphic novel different? Because this new wave arrives when the ascendancy of the image – presciently described by George Steiner, in 1971, in his book *In Bluebeard's Castle* – has begun to dwarf the power of the word. The visual arts are booming. The screen fills our lives through television, cinema, and computers. Thanks to computers, even when we are obliged to read words, we expect them to be arranged in helpful modules, with plenty of graphics. The computer normalises the graphic novel as a form. The graphical user interface may one day be seen as the most important invention of our time. Through such devices, the imperial image reigns and is, more successfully than ever before, invading the book.

Good thing, bad thing? Who knows? For me, these books are hard work. I can't relax into their images in my mind, as I do with a conventional novel. The author's versions keep dragging me back. But I guess they're not for me. They're for the kids sprawling in the graphic-novels section.

They, and Comic Book Guy, own the image-soaked future.

---

3 'Now Showing' is an exhibition of
   A vintage illustrative film posters.
   B reproductions of old posters.
   C new posters designed for old films.
   D film posters of the 1980s.

4 The writer's idea for the project was born out of
   A a desire to recapture the essence of the film poster as an art form.
   B his love for vintage film posters of the 1980s.
   C a strong aversion to contemporary, photography-based film posters.
   D a desire to promote screenprinted artwork.

5 The writer suggests that the present revival of the graphic novel
   A has been inspired by the words of the writer, George Steiner.
   B is a direct result of the ascendancy of visual arts in our lives.
   C diminishes the power of language to inspire us.
   D is supported by the pervasive influence of graphic computer images.

6 Which word best sums up the writer's attitude towards the graphic novel?
   A indifference
   B resignation
   C pleasure
   D bewilderment

Language development: compound words

1 Match the beginnings of the sentences with their correct endings.

1 The bird flew over the roof

2 Paul's got this great new computer

3 The bride's brother had to act as stand

4 Peter used a paper

5 The children ran around the garden, making foot

6 Surfing the Internet is a pleasant, time

7 Harry's secretary has beautifully manicured finger

8 Mary hates the every

a wasting activity for students who are supposed to be studying!

b clip to attach the students' compositions together.

c tops, until it came to some green fields.

d prints in the snow.

e day chores of cooking and commuting.

f controlled vacuum cleaner which does the housework at the press of a button!

g nails that she's forever polishing!

h in photographer, as the one they had hired was suddenly taken ill.

Key word: *pay*

2 Match the phrases with *pay* in column A with their meanings in column B.

A	B
1 pay attention to	a say something good about someone's work
2 pay tribute to	b make someone suffer for doing something wrong
3 pay homage to	c experience something unpleasant because you have done something wrong
4 pay someone back for	d listen to and watch someone or something carefully
5 pay someone respect	e pay more for something than it is really worth
6 pay someone a compliment	f visit or send a polite greeting or wishes to someone
7 pay my respects to	g pay for everything without depending on anyone else
8 pay the penalty	h be polite and considerate towards someone
9 pay my way	i say something good about someone's appearance or character
10 pay through the nose	j do something to show your admiration for someone or something

3 Complete the following sentences with a suitable phrase from exercise 2.

a It's not like Alan to _____ on my appearance! I wonder what he wants?

b She _____ for that dress, and it's not even well-made!

c That was a horrible thing to do! I'll _____ you _____ for that!

d I must go and _____ to Mrs Smith, whose husband died last week.

e In his speech, the Managing Director _____ the innovative work of the design team.

4 Replace the underlined phrases in the following sentences with a suitable phrase with *pay*.

1 I promise I'll <u>give back the money I owe you</u> by the end of the week.

2 This week I had to <u>distribute</u> 500 in bills.

3 While you're in town, could you <u>deposit this cheque into</u> my bank account?

4 The company was prompt in <u>settling</u> my insurance claim.

5 She wasn't happy with the plumber's work, so she <u>gave him the money for what he'd done and asked him to leave</u>.

Listening: understanding stated opinion

1 🎧 **9.1 Listen to the recording script for the exam task below, and list five things the consultant thinks are important when designing a website.**

1 Include _____

2 Don't write _____

3 Place _____

4 Avoid _____

5 Provide _____

2 🎧 **9.1 PAPER 4, PART 3 Complete the exam task below.**

> You will hear part of a radio programme in which a web design consultant is giving advice on designing successful websites. Listen to the interview again. For questions 1–6, choose the answer (A, B, C or D) which fits best according to what you hear.

1 When designing a website, Alex suggests it is best to consider
  A the fact that people have different expectations.
  B the value of inserting a sophisticated search engine.
  C the respect that needs to be shown with regard to users' personal details.
  D the person who is most likely to have difficulty using the site.

2 Alex implies that long texts are
  A useful for elderly users.
  B unlikely to be read.
  C eye-catching.
  D easy to read online.

3 According to Alex, including the company logo on every page is advisable in order to
  A aid the user in navigating the site.
  B remind the user which product he is looking at.
  C maintain the user's attention.
  D protect your copyright.

4 In Alex's opinion, PDFs should be reserved for documents
  A which may need printing.
  B that contain general product information.
  C containing price lists.
  D which include visual materials.

PAPER 4, PART 3 Understanding stated opinion

Remember:
• In this part of the Listening Paper, you need to follow the development of the discussion. It's also very important to ascertain the main speaker's attitude towards the subject.

Tips
• Before listening, concentrate on the question stems, to give you an idea of what specific information you should listen for.

• When you listen for the first time, note the relevant points the main speaker makes.

• Try to understand any opinions that are expressed.

Practise:
• listening to BBC World service interviews and discussions, and make notes on the main points raised;

• building up a list of useful vocabulary connected with expressing ideas, feelings and opinions.

5 She advises against including
  A a large number of visuals on the site.
  B many photographs on the same page.
  C a price list of your products.
  D zoom-able photos of a product.

6 Overall, Alex seems to think the basic principle in web design is to
  A offer useful links to other sites.
  B make the website user friendly.
  C follow general trends in design.
  D use lots of graphics on the page.

Grammar: changing sentence structure: a change in emphasis, or meaning?

1 Rewrite the sentence below from Text 3 on page 67 so that computers are no longer emphasised.

'Thanks to computers, even when we are obliged to read words, we expect them to be arranged in helpful modules, with plenty of ...'

_____

2 Match each picture to one of the sentences in the following pairs.

1

a They bought the dog, which had funny ears.

b They bought the dog which had funny ears.

2

a As I'd expected, he didn't have a driving licence.

b He didn't have a driving licence as I'd expected.

3

a The artist, whose exhibition starts on 12 June, is from Cuba.

b The artist whose exhibition starts on 12 June is from Cuba.

I'm from Cuba

3 Invert the word order in the sentences below to make them more emphatic.

1 I don't know how he manages to run six miles after a full day's work.

_____, I just don't know.

2 Although it may seem like an easy job, it does have its challenging aspects.

_____, it does have its challenging aspects.

3 This is what you should do. Buy a computer, fax machine, and printer, and work from home.

_____ a computer, fax machine and printer, and work from home.

4 It's quite simple. You just need to get some paper, paints, and a place to work, and start painting.

_____ get some paper, paints and a place to work, and start painting.

5 I've no idea where he gets his bad temper from!

_____, I've no idea!

4 Write the questions to the following answers.

a _____?

What Sarah did was steal a dress from the boutique on the corner.

b _____?

It was a dress that Sarah stole from the boutique on the corner.

c _____?

It was the boutique on the corner that Sarah stole a dress from.

d _____?

It was Sarah who stole a dress from the boutique on the corner.

e _____?

The young sales assistant saw Sarah take the dress.

f _____?

Sarah hid the dress inside her large, leather handbag.

Use of English: key word transformations

SPOTLIGHT CHECKLIST

PAPER 3, PART 5 Key word transformations

Remember:
- To check for negative ideas in a sentence.
- To check whether negative ideas need to become positive when transformed.
- That some sentences may require inversion.
- To check that what you have written has a similar meaning to the initial sentence.

Practise:
- writing sentences in different ways;
- transforming sentences using inversion, reported speech, passive etc.

1 **PAPER 3, PART 5 For questions 1–8, complete the second sentence so that it has a similar meaning to the first sentence, using the word given. Do not change the word given. You must use between three and six words, including the word given.**

1 You just tell him you don't want to go when he arrives.
ALL
When he arrives, _____ you don't want to go.

2 In his speech, the College Principal spoke highly of the third year science students who had won an award.
PAID
The College Principal _____ the award-winning third year science students in his speech.

3 'Harry didn't write that poem, Peter did,' said Mandy.
WAS
According to _____ who wrote the poem.

4 Although she is clever, she is very arrogant.
MAY
Clever _____ she's very arrogant.

5 I like all kinds of sweets, but my favourites are lemon sherbets.
MOST
Although I like all kinds of sweets, _____ are lemon sherbets.

6 If Mr Smith hadn't intervened, the boys would have seriously hurt each other.
BUT
The boys would have seriously hurt each other, _____ intervention.

7 I've never been so moved by an opera, and I've seen quite a few.
BEFORE
I've seen many operas, but _____ so moved by one.

8 The last time she spoke to her grandfather was five years ago.
SPOKEN
She _____ for five years.

Speaking: problem-solving

SPOTLIGHT EXAM GUIDANCE

PAPER 5, PART 3 Problem-solving

In this part of the interview, you and your partner talk together. The task requires you to discuss something, and then try to reach a decision. It isn't necessary to actually reach an agreement. You have four minutes for this part.

Tips
- Make notes of useful functional language for expressing ideas, justifying, agreeing and disagreeing.
- Avoid simply agreeing with your partner, but be able to add something.
- Never start your conversation with 'I think this is the best picture', but evaluate all the pictures in turn before reaching a decision.

1 ⌒ 9.2 Listen to a sample Paper 5, part 3. Note down the two parts of the task the students must complete.

First, _____

Then, _____

2 **Listen again, and write down some of the ways in which they ask each other questions.**

_____
_____
_____

3 **Write down some phrases they use to disagree with each other.**

_____
_____
_____
_____
_____

Writing: competition entry

1 Read the task below, and the sample answer at the top of the right-hand column. Make a list of the reasons the writer gives for nominating this particular person, and how she justifies each point.

Reason 1 _____

Justification: _____

Reason 2 _____

Justification: _____

_____

Reason 3 _____

Justification: _____

_____

PAPER 2, PART 2

You have seen the following announcement in your local newspaper and have decided to enter the competition.

Best graphic artist competition!
Wellington Art Gallery are housing an exhibition of graphic art at the end of September. Readers are invited to nominate their favourite graphic artist, giving a brief description of their work, and explain why they think they deserve to be chosen for the exhibition.

In my opinion, an exhibition of graphic art would not be complete without examples of the work of Masashi Kishimoto. A writer and illustrator of graphic novels, his imaginative artwork for the Naruto books has led to these stories being among the most popular in the world today.

Graphic novels have a greater following today than ever before, and although they are mainly read by teenagers, a growing number of serious graphic novels for adults are appearing on the market, and so deserve to be represented in the exhibition. Graphic illustrators have developed some very exciting styles, with the help of technology, and Masashi Kishimoto's work is considered to be among the best. He admits that as a boy he was inspired by Akira Toriyama, who wrote and drew the well-known 'Dragonball' series. However, there is no doubt that he has taken this style of cartoon drawing and made it his own. His characters are well-developed, each one having their own distinctive style, and his designs for each picture in his books are amazingly complex. Posters from his stories cover many teenagers' bedroom walls, including my own. His Naruto stories can now be read on the Internet, and the number of related websites shows just how popular they are. Many young people try to copy his style of drawing, so Kishimoto is now inspiring other young artists!

For these reasons, I have no hesitation in nominating Masashi Kishimoto for inclusion in your exhibition, as I feel he is a very strong candidate.

2 Now look at the task below, and choose what you would nominate for the competition. Make a list of reasons to justify your choice similar to the one in exercise 1.

PAPER 2, PART 2

You have seen the following announcement in your local newspaper and have decided to enter the competition.

Favourite everyday designs competition!
We are running a feature on the most popular designs of everyday objects. Readers are invited to nominate their favourite design of anything from kitchen utensils to mobile phones, giving a brief description of their design and function, and explaining why they think they deserve to be included in the feature.

3 Write your **competition entry** (220–260 words).

10 The good life

EXAM MENU

Reading: Paper 1, part 2
Listening: Paper 4, part 4
Speaking: Paper 5, part 2
Use of English: Paper 3, part 4
Writing: Paper 2, part 2

Getting started

1 Complete the sentences below with a suitable phrase from the box below.

> a happy family   good health   personal success
> a good job or career   material wealth   social standing

To me the most important thing is ... (a) _____ because I would be able to afford anything I wanted. (b) _____ because I would have a long life free from pain and suffering. (c) _____ because I would be respected by other members of the community. (d) _____ because I would be happy doing what I do. (e) _____ because I would be able to watch my children laugh every day. (f) _____ because I would feel good about fulfilling my own dreams.

2 Answer the questions with the answer that is truest for you.

Quiz: How environmentally conscious are you?

1 You have just been to the supermarket and unpacked your shopping. Do you ...?
  a throw away all the plastic bags (they are free anyway).
  b reuse your own homemade shopping bags which you made yourself from old clothes.
  c store the plastic bags to reuse again next time you go shopping or as rubbish bags.

2 You feel hungry and want a quick snack. Do you ...?
  a eat a healthy nut bar and drink some orange juice.
  b buy a packet of crisps and fizzy drink from the supermarket.
  c pick some organic fruit from your own garden.

3 When you wash, do you ...?
  a fill the bath to the top with hot water, lots of bubbles, and bath salts.
  b recycle rainwater you've collected from the garden and have a sponge bath.
  c have a quick shower, switching the water off while you shampoo.

4 It's time for bed. Do you ...?
  a let the lights fade out by themselves – they're solar powered anyway.
  b leave all the lights and the TV set switched on to scare off intruders.
  c switch off everything on standby.

5 You don't have a washing machine. Do you ...?
  a buy the flashiest, most impressive model you can find.
  b buy an ecologically approved, low energy model.
  c buy neither because you wash everything by hand.

6 You want to cut down on your electricity bills. Do you ...?
  a install another photovoltaic panel on the roof to supplement your wind turbine power.
  b avoid playing your stereo at the same time the TV is on.
  c use low energy appliances and light bulbs and switch to natural gas heating.

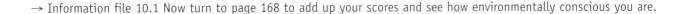

→ Information file 10.1 Now turn to page 168 to add up your scores and see how environmentally conscious you are.

Reading: gapped text – text structure, paragraph cohesion and coherence

1 PAPER 1, PART 2 Choose from paragraphs (A–G) the one which best fits each gap in the text (1–6). There is one extra paragraph which you do not need to use.

Negotiating Animal Rights

The animal rights movement confronts us with an important critique on a range of human practices that involve the use of animals, raising genuinely difficult ethical concerns. And it challenges us, if we are open to it, to rethink our worldview; to reassess how we see ourselves as humans in the bigger scheme of things.

1 [...]
What different parties in the debate mean by 'decent treatment', and to what extent this is translated into practice, is another matter. From within the research industry, decent treatment typically means keeping animal pain and distress to a minimum; keeping careful guard against unnecessary experiments, such as those that duplicate research findings; and using non-sentient animals when possible.

2 [...]
The whole institution of animal-dependent research is held to be profoundly unjust, and a parallel is sometimes drawn with slavery. It's argued that as with slavery, the ethically appropriate action isn't simply to tidy up the institution by reducing suffering; the only ethically sound course of action is to abolish the practice altogether. From this perspective the decent treatment of animals means that they shouldn't be used as means to our ends at all.

3 [...]
This all sounds straightforward enough. But in fact, given the way we currently keep and use animals, translating the five freedoms into practice is extremely challenging. This is especially true of the freedom to perform behaviour in their natural repertoires.

4 [...]
It is still true, in general, that humans routinely inflict pain and suffering on animals, across a whole range of different contexts, including those in which there is a genuine commitment to 'decent treatment'. This is where the concept of rights comes into its own.

5 [...]
Combine the idea of animal rights with that of the five freedoms, and we have a powerful interpretation of what the decent treatment of animals, in any context, should actually involve. Assuming that we are going to carry on using animals, then those animals should enjoy freedom from hunger, thirst, fear and suffering, and freedom to perform behaviour in their natural repertoires.

6 [...]
The capacity for responsibility should, in any case, be irrelevant. Given that rights are granted to protect fundamental quality of life, the prerequisite for having them is, surely, the capacity to have a quality of life. This is a capacity that humans and many other animals share, and it can be present whether or not a creature has the capacity to take responsibility for their behaviour.

A

There are vociferous opponents of extending rights to animals. A common argument against the notion is that rights go with responsibilities. In other words, a person can't be given rights unless they can be held responsible for respecting the rights of others. Animals cannot be held responsible; therefore animals cannot have rights. But rights are not withdrawn from humans who, for whatever reason, have a restricted capacity for responsibility (for example, human babies are granted rights). So why should they be withheld from non-human animals for the same reason?

B

The 'five freedoms' provides a powerful way of moderating between those who are for and those who are against the use of animals for human ends. They are: freedom from hunger, thirst, fear, suffering and freedom to perform behaviour in their natural repertoires. The latter refers to the range of behaviours that animals perform if unrestricted, like grooming, grazing, roaming, flying, nesting, spending time with other animals of the same species, digging, burrowing and so on.

C

From the farther end of the animal rights spectrum, the issue is not just that we sometimes inflict pain and suffering on the animals we use, but that we use them at all. From their perspective, treating sentient animals simply as a means to human ends, like any other item of laboratory equipment, is unacceptable no matter how carefully they are treated.

D

Every animal was thus intended to serve some human purpose, if not practical, then moral or aesthetic. Horse-flies, guessed the Virginian gentleman William Byrd in 1728, had been created so 'that men should exercise their wits and industry to guard themselves against them'. As for cattle and sheep, Henry More in 1653 was convinced that they had only been given life in the first place so as to keep their meat fresh 'till we shall have need to eat them.'

E

The term 'rights' is used in a variety of ways, but the core idea is that a right is like a protective fence around an individual. Rights protect those things that are fundamental for the animal (human or otherwise) to lead a life of basic quality. Thus, Animal rights would protect those things established as fundamental to good animal welfare – the five freedoms.

F

First, it is worth noting that we don't need the language of rights to argue that having bought non-human animals into human social and economic systems, we should treat them decently. More or less all parties in the debate over the use of animals in medical and scientific research in fact agree that sentient animals (those capable of experiencing pain and pleasure) are owed such treatment.

G

Interestingly, the use of animals in research falls short perhaps most consistently with regard to this freedom as well. While the UK research industry is, in the main, conscientious about limiting suffering with the use of anaesthesia, the majority of research animals are kept in barren cage environments, in isolation from other animals of their own kind.

Language development:
fixed phrases

1 Complete the sentences below with a suitable word to complete the expressions.

1 Martha couldn't cope with the *stresses and* _____ of being the head of a dance company, so she decided to retire early.

2 When Mike came home from school with a black eye for the second time in a month, _____ *bells started to sound.*

3 Pete and I have decided to _____ *sticks* and move to Australia.

4 *The bottom* _____ is that if we don't do something about it now, we won't be able to protect the most endangered species.

5 Years of looking after her disabled daughter finally started to *take its* _____ and that's when the family decided Claire needed some kind of psychological support.

Key word: *pull*

2 Write the phrasal verb with *pull* that matches the definitions below. Write one example sentence for each in your notebook.

a to stop doing something or being involved in it

b to take hold of something and pull it several times

c to succeed in doing something difficult

d to destroy something, such as a building or to make someone less successful or happy

e to drive to the side of the road and stop

f to start to drive away from a place where you had stopped

g to improve something by organising it more effectively

h to stay alive or survive a difficult experience

i to get out of a bad situation or dangerous place

j to carefully examine something or someone, in order to criticise it or them

Listening: 'who says what'

PAPER 4, PART 4 Identifying speakers

Tips

- Make sure you know what each task is asking you.

- Focus on the key words in each option.

- Listen to the gist of what each speaker says – pay less attention to detail than you would in parts 1 and 2.

1 ◯ **10.1 PAPER 4, PART 4 You are going to hear five people talking about major lifestyle changes.**

Task One

For questions **1–5** below, choose from the list **(A–H)** the person who is speaking.

A someone that sold up and moved to the country

B someone who helps children with special needs

C someone that campaigns for animal rights

D someone who decided to become vegan

E someone that joined 'doctors without borders'

F someone that donated an organ to save a life

G someone that set up their own alternative power supply

H someone that decided to adopt orphaned children

Speaker 1 [ ] 1

Speaker [ ] 2

Speaker [ ] 3

Speaker [ ] 4

Speaker [ ] 5

Task Two

For questions **6–10**, choose from the list **A–H** the reason that the speaker expresses for the change.

A being fed up with waiting for politicians to get things done

B a desire to accomplish more creatively

C wanting to get out of a financially motivated system

D wanting to make more money

E wanting to do something with excess free time

F disgust at the way someone or something is treated

G wanting to help others improve their lifestyles

H wanting to get away from a potentially unhealthy lifestyle

Speaker 1 [ ] 6

Speaker 2 [ ] 7

Speaker 3 [ ] 8

Speaker 4 [ ] 9

Speaker 5 [ ] 10

Grammar: direct and reported speech

1   Rewrite the following sentences as reported speech.

1   Jenny said to Ed: 'I wish we could go on holiday next week.'

_____

2   'Can I have a salad for lunch?' Michael asked.

_____

3   'Haven't you got any homework to do?' Mum wanted to know.

_____

4   Philip said, 'This is the best meal I've eaten this year.'

_____

2   Rewrite the following sentences as direct speech.

1   Miriam denied breaking the porcelain vase.

'It _____!'
exclaimed Miriam.

2   Samuel insisted on paying for lunch and added that it was his birthday.

'_____.'

Anyway, _____,'
announced Samuel.

3   Rebecca blamed me for spoiling the surprise party we had planned for Dad.

'You _____,'
whined Rebecca.

3   Choose the best reporting verb for each of the sentences below and rewrite the second sentence so that it means the same as the first.

admit	advise	beg	blame
complain	encourage	threaten	

1   'Please, don't leave me!' said Matthew to Sara.

Matthew _____ him.

2   'You do that one more time and I'm telling Mum!'

She _____ if he did it again.

3   'If I were you, I'd get that arm seen by a doctor,' Mike said to Jim.

Mike _____ by a doctor.

4   'It's true – I did have a snack before lunch,' Arnie told his mum.

Arnie _____ a snack before lunch.

5   'Come on Susan, I know you'll pass the test if you take it!' her mother said.

Susan's _____ the test.

6   'It's your fault that we missed the bus!' Sally said to Tony.

Sally _____ they had missed the bus.

7   'I'd like you to bring me another beer – this one is warm!' Mr Roberts told the waiter.

Mr Roberts _____ and asked the waiter to bring him another one.

4   Read the dialogue below. Then read the summary that follows and complete each gap with a word or short phrase. Make any changes that are necessary.

It was the night of the dinner party. Mike entered the bedroom wearing a bright red jacket.

'You're not going to wear that are you?' asked Julia, looking dismayed.

'Yes. Why not? I like this jacket,' Mike replied, feeling slightly hurt by her reaction. 'I can't see what the problem is.'

'But I've already decided I'm going to wear my pale green silk dress. We can't go to a formal dinner party in such different colours!' Julia exclaimed.

'Oh come on!' said Mike, annoyed. 'There are so many other dresses you could wear, anyway.'

'Don't be ridiculous Mike,' Julia retorted. 'If you're going to wear that awful jacket, I'm not going!'

On the night of the dinner party, Mike had
(1) _____ his red jacket.
When he walked into the bedroom Julia expressed
(2) _____ thinking of wearing
it. (3) _____ by her reaction,
Mike told her (4) _____
the jacket and (5) _____
the problem was. Julia informed him
(6) _____ her pale green silk
dress and said (7) _____ to
a formal dinner party in such different colours. Mike
got (8) _____ and pointed out
that (9) _____ to choose from.
Julia told (10) _____ and said
(11) _____ his red jacket she
(12) _____ to the party!

Speaking: organising a larger unit of discourse

1   ⌒ 10.2 Listen to two students doing part 2 of the Speaking Paper. Note down the expressions each uses to perform different functions. Complete the table below.

Function	Student 1: Elisabeth	Student 2: Giovanni
Compare	Both of these pictures show ... In both of these situations ...	
Contrast		On the other hand this picture shows a completely different environment ...
Describe	I can see a man ... It looks like he is on a train ...	
Express an opinion		I think this man likes it though ...
Speculate	He must be a businessman I think ... He is probably travelling ...	

PAPER 5, PART 2 Organising a larger unit of discourse

Remember:

- You'll be given the opportunity to speak for one minute without interruption.

- You'll have the opportunity to show your ability to organise your thoughts and ideas and express yourselves coherently in appropriate language.

- You should listen while your partner is talking but do not interrupt. You will be given a chance to comment at the end of your partner's turn.

Tips

- Do not waste time explaining which pictures you are going to talk about.

- Do not adopt 'closure' techniques – you should keep talking until the interlocutor indicates you should stop.

- Try to speculate about something which relates to the focus of the visuals. You will never be asked to merely describe the visuals.

Practise:

- talking about a variety of subjects for one minute;

- timing yourself to see how long one minute lasts for.

2   Write down the subject of each of the pictures the students described. The first one has been done for you.

a Elisabeth's pictures

   1 *a business man wearing a suit, sitting on a train. He has an open laptop computer and is talking on his mobile phone.*

   2 _____

     _____

     _____

b Giovanni's pictures

   1 _____

     _____

     _____

   2 _____

     _____

     _____

Use of English: gapped sentences

SPOTLIGHT EXAM GUIDANCE

PAPER 3, PART 4 Focusing on lexical contexts

The focus of the task is lexical and it aims to test your knowledge of lexical patterns such as collocation, phrasal verbs, and other word combinations. The task tests whether you know items of vocabulary in a range of contexts and with a range of meanings.

Tip
• Make a note of every new meaning of a word when you come across it.

1 Use a dictionary. Write an example sentence for each of the definitions provided below.

order (n)

• the sequence in which things or events are arranged, in ~ / out of ~.

  Example _____

• an instruction to do something that is given by someone in authority.

  Example _____

• a request for food or drink in a restaurant or bar.

  Example _____

present (v)

• to give something to someone, usually at a formal occasion or event, as a prize.

  Example _____

• to show something such as a document or ticket to someone in an official position.

  Example _____

• to formally introduce someone to another person, usually of much higher rank.

  Example _____

2 PAPER 3, PART 4 For questions 1–6, think of one word only which can be used appropriately in all three sentences.

1 Give them a/an _____ and they'll take a mile!

  Peter is six foot and one _____ tall.

  To avoid being seen, they moved forward one _____ at a time.

2 It was a stroke of _____ that Martin came by when he did.

  I was sorry to hear about the race – better _____ next time!

  Sorry mate – you're out of _____; I just sold the last turkey.

3 Gillian has been diagnosed as suffering from a form of _____ illness.

  Kim made a _____ note to talk to her brother when she got back from college.

  When I told Dad I'd crashed the car he went absolutely _____ at me.

4 Nobody thought the new business would be successful, but they managed to _____ it off.

  I grabbed hold of the end of the rope and started to _____ as hard as I could.

  Roman tried to _____ a fast one on me, but I could tell it was a plastic spider!

5 The company produces a wide _____ of products all made from organically grown plants.

  Her vocal _____ is absolutely amazing – only a few people can hit that many notes.

  We could see the entire mountain _____ from our window.

6 Arnold _____ his fist at the boys who ran off when they kicked their ball through his window.

  Timmy _____ with fear – what was that dark shadow in the corner of his room?

  It _____ him up a bit when he found out that his Mum and Dad were getting a divorce.

Writing: an information sheet

1 PAPER 2, PART 2 **Read the exam question below and answer the questions that follow.**

> Your local council has decided to produce an information leaflet for residents explaining why it is important to cut down on the overuse of water. They have asked you to write the leaflet and focus on the different ways in which residents can save water so that there will be enough for future generations.

a What two functions are you being asked to do in this task?

_____

b Who are you writing the information leaflet for?

_____

c What register should you use?

_____

2 **Brainstorm headings that you could use in your leaflet.**

3 **Read an answer to the question below.**

4 **List the tips that the writer gave to residents to save water ...**

a in the home

b in the garden

c in the community

5 Now write your own answer to the question on the left, but substitute the word 'electricity' for 'water'. Some tips for saving electricity are given below, though you don't need to use them all.

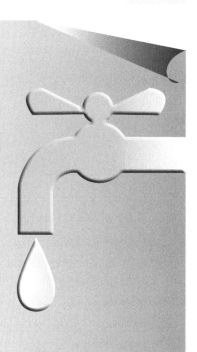

┌───┐
Tips for saving electricity (at home, school, or work)

→ switch off unwanted lights

→ switch off appliances at the mains or don't leave on standby

→ do things by hand whenever possible (ie: sweep instead of use the vacuum cleaner)

→ install a wind turbine or solar panels
└───┘

The importance of saving water

Water is not an infinite resource and in today's ever-warmer environment, with modern needs increasing, it is becoming increasingly hard to find renewable sources of water. Our reservoirs are drying up and many natural lakes and rivers have been depleted which has a disastrous effect on local wildlife.

Saving water in the home

There are a number of ways we could save water in the home. First, we should ensure that we take showers rather than baths, and that we turn off the water when we are soaping ourselves. Secondly, we should use the washing machine less frequently and always make sure it is full. We should only use washing machines and dishwashers that have a good water economy programme. Another idea is to use water that we have collected from washing our hands to flush the toilet with.

Saving water in the garden

It is important to reduce the amount of water we use in the garden. We should avoid using a hose in hot weather, or watering during the day when much of the water evaporates. We should avoid washing the car or the yard unless it is absolutely essential, and then only with a bucket. We could also collect water from rainfall by installing water butts around the house at the bottom of each drainpipe.

Saving water in the community

We should all aim to save water every day. Pass this leaflet on to your friends and neighbours so that everyone can participate in our water saving effort for the community.

11 Making ends meet

EXAM MENU

Reading: Paper 1, part 3
Listening: Paper 4, part 2
Use of English: Paper 3, part 1
Speaking: Paper 5, part 4
Writing: Paper 2, part 1

Getting started

1 Match the clues below with their answers in the 'find a word' puzzle. Write them in the appropriate column.

a someone who works all the time and hardly ever rests _____

b someone who buys and uses goods _____

c money owed _____

d act of stealing someone's personal details in order to use them illegally _____

e total amount of money spent during a particular period of time _____

f process of buying and selling _____

g someone whose job it is to check money spent and earned by a particular business _____

h act of illegally using someone else's credit card to buy goods _____

i management of money by governments and large organisations _____

j buy shares in a property or organisation because you hope to make a profit _____

T	T	F	E	H	T	Y	T	I	T	N	E	D	I	D
R	U	V	Q	S	I	I	K	M	U	T	Y	B	R	F
E	M	G	E	O	D	R	V	I	O	R	F	H	W	M
N	N	F	L	R	E	M	U	S	N	O	C	U	U	B
O	D	E	B	T	N	E	E	E	J	P	E	M	S	B
I	W	J	L	R	T	X	C	X	Q	P	U	M	O	C
T	O	V	G	B	I	R	N	D	I	X	Z	R	Q	V
C	R	E	D	I	T	C	A	R	D	F	R	A	U	D
A	K	C	A	R	Y	L	N	B	Y	X	X	Q	T	T
S	A	B	F	Q	F	Z	I	W	M	A	P	S	B	U
N	H	M	E	P	R	S	F	L	J	Z	E	X	A	S
A	O	E	Z	G	A	S	G	T	Y	V	Y	Z	N	E
R	L	U	E	R	U	T	I	D	N	E	P	X	E	X
T	I	S	S	Y	Y	J	X	I	B	R	E	S	D	Y
A	C	C	O	U	N	T	A	N	T	Z	M	E	Y	U

81

Reading: interpreting literature

1 **PAPER 1, PART 3 You are going to read an extract from a novel (on page 83). For questions 1–7, choose the answer (A, B, C or D) which you think fits best according to the text.**

1 We can infer from the first two paragraphs that Marty
   A is from a wealthy background.
   B feels very confident about winning.
   C has a strategy for playing the game.
   D does not believe he is lucky.

2 In the second paragraph, the writer implies that Marty
   A never listens to other people.
   B is deep in concentration.
   C has an arrogant attitude towards the host.
   D doesn't like being on the show.

3 Before making his discovery, Marty seems to have considered the possibility that
   A the game show host knew the flashing sequence on the board.
   B the lights were programmed to flash around the board in a certain way.
   C it would be easy to memorise how the sequence patterns worked.
   D it would be difficult to win a large amount of money on the show.

4 Once he discovered the truth, Marty
   A expected to be proved right in his suspicions.
   B thought it would be easy to go on the show and win lots of money.
   C knew that by playing clumsily, he would get caught.
   D was certain he wouldn't get caught.

5 As he begins to play, Marty feels
   A miserable.
   B determined.
   C over-confident.
   D threatened.

6 The writer implies that Paul Thomas
   A is amazed that Marty hasn't stopped playing.
   B is angry at Marty's stupidity.
   C believes Marty is bound to lose.
   D believes Marty is cheating.

7 In the final paragraph, Marty
   A wins over $100,000.
   B misses the Blooper.
   C has regained control.
   D beats the system.

PAPER 1, PART 3 Indirect meaning in literature

Remember:
- You're sometimes required to read an extract from a novel, or a short story in this part of the Reading Paper.

- In order to answer some of the multiple choice questions, it may be necessary to understand indirect meaning within the text. The stems of such questions sometimes read *'The writer implies in the second paragraph that …'* or *'We can infer from the last paragraph that …'*

- Literary extracts usually focus on characters' feelings and attitude towards the situation they are in.

Practise:
- reading unabridged short stories or novels, to get used to different literary styles;

- reading globally, to gain understanding of a text without needing to understand every single word;

- developing skills to infer underlying meaning in the text, particularly where attitude or feeling is not directly expressed.

2 **Find a word or phrase in the extract which means the following:**

a the order in which something occurs *[para 1]*
b turn around very fast *[para 2]*
c a large amount of money *[para 2]*
d without much meaning or importance *[para 2]*
e without thinking *[para 2]*
f supposedly true *[para 3]*
g in no particular order *[para 3]*
h possible future effect *[para 3]*
i skilful *[para 3]*
j unable to believe *[para 5]*
k near disaster *[para 6]*
l self control *[para 7]*

Spinning a fortune

'OK. This is it … Now, don't blow it, just act cool … Easy does it …' Sweating slightly, Marty Lane wiped the palms of his hands against his cheap, supermarket trousers, as Paul Thomas, the game show host, turned his attention towards him. The atmosphere in the studio was tense, and Marty could feel everybody's eyes upon him. He struggled to focus. 'Concentrate, Marty, concentrate … Think of your timing … remember those sequences … get ready now …'

He barely noticed that Thomas was talking to him. 'So, Marty! At the end of round one, you're in third place, with only $2500! You were pretty unlucky there, buddy, hitting that 'Blooper' square on just your third go. But here's your chance now to make up some of that money. So, are you ready to … 'Spin Your Fortune'? Marty placed his hand over the red button in front of him. 'Ready when you are, Paul!' he said, with a confidence he didn't really feel. The second round began with some inane questions from Thomas, which Marty answered mechanically, his mind fixed on the eighteen boxes with cash prizes hidden under them.

He went through the sequences again in his head. For six weeks, he had watched the game show, 'Spin Your Fortune', religiously videotaping every episode and playing it back, frame by frame, to see if the ostensibly random lights that flashed on different squares around the board were indeed random. He was amazed to discover they were in fact a series of sequence patterns. After contemplating this little gem of information for a while, and the implications of someone being able to memorise those sequence patterns, a plan began to form in his mind. He began to practise while watching the show, and soon became adept at pressing the button at just the right moment to land on a square with lots of money and an extra spin of the wheel. Marty needed to make sure that he got the extra spin, so he could keep playing. It worked!

That was it! He would go on the show, earn lots of money, and not only pay off all his debts, but come away rich! The TV company must never suspect him though, or they would stop the game. He'd have to plan his strategy carefully, perhaps play clumsily in the beginning, look like he was a sure loser … Yes, that was it. If he played badly in the first round, and made sure he ended it in last place, then he would be the one to start the second round, where there was more money on the board. Marty spent ages working out exactly how he was going to play, until he was certain he was ready. It would be easy. He would go on the show and catch them unawares. So, he applied, and was booked.

Now, here he was, with a chance of making big money for the first time in his miserable life, and he wasn't going to waste it! He began to play, making sure to hit the small bucks square at first, until he got into his stride, and started raking in the large amounts. As his total rose above the $25000 mark, Thomas became incredulous. He couldn't believe that Marty still wanted to carry on playing. Surely the guy knew that it was only a matter of time before he hit a Blooper and lost it all? But Marty carried on, and kept landing on the money. $40000, $50000, $60000 … He was on a roll! The audience were going wild … He'd already won more money than he'd ever had in his life!

The rush of adrenalin threatened to overwhelm him, and Marty began to falter. Suddenly, he could no longer focus, and started taking longer spins. 'C'mon! Don't lose it now … Not yet, not yet … now, no!… Steady … Now!' Desperately, he pressed the button, and closed his eyes as he realised he'd missed the sequence. Luckily, he won some more money. He was out of the woods, but it had been a close shave, for the very next square had been a Blooper. He might have lost over $80000! Somewhat shaken and annoyed with himself, he quickly passed his remaining spins to one of the other contestants, and took a break to pull himself together.

So engrossed was he in regaining his composure, that he barely noticed his opponent hit a Blooper. Before he knew it, it was his turn to play again. The atmosphere in the studio was electric. Marty had the chance to make over $100000 and knew he was about to make game show history, for no one had managed to make so much money in one game before. If he succeeded, he would also be the first person to beat the system, but that would have to remain his secret. The wheel began to spin, and the studio fell silent. Marty watched the lights flash around the board. Could he do it? 'C'mon! 2 … 4 … 6 … 3 … 7 … Careful! Not yet! Wait for it!… Now!' Marty pressed the button …

Language development:
idiomatic phrases with *out* and *money*

1 Circle the correct phrase in italics to complete the following sentences.

a You must be out of *this world / your mind* to go bungee jumping off a bridge!

b I felt really out of *place / order* at the party, since I didn't know anyone.

c Sorry, but I can't come to the cinema; I'm out of *it / money* at the moment.

d I hadn't heard from her in months, when she phoned me out of *the blue / control* and asked me to lend her £500!

e 'Sorry,' I said, 'but I can't lend you £500. You're out of *luck / the question*, I'm afraid.'

2 Complete the sentences below with one of the following phrasal verbs with *out*.

find out	hand out	put out
sort out	work out	

1 'With such strong winds, it will be difficult for the firemen to _____ the fire.'

2 'Ursula, can you _____ if Mrs Keene would like cream or milk with her coffee?'

3 David spent all evening trying to _____ how much it would cost to build an extension onto the back of the house.

4 'Ian, can you please _____ the photocopies to the rest of the class?'

5 'Mum, we need to _____ the rubbish for the recycling bins.'

3 Use a dictionary to add compound words with *out* to the lists below.

a **Nouns**   b **Verbs**   c **Adjectives**

outbreak   *outdistance*   *outdated*

outcast   *outdo*   *outdoor*

_____   _____   _____

_____   _____   _____

_____   _____   _____

_____   _____   _____

d Write a sentence using 'outdoor', and another using 'outdoors'.

_____

_____

Key word: *money*

4 Complete the sentences with a suitable phrase with *money* from the box below. Make any grammatical changes necessary.

get (your) money's worth	have money to burn
money is no object	money talks
not made of money	pump money into
put your money where your mouth is	raise money
save money	throw money

a The school is holding a sponsored walk round the town to _____ for charity.

b 'I can't afford to buy you that car; I'm _____, you know!'

c My father _____ my graphic design company to help me get started.

d 'You can _____ on clothes by recycling old outfits.'

e 'Here's my credit card, so go and buy what you like. Honestly, _____!'

f 'If you really believe that, why don't you _____, and show me!'

g They've just come back from a week in Paris, and now they're off to Lisbon, so they must _____!

h 'I'm sure if you give the waiter a good tip, he'll get us the best table. _____, you know.'

i That restaurant was quite reasonable, and we really _____ at the salad bar, where we filled our plates for €2!

j 'James, don't _____ at her, as it won't make her love you any more.'

Listening: sentence completion

SPOTLIGHT CHECKLIST

PAPER 4, PART 2 Listening for dates, statistics, and/or figures

Remember:

- The gaps usually require no more than three words.

- Use actual words you hear in the recording

Tips

- Write your answers clearly, in CAPITAL LETTERS.

- Do not leave blanks – you may make a lucky guess!

Practise:

- listening to interviews and discussion programmes on a variety of topics;

- listening to different accents;

- predicting the type of word or information needed in each gap before you listen (noun, verb, date, number etc);

- checking that your answers fit grammatically – is the noun singular or plural; which tense should the verb be in?

1 ⋒ 11.1 PAPER 4, PART 2 **You will hear part of a talk in which a financial management specialist gives advice on family spending. For questions 1–8, complete the sentences with a word or short phrase.**

According to the speaker, the family should make sure they live within their (1) _____.

Consideration should be given to the possibility of (2) _____, such as accidents or sudden health problems.

The speaker states that in order to create a spending plan that works, there are (3) _____ steps to take.

She suggests completing a (4) _____ listing the family goals to be achieved over a given period of time.

The total family monthly (5) _____ should be calculated, so that everyone knows how much money is available.

The speaker identifies (6) _____ main categories of expenses the family should consider.

Family members need to adopt good (7) _____ with regard to limiting their spending.

The speaker suggests that having a monthly (8) _____ will help families remain in control of their finances.

Grammar: modal auxiliaries (2)

1 Match the function in the box to each of the sentences below.

annoyance	criticism	plan
prediction	resignation	

1 'They're not going to score now, so we may as well leave.'
2 'I think Liverpool will win the Champions League this season.'
3 'Be gentle! You might have broken the cat's leg!'
4 'Daniel will keep leaving his toy cars in the middle of the hall for me to trip over!'
5 'I think I'll bake an apple pie and take it to my aunt's this afternoon.'
6 'You could at least apologise to her for being so rude!'
7 It's raining, so I might as well do my homework.
8 'Oh no! You would get sick the day before the competition!'
9 'I know! For Tina's birthday, I'll buy her that new Amy Winehouse CD!'
10 'Mark my words, it will snow tomorrow now that we've planned this picnic.'

2 Complete the following email with the correct form of a suitable modal auxiliary, similar to those in exercise 1.

New · Reply Reply All Forward Print Delete Send & Receive

Hi Mike,

Why didn't you turn up yesterday? I waited all evening! I do think you (1) _____ phoned to say that you (2) _____ coming. You (3) _____ do this to me when I'd prepared your favourite spaghetti dish!

No doubt you've got your reasons, but you (4) _____ at least talk to me about it, or send me an email. I (5) _____ be in The Coffee Shop this afternoon at around 4pm, if you want to come and talk.

Take care,

Sue

3 Complete the captions below with a suitable modal phrase.

A Lovely Day Out

1 'It _____ a beautiful day!'

2 'I know! I _____ her some flowers!'

3 'We _____ a wonderful time!'

4 'Watch out! You _____ that poor kitty!'

5 'Your mother _____ interrupting when I'm trying to talk to you!'

6 'Oh well! I _____ read the paper!'

Use of English: multiple-choice cloze

1 **PAPER 3, PART 1 For questions 1–12, read the text below and decide which answer (A, B, C or D) best fits each gap.**

Taking Pride In Their Work

Everything (1) _____ in Cairo, every newspaper, torn pair of trousers or slice of bread, starts on a secret journey from the moment it is put in the bin. It is not a trail of chaos – but of professionalism, ingenuity, and imagination, crystallising into an industry as efficient as it is (2) _____ .

The zabaleen (rubbish collectors) are one of a (3) _____ of autonomous groups that keep the city (4) _____ of rubbish while at the same time making a living. Traditionally, the main division is between the zabaleen and the wahiya (oasis people). The (5) _____ came around 1900 and took on responsibility for household waste disposal, selling it as fuel either to heat the public baths or for cooking. The arrival of the zabaleen about fifty years later from villages in Upper Egypt pushed the wahiya up (6) _____ . Now the wahiya are middlemen, (7) _____ the rights to service buildings and selling collection routes to the zabaleen. Zabaleen make money from feeding the organic waste (about two thirds of the total) to their (8) _____ and recycling the rest.

The women of the household sort out the (9) _____ categories – plastic, glass, metal, paper, and textiles. It's hard work – but more environmentally friendly than the mechanised garbage crushing trucks from Europe that the municipality brought in about ten years ago. Once rubbish has been (10) _____ compressed, no recycling is possible. It can only be dumped. One zabaleen woman called Layla empties bags on the floor for her four daughters to (11) _____ through. She sees her job as vital for the city's survival.

'We don't like attention. Rubbish is never attractive and we're quite happy (12) _____ quietly ... but our work supports a whole industry that's virtually invisible to most people.'

	A		B		C		D	
1	A left behind	B disregarded	C put aside	D thrown away
2	A unheard	B unknown	C unaware	D unimportant
3	A number	B group	C tribe	D sector
4	A devoid	B vacant	C clear	D deprived
5	A former	B latter	C previous	D concluding
6	A a portion	B a pinch	C an ounce	D a notch
7	A presenting	B taking	C acquiring	D providing
8	A livelihood	B household	C livestock	D smallholding
9	A varied	B various	C varying	D variable
10	A technically	B metallically	C mechanically	D technologically
11	A rummage	B see	C glance	D browse
12	A going on	B moving off	C settling in	D carrying on

Speaking: disagreeing with someone else's opinion

1 **List useful phrases for expressing …**

a partial agreement with your partner's views

_____

_____

_____

b polite disagreement

_____

_____

_____

2 **⌂ 11.2 PAPER 5, PART 4 Listen to Raul answer the following question, and think about your own views.**

> Do people care about their work ethically any more?

3 **Do you agree with Raul? Write down your responses to the points he makes. Use some of the phrases you noted in exercise 1.**

1 The value of doing a job well:

_____

_____

_____

2 A job is a means to gain money, nothing more:

_____

_____

_____

3 Respect:

_____

_____

_____

Writing: a report

SPOTLIGHT CHECKLIST

PAPER 2, PART 1 Being concise when writing a report

Practise:

- writing brief introductions and conclusions, to allow yourself more to say in the main paragraphs;

- restricting yourself to three main points;

- paraphrasing and summarising texts in order to train yourself to be concise.

1 Read the following examination task on the right, and then the sample answer below.

2 The sample answer in exercise 1 below is too long. Rewrite it more concisely, ensuring that your version falls within the required number of words. Use the following tactics to help you.

a Look for unnecessary phrases, and repeated points.

b The introduction should be two lines long. What information is unnecessary?

c For a task of the required length, there are too many paragraphs in the answer below. Can some points be joined together and mentioned as one point?

d Reduce the length of the conclusion by omitting unnecessary detail.

You are the assistant manager of a paint factory. You have received the email below from the manager.

Read the email, and the notes you have made on it, and, using the information provided, write a report. (180–220 words)

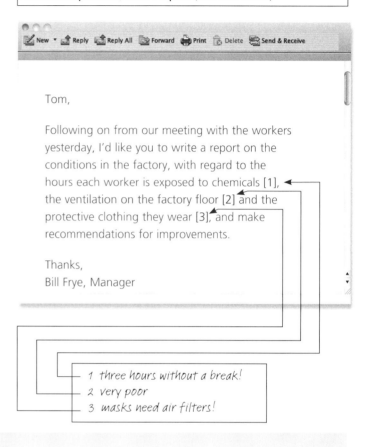

New · Reply · Reply All · Forward · Print · Delete · Send & Receive

Tom,

Following on from our meeting with the workers yesterday, I'd like you to write a report on the conditions in the factory, with regard to the hours each worker is exposed to chemicals [1], the ventilation on the factory floor [2] and the protective clothing they wear [3], and make recommendations for improvements.

Thanks,
Bill Frye, Manager

1 three hours without a break!
2 very poor
3 masks need air filters!

Introduction

The aim of this report is to examine the issues surrounding the workers' complaints, and to make some recommendations for improving the current situation. We asked workers their opinion on the following areas: the number of hours workers have to work with hazardous chemicals, the lack of sufficient ventilation on the factory floor, and inadequate protective clothing, and gathered the information set out in this report.

Exposure to chemicals

It was discovered that due to production demands and the fact that there have been recent cutbacks in the number of employees, workers are now working for more than three hours at a time without a break. During that time, they are constantly exposed to fumes from the paint chemicals. We need to reassess the number of workers needed during a shift, in order to ensure that workers have a fifteen-minute break every one and a half hours, during which they should leave the factory floor.

Ventilation

Research also revealed that, due to neglect, the filters in the ventilation system have become damaged, and as a result, the air is not circulating effectively on the factory floor. To combat this, the filters must be replaced, and a person allocated to be responsible for cleaning the new ones regularly.

Protective clothing

The problems mentioned above have been made worse by the fact that the clothing currently provided to the workers for their protection is sadly inadequate. The orange overalls are faded and worn, and the facial masks fail to give workers sufficient protection from the hazardous fumes. It would therefore be advisable to order new sets of overalls, and more modern masks with air filters, to ensure that workers are not affected by chemical fumes while they are working.

Conclusion

As can be seen from the points raised above, there are several problems facing workers at present. However, with the implementation of the improvements suggested, the situation will soon improve, to the satisfaction of workforce and management alike.

Getting started

1 Use the clues provided to find the missing words in the word box below. Find the word in the central column that is another word for *filmmaking*.

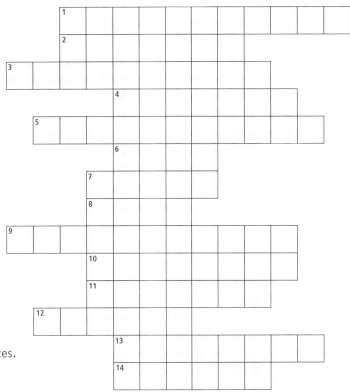

1 A film that is a huge box office success.

2 A film or play that tells a story to music.

3 The story as it is written for the screen.

4 The place where a film or scene is supposed to be taking place.

5 A film that contains information or facts.

6 All the actors and actresses in a film or play.

7 A person who makes a living out of appearing in films or on stage.

8 The development of a story in a film, play, or book.

9 The pictures or stills that are used in a film.

10 The person who is responsible for telling the actors how to act.

11 A short preview of a film that aims to sell it to audiences.

12 The written dialogue for a film or play.

13 A film or story that contains action, suspense and mystery.

14 The words of a song.

Reading: gapped text

1 Complete the missing words in the definitions below.

> **a** _____ (n) a subtle form of humour which involves saying things that you do not mean or the opposite of what is true. E.g. *'Hello, Mr Brown … I see you're nice and early for a change!'*
>
> DER _____ (adj), _____ (adv)

> **b** _____ (n) speech or writing which actually means the opposite of what it seems to say, and is sometimes intended as a joke or to mock or insult someone. E.g. *'I love Julie's new blonde hair – isn't she just like Marilyn Monroe!'*
>
> DER _____ (adj), _____ (adv)

2 **PAPER 1, PART 4 You are going to read an article (on page 91) containing interviews with four people who work in the film industry. For questions 1–15, choose from the interviews (A–D). The reviews may be chosen more than once.**

In which interview does the speaker …?

- insist that background research is an essential part of the job   1 ____
- use their craft to forge a link between data and emotions   2 ____
- feel proud of the developments that have occurred in recent years   3 ____
- acknowledge that the best in the field come via another medium   4 ____
- point out that success in the industry has created more opportunities   5 ____   6 ____
- look for inspiration to achieve his/her goals in another industry   7 ____
- express a wish to diversify more in his/her work in the future   8 ____
- claim one cannot begin to work until the groundwork is laid   9 ____
- feel frustrated by the wrong kind of media attention   10 ____
- despise the more naive approach others in the field tend to have   11 ____
- explain that the industry has undergone a complete revolution   12 ____
- not believe there is much long term security in their line of work   13 ____
- believe the best way to learn is by working with the masters   14 ____
- claim that innovations in the industry have paved the way for others   15 ____

PAPER 1, PART 4 Skimming and scanning

In this part of the exam you're required to match questions with the relevant information from the text. To do this, you need to locate a section of text where that idea is expressed, discounting ideas in other sections which may appear similar, but which do not reflect the whole of the question accurately.

3 Scan the texts to find an expression which means …

1 put oneself in a position of control *[text A]*
2 get something on paper *[text B]*
3 a way of achieving something *[text B]*
4 to make a connection between two things *[text B]*
5 work one's way to the top *[text C]*

4 Which of the following words from the text is used to describe …?

apprentice   digital   dot-com
genre   period-piece

1 a film set in a historical time
_____

2 something associated with Internet business _____

3 something associated with electronic technology
_____

4 a particular style of art or literature _____

5 a person who learns a trade or craft by working with a teacher
_____

A

Bollywood actor, Prabir Amar talks about his latest film in which he stars against his real-life love interest Kalika Chandana, and about the growth of the Hindi film industry.

'My role in the film is not that of a Casanova as the title hints. I play the boy next door and the film is about his love life at different phases of life. It's an interesting role though I would not like to be confined to a lover-boy role in all my films. The frustrating thing is the interest people are taking in linking our personal lives with the romance on-screen. Kalika and I would appreciate it if the press would take an interest in the film and our characters instead.

'Bollywood has never been so competitive. The Hindi film industry has grown so much in the last couple of years and as a result all actors have to constantly reinvent themselves. Every day a new actor takes the reins.'

B

Bruce Sterling, talks about being a science fiction writer, and what gives him inspiration.

'I call myself a science fiction writer because that's the name of my genre, but when I'm trying to pin a scene down on the page, I'm really writing "design fiction". I spend a lot of time thinking about imaginary industrial products, cyber products, and post-industrial products. Design thinking has become a powerful means to an end. I write fiction about science. I grapple with scientific knowledge from a literary perspective. I am using literary techniques to bridge the gap between what we have come to know about the universe, what that knowledge means to us and how that knowledge feels. In doing so, I've found that a designer's approach is fruitful. It is more productive, more authentic, more convincing and more moving than the wide-eyed approach of a sci-fi visionary, a new-age guru, a pop-science Mr Wizard figure or even a dot-com stock promoter.'

C

Ivana Primorace, whose films include and, talks about being a movie make-up artist.

'The job of the make-up artist and make-up designer is quite a lengthy process. You start with an initial idea or a script and then you research it, especially if it's a period piece such as *The Other Boleyn Girl*. You have to go into quite a lot of historical detail – not just make-up. You properly research the period. Then you discuss with the director and the actors what you are trying to achieve. And then, and only then, you decide what these people should look like.

'It's difficult to give advice to aspiring make-up designers. It's an apprenticeship and I think what young people don't realise is that it takes five or six years. People would like to speed up that process but you can't, so the best thing to do is to work with the designers and climb through the ranks. Theatre gives the best training, because there are quick changes. The best-trained people come from theatre to this day.'

D

Gillian Roderick talks about the changes that have been brought about in the film industry by computer graphics.

'Hollywood has gone digital, and the old ways of creating visual effects are dead. As film editors we used to painstakingly cut and glue film segments together. Now we sit in front of computer screens, editing entire feature-length films, while adding digitally-created sound. Film-goers can now witness the results of CG technology in full-length animated feature films all done on a computer; or lose themselves in special effects sequences in movies that could never have been achieved with such a degree of realism using conventional methods. At last, Hollywood has acknowledged that the digital age has finally arrived to stay and as a result, the number of well-trained animators and programmers has increased dramatically. All these factors have led to an explosion in both the size of existing studios and the number of new enterprises opening their doors.'

Language development:
modifying and intensifying adjectives with adverbs

1 Complete each sentence below with an appropriate word.

1 I had to have a tooth taken out yesterday – it was excruciatingly _____.

2 Have you seen Carl's new girlfriend? She's stunningly _____.

3 I had to help George with his homework but he is painfully _____ at maths.

4 I wouldn't advise going to see that four hour play – it was mind-numbingly _____ in my opinion!

5 Jemima is hopelessly _____ to her big brother Ted – she follows him everywhere!

6 Michael wants to become a surgeon like his mother, which is perfectly _____ under the circumstances!

Key word: *quite*

2 In the sentences that follow, decide if the meaning of *quite* is …

a fairly or rather

b extremely or absolutely

c to emphasise that a person or thing is very impressive or unusual (in front of a noun group)

d for emphasis

e to make what you are saying less emphatic or weaker (after a negative)

1 I think you are *quite* right to call off the wedding.

2 He didn't *quite* manage to pull it off as a film director.

3 The weather's *quite* warm at the moment.

4 We've had *quite* a day of it today!

5 Did you see that documentary yesterday? It was *quite* ridiculous.

3 Read the passage that follows and complete the gaps with a suitable phrase from the box below.

- baffling decision • coldly suppressed rage • conventional action • cool, cruel presence • coolly ruthless agent
- crash-bang Bond • deafening episodes • especially underpowered • indefinably difficult task • perpetually semi-pursed
- perplexingly named • short, sharp, bone-cracking bursts • similarly powered vehicle • smart elegance
- some new nastiness • thrilling music

Quantum of Solace

A review by Peter Bradshaw

He's back. Daniel Craig allays any fear that he was just a one-Martini Bond, with this, his second 007 adventure, the (1) _____ *Quantum Of Solace*. I've got to admit that this didn't excite me as much as *Casino Royale* and the villain is (2) _____. But Craig personally has the chops, as they say in Hollywood. He's made the part his own, every inch the (3) _____-cum-killer, nursing a broken heart and (4) _____. This is a (5) _____, high on action, low on quips, long on location glamour, short on product placement.

Under the direction of Marc Forster, the movie ladles out the adrenalin in a string of (6) _____: car chases, plane wrecks, motor boat collisions. If it's got an engine, and runs on fuel, and can crash into another (7) _____, with Bond at the wheel, well, it goes in the movie. As in *Casino Royale*, the famous John Barry theme tune is saved up until the end; a (8) _____, I always think, not to use this (9) _____ at the beginning of the film.

Bond has hardly got his 007 spurs, when he's infuriating M, Judi Dench, with his insolence and insubordination. Out in the field, he's whacking enemy agents in (10) _____ of violence when he should be bringing them in for questioning. But set against this is the (11) _____ of Craig – his lips (12) _____, as if savouring (13) _____ his opponents intend to dish out to him, and the nastiness he intends to dish out in return. *Quantum of Solace* isn't as good as *Casino Royale*: the (14) _____ of Craig's Bond debut has been toned down in favour of (15) _____. But the man himself powers this movie; he carries the film: it's an (16) _____ task for an actor. Craig measures up.

Listening: understanding purpose and function

1   🎧 12.1 PAPER 4, PART 1 You'll hear three different extracts. For questions 1–6, choose the answer (A, B, or C) which fits best according to what you hear. There are two questions for each extract.

Extract One

You hear part of an interview with a songwriter.

1   Claudia says she wrote the musical because
   A   she was bored with seeing the same kind of musical all the time.
   B   she was inspired by other rock stars who had done the same thing.
   C   she wanted to see her songs used to tell a story visually.

2   The reason for choosing her particular subject matter was to
   A   discourage teenage girls from leaving home too young.
   B   examine black teenage problems from a new perspective.
   C   give black women more chances to star in musicals.

Extract Two

You hear two people talking about a film they've just seen.

3   The speakers agree that the film was
   A   confusing.
   B   funny.
   C   strange.

4   According to the speakers, the humour in the film
   A   did not translate to other cultures.
   B   was practical rather than linguistic.
   C   was very old-fashioned.

Extract Three

You hear a conversation in which a director is talking to a set designer.

5   The set designer implies that the director
   A   has never worked in the theatre before.
   B   doesn't know anything about the theatre.
   C   has impractical ideas for a stage design.

6   The set designer suggests that he
   A   needs to be given free materials.
   B   feels creatively restricted by the director's ideas.
   C   could build a better set in a different theatre.

Speaking: exchanging ideas (parts 3 and 4)

PAPER 5, PARTS 3 and 4 Exchanging ideas

Remember:
- In both parts 3 and 4 you will be given the opportunity to show your range of language and your ability to invite the opinions and ideas of your partner.
- You'll be expected to share the interaction with your partner and to initiate and respond appropriately.
- You'll be assessed on your ability to use the language of negotiation and collaboration.

Practise:
- discussing topics as often as you can;
- debating controversial issues with your friends.

1   🎧 12.2 PAPER 5, PART 3 Listen to two students answering part 3 of the Speaking exam. What do you notice? As you listen, note down the pictures that Roberta and Marcel mention.

Picture 1: _____

Picture 2: _____

Picture 3: _____

Picture 4: _____

Picture 5: _____

Picture 6: _____

2   Turn to page 161 and look at the tapescript. Decide at which points Marcel could have interrupted and at which points Roberta could have passed her ideas over to him.

3   Rewrite the dialogue so that it is more balanced.

4   PAPER 5, PART 4 Write two discussion questions that could be asked as a follow on to the questions in part 3.

Grammar: participle clauses

1 Match the uses of the present participle to the examples that follow.

The present participle can be used:

1 as an adjective

2 to form continuous tenses

3 after verbs of sensation

4 after *catch/find* + object

5 after *have* + object

6 *spend/waste*

7 after *be busy*

8 to introduce a statement in indirect speech

a *I felt him **touching** me.*

b ***Refusing** the offer of a lift he picked up his coat and left.*

c *I found him **going** through my things.*

d *I'm busy **working** right now.*

e *It was an **exciting** moment.*

f *Paul is **watching** you.*

g *I'll have you **riding** horses again before you know it.*

h *He wastes his time **playing** video games.*

2 Match the rules below to the example sentences on the right.

A present participle can replace a sentence or main clause:	
1 when two actions by the same subject occur simultaneously	a *They rushed into the house, **leaving** muddy footprints on the carpet.*
2 when one action is immediately followed by another and is performed by the same subject	b ***Clutching** the baby in her arms, she rushed out of the house.*
3 when the second action is caused by, or is a result of, the first action	c ***Putting** down his briefcase, he walked over to the window.*
A present participle	
4 can replace a subordinate *clause with as/since/ because* + subject + verb	a *The food **being** cold, we decided to warm it up*
5 can be used when the subject of the participle clause is different from the subject in the main or subordinate clause.	b ***Knowing** that it would rain, she took an umbrella.*
6 can be used in a clause that follows another participle clause	c *Anyone **wanting** pizza should order it now.*
7 to replace a relative clause (reduced relative clauses)	d ***Being** the last to arrive, and not **wanting** to keep them waiting, I offered to drive*
The perfect participle can be used:	
8 to more clearly show that one action had finished before another began	a ***Having been lied** to before, he found it hard to trust me.*
9 to emphasise that an action expressed by the participle happened before the action expressed by the next verb (passive)	b ***Having been** to Spain twice before, he wanted to go somewhere new.*
10 to form the passive voice	c ***Having been designed** by a top Italian architect ...*
The past participle can be used:	
11 as an adjective	a ***Designed** by Sir Christopher Wren ...*
12 to form the perfect tenses	b *To have **slept** on a bed of roses ...*
13 to form infinitives	c *She had **fallen** asleep.*
14 to replace a subject + passive verb	d *She recognised it as a **stolen** car.*

3 Read the text below and replace the underlined parts of each sentence with a participle or participle clause. Reduce any clauses that can be reduced or joined together.

A Film to Remember

Last week during the film festival, (1) <u>Cynthia and I, who are both fans of the cinema</u>, decided to go and see a film. (2) <u>The film had been directed by Woody Allen. It had received quite good reviews.</u> (3) <u>Because we had been given</u> the afternoon off, we decided to see a matinee. (4) <u>As we were crossing the road</u> outside the cinema we bumped into (5) <u>Dick and Isabella, who are good friends of Cynthia's. We invited them</u> to come too. (6) <u>When we arrived at the cinema</u>, we saw that we had missed the start of Woody Allen. (7) <u>As we didn't want to go</u> in late, I suggested going to see the film with George Clooney instead. (8) <u>Since Isabella had already seen the film she</u> didn't want to see it again. (9) <u>Seeing as we didn't want</u> to see any other film, we decided to go for a meal at a (10) <u>nearby restaurant, which was run by an Italian couple.</u> You'll never believe who we saw having dinner in that restaurant: Woody Allen and George Clooney!

Use of English: open cloze

1 Read the text below all the way through, ignoring the gaps, and answer the following question:
What does the writer think of the film?

2 Read the review again and identify the following parts of speech needed to fill each gap. Tick them off the list below.

adjective after noun	particle after noun	adjective (defining adjective before noun)
adjective before noun	particle before noun	adjective (preceded by a possessive)
adverb	preposition	conjunction (particle expressing comparison)
auxiliary verb	preposition of time	particle (forming phrasal verb)
modal auxiliary	relative pronoun	verb (simple present, third person plural)

3 PAPER 3, PART 2 For questions 1–15, read the text below and think of the word which best fits each gap. Use only one word in each gap.

Snow White and the Seven Dwarfs

Some films are beyond cynicism. A real classic influences the hearts and minds of audiences, even generations (1) _____ its creation. Some classics like *The Wizard of Oz* hold (2) _____ value that they become indelibly etched in the minds of movie-goers from every walk of life. Disney's *Snow White* is another such film that has earned a tender place in our hearts.

Indeed, (3) _____ Miss White and her band of little men, Disney's moneymaking empire of full-length animated films might never (4) _____ existed. Films that generation after generation of children have laughed and cried over might never have been. But *Snow White* is more (5) _____ the grandfather of full-length animated films; it is a genuine classic in its (6) _____ right.

Disney's adaptation (7) _____ this classic, star-crossed fairy tale (originally a Brothers Grimm fable), manages to transcend cultural and social barriers to tell an honest and heartfelt story about loss and love. In fact, so successful (8) _____ Disney's version at rousing our emotions, that most people think of nothing (9) _____ when they think of *Snow White*. With the new box-set DVD we can once (10) _____ find delight in the magic of the film, cringe (11) _____ terror at the evil deeds of the wicked queen, and laugh and smile at the antics of the loyal seven dwarfs. *Snow White* brings everything (12) _____ in one beautifully rendered (and of course, hand-drawn) package.

However you view the film, *Snow White and the Seven Dwarfs* (13) _____ be acknowledged as an icon, its characters standing alongside Dorothy, Superman, and a host of (14) _____ cinematic creations (15) _____ have indelibly left their mark on every aspect of western movie-going culture.

Writing: a review

PAPER 2, PART 2 Planning a review

Tips

- Read the question carefully, making sure you understand what is required.

- Underline the key points to help you focus.

- Think of the style, structures, and vocabulary you will need and make sure you feel confident about answering the particular question.

- After you have written, check that your style and content are relevant to the question.

Practise:

- reviewing films, books, plays, CDs, concerts as often as you can.

- reading as many entertainment reviews as you can.

1 Look at the following question.

PAPER 2, PART 2

> A film review website has invited its visitors to send in reviews of their favourite animated films, briefly outlining the plot, saying what they liked most about it and giving their opinions on any elements of the film that made it stand out from the others. You have decided to write a review.

2 Write a paragraph plan and decide which of the following elements you would write about.

- an outline of the story
- details of the plot
- a description of the characters
- what you liked about it
- what you disliked about it
- background information
- the writer, director or actors
- the setting or costumes
- what awards it won or how successful it was
- when it was written, made or performed
- your recommendation

3 Read the film review on the right and tick the points in the box above that have been mentioned.

4 The paragraphs are mixed up. Number them in the correct order.

1 _____ 2 _____ 3 _____
4 _____ 5 _____

Toy Story

a The film was the combined effort of two studios: Pixar and Disney, and it (1) _____ computer graphic films which were soon to dominate the market. Films such as *Finding Nemo, Ice Age,* and *Shrek* soon followed and were all huge box office hits. The voice talents of Tom Hanks and Tim Allen helped to draw the crowds.

b Most of all I loved the humour. The script (2) _____ that never become corny. It can be enjoyed by both adults and children alike; and I'm sure many generations of children will continue to take delight in it.

c At first Woody is miffed to find himself (3) _____, and the other toys unjustly accuse him of trying to get rid of Buzz, but this misunderstanding takes Woody and Buzz on an adventure that will eventually unite them.

d *Toy Story* has got to be (4) _____ _____. It's also the first full-length computer animated film which is an achievement (5) _____.

e It tells the story of Woody, a wooden toy cowboy that belongs to a little boy named Andy. When Andy is not in the room, Woody and the other toys come to life and have a lot of fun. But all this changes when Andy is given a new toy for his birthday – a spaceman called Buzz Lightyear, who (6) _____ _____ the more traditional 'Woody'.

5 Complete the gaps in the review above with one of the following phrases.

a is loaded with hilarious one-liners

b sports many more gimmicks and novelties than

c no longer foremost in Andy's affections

d in its own right

e paved the way for

f one of the all time animated greats

6 PAPER 2, PART 2 Write a review of your favourite animated or children's film.

EXAM MENU

Reading:	Paper 1, part 2
Listening:	Paper 4, part 4
Use of English:	Paper 3, parts 2 and 4
Speaking:	Paper 5, part 3
Writing:	Paper 2, part 2

Getting started

1 The words below are hidden in the box. They may be placed vertically, horizontally, diagonally, forwards or backwards. See how many you can find.

broadcast	clarify	communicate	convey
exchange	explain	impart	information
instil	knowledge	message	publish
reveal	send	share	transmit

C	O	M	M	U	N	I	C	A	T	E	N
R	O	T	H	I	N	N	E	E	X	X	I
C	U	N	O	T	P	F	E	D	H	C	S
L	A	E	V	E	R	O	W	I	E	H	A
A	M	X	P	E	E	R	P	X	A	A	D
R	K	P	U	M	Y	M	H	R	Z	N	C
I	Q	L	J	R	L	A	E	W	E	G	B
F	D	A	N	T	E	T	R	E	X	E	O
Y	A	I	S	O	P	I	N	S	T	I	L
O	W	N	Y	T	S	O	U	I	R	Z	R
E	F	I	T	D	K	N	M	C	A	J	F
D	M	Q	N	V	A	E	B	I	N	E	T
J	E	E	O	W	P	I	A	L	S	U	S
T	S	A	C	D	A	O	R	B	M	T	A
R	S	S	T	R	E	M	Y	U	I	K	M
A	A	H	S	I	L	B	U	P	T	T	N
P	G	R	Y	E	A	X	N	G	N	U	T
M	E	K	N	O	W	L	E	D	G	E	U
I	R	A	W	P	N	O	P	L	E	R	V

2 Find the word hidden in the box which means to make a fact or event widely known to the public.

Reading: predicting information

SPOTLIGHT EXAM GUIDANCE

PAPER 1, PART 2 Predicting information

Read the text as a whole to get an idea of how the theme develops before attempting the task. Try to predict what kind of information will follow a paragraph. For example, do you expect to see an example of a point made, a further supporting point, or perhaps an opposing argument?

Tips
- Pay careful attention to names mentioned before the gap.

- Look at the paragraph which follows the gap. Is the same person speaking, or has this changed?

- Think about what information the missing paragraph needs to include to enable the paragraphs to flow.

1 PAPER 1, PART 2 Choose from paragraphs (A–G) the one which best fits each gap in the text (1–6). There is one extra paragraph which you do not need to use.

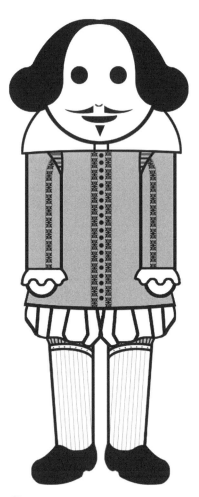

English as she will be spoke

On 23 September 1938, engineers from the Westinghouse Electric and Manufacturing Company sank a time capsule deep into the ground at Flushing Meadows Park in New York City, venue of the 1939 World's Fair. Among other artefacts, the capsule contained a printed 'key to English' that described the words, sounds, and grammar of twentieth-century American English to help its discoverers, 5,000 years in the future, understand a language that presumably would be as foreign to them as Hittite is to us.

1 [...]

10 Will it be like this: 'I punya manglish iz wely chekai wan lah, singlish lagi terok, i tok chinglish beter'?[1]

Or this: 'Our Father, who comes to us from above, your name is holy'?[2]

Or this: 'It musve ben some girt jynt thing hy hy up and with a shyning and a flashing to it time back way back when they had boats in the air and all the res of it'?[3]

2 [...]

Historical trends are a useful guide to the future. One common prediction is that Modern English is following the same path as classical Latin – a global language belonging to
20 a powerful empire which evolved gradually, broke apart and was eventually buried by its progeny. According to language historians, as early as AD 300 the Latin of the masses had a vocabulary, pronunciation, and grammar largely distinct from the elite's classical Latin. Over the next 500 years this 'vulgar' Latin split into increasingly distinct regional dialects, and by AD 800 it had evolved into a family of mutually unintelligible languages – the forerunners of today's Italian, Spanish, French and other Romance languages.

3 [...]

What seems certain is that new words will form, meanings
30 will migrate, and obsolete words will die out. These are the facts of life for any language. Vocabulary changes not so much because new words are invented but because words take new meanings and are combined in new ways. For this reason, 'most likely the English of 2300 will be harder for us to understand than the English of 1700,' says Edwin

Duncan, a historian of English at Towson University in Maryland. He points out that Shakespeare knew the words 'hot', 'dog', 'ice' and 'cream', but he wouldn't know what we mean by 'hot dog' and 'ice cream'.

4 [...]

The momentum of this shift is still being felt. Marckwardt [40] predicted that some vowels of English will continue to evolve. The word 'home' – pronounced 'heim' in Germanic, 'hahm' in Old English and 'hawm' in Middle English – might some day be 'hoom'. Some vowels, however, appear immutable: those in 'ship', 'bet', 'ox' and 'full' have remained the same for centuries.

5 [...]

His predictions for grammar were more radical. His main prediction was that more and more English words would lose their inflections, in keeping with long-term trends. Old English had a rich system of inflections for conjugating [50] words (for example sing, sang, sung) and marking nouns with inflections to indicate such things as possessive, indirect objects, or the objects of a preposition. Then, about 900 years ago, the system began to collapse, mainly because words borrowed from Latin, French, and Norse had stress on their first syllables, which de-emphasised the final syllables where the inflections were. Norse speakers also introduced new endings. English began its life as a language like Latin, where one word mattered little because inflections kept meaning and syntax straight, but [60] ever since 1066 it has been on a slow path to becoming a language like Chinese, where word order is fixed because the language has no inflections at all.

6 [...]

Any changes that do occur to our language will probably be quite slow. Last October, 'Nature' published a paper about the pace at which irregular English verbs such as 'run/ran' regularise by acquiring '-ed' to mark them as past tense. This has been happening gradually over the past 1200 years as modern English evolved from its Germanic roots. As one example, what we know as [70] 'helped' was 'holp' in Middle English.

---

1   Malaysian English: 'I can't speak Malaysian or Singaporean English very well, but I speak Chinese English better.'
2   Globish, developed by Jean Paul Nerriere
3   From 'Riddley Walker' by Russell Hoban, set in a post-apocalyptic future England.

A Predicting future vocabulary is difficult, but how will the language be pronounced? How will words be put together, and what will be the shape of sentences? Nearly fifty years ago, Albert Marckwardt, a linguist at the University of Michigan, predicted some characteristics of the English to come based on where it had been. Take, for instance, the shifting sands of English vowels. From around the twelfth century until the sixteenth century, English underwent the 'great vowel shift'. This shortened some vowels – like 'ee' to 'aye' as in 'mice' – and pushed others to the front of the mouth, for example the Middle English vowel pronounced 'oh', which became 'oo' as in 'boot'.

B It's a safe bet that the discoverers of the Westinghouse time capsule will need to use Harrington's key, because 5,000 years is a long time in the life of any language. Only 1,600 years ago, the people who spoke the languages that would form the core of English had not yet migrated to England. A thousand years ago, English was a language so different from our own you'd have to learn it as a foreign language; very few people can understand 'Beowulf' in its original Old English. The fourteenth-century Middle English of Chaucer's *Canterbury Tales* needs to be updated to make it fully intelligible. Even the unmistakably modern English of Shakespeare can be hard to understand, and that's only 400 years old.

C The fate of the few remaining inflections (including the plural -*s*, the possessive -'*s*, the past tense -*ed* and -*ing* on verbs) is up in the air. Some show signs of changing. Words like 'messier' and 'messiest' are giving way to 'more ...' and 'most messy', while the possessive is being replaced by phrases with 'of'. English speakers used to be able to say 'our's one'; now we say 'one of ours'. The verbal inflections (-*ed* and -*ing*, among others) seem more stable. 'I really think these won't drop,' says Geoff Pullum, a linguist at the University of Edinburgh, UK, and co-author of 'The Cambridge Grammar of the English Language'. 'Not in hundreds of years.'

D The author of the document, John Harrington of the Smithsonian Institution in Washington DC, presumed that modern English would be radically changed by the year 6939. But how? Is it possible to say what English will be like 5,000 years from now, or even 500?

E Compared to vowels, English consonants have always been fairly stable. There have been some notable changes – the 'k' in 'knife' was once pronounced, 'nature' was 'natoor', 'special' was 'spe-see-al', and there have also been some shifts in how people say 'r' and 'l'. But Marckwardt was confident that English consonants would stay the same.

F Of the 177 verbs Lieberman tracked, seventy-nine have now regularised. So what is to become of the remaining ninety-eight? They are not going to follow suit any time soon. Lieberman predicts that only 10 more will become regular by 2500. The next candidate is 'wed', whose past tense ('wed') is already giving way to 'wedded'.

G But history can only take us so far. The worldwide success of English, which puts it on many more lips and tongues than are found in its native-speaking homelands, and the development of global communications mean that the forces acting on the language are unlike anything seen in the past. Fortunately, recent research into language evolution can help.

Language development: nouns followed by particles

1 Complete the following sentences taken from the text on pages 98–99, with the correct particle.

   a Historical trends are a useful guide _____ the future. [line 17] _____

   b His predictions _____ grammar were more radical. [line 47]

   c Old English had a rich system _____ inflections for conjugating words ... [line 49]

   d Some show signs _____ changing. [para C]

   e Fortunately, recent research _____ language evolution can help. [para G]

2 Complete the following sentences with a suitable particle from the box below. Words can be used more than once.

for	to	of	over	with

   1 I have a terrible fear _____ heights.

   2 We need to find a solution _____ this problem quickly!

   3 Access _____ the building is situated down that alleyway round the corner.

   4 Isn't there any alternative _____ having an operation, doctor?

   5 The fire officer was given an award in recognition _____ his services to the community.

   6 The writers are working in collaboration _____ scientists in order to produce a comprehensive book on space exploration.

   7 She was on the verge _____ tears, so I asked her what was wrong.

   8 The city council and refuse collectors are in dispute _____ wages again.

Key word: *set*

3 The past participle form of the verb *set* can also be used in certain phrases. Explain the meaning of the phrases in italics in the following sentences.

   1 'Don't ask her to change now. She's too old and *set in her ways.*'

   2 'Jane's parents are so *set against* her marrying Kevin that they may not go to the wedding.'

   3 'Oliver's *set to* start university in September.'

   4 'This hotel has a very good *set menu,* but if you want more choice, there's a great restaurant down the road.'

   5 'Claire's s*et on* coming to stay for Christmas, so I can't say no to her.'

4 Match the following phrasal verbs with their definitions.

A

1	set about	6	set down
2	set someone against someone	7	set in
3	set apart	8	set off
4	set aside	9	set out
5	set back	10	set up

B

   a delay the development of something

   b cause someone to start a fight with someone else

   c make an alarm start ringing

   d keep something such as money for a particular purpose

   e write something down in order to keep a record of it

   f start doing something which takes time and effort

   g (of a period/season etc) start and seem likely to continue for a long time

   h begin with the intention of doing something specific

   i start a business

   j make someone look different or special compared to others

5 Complete the sentences with a suitable phrasal verb from exercise 4. Make any grammatical changes necessary.

   1 It suddenly went very cold in November, as winter _____.

   2 Billy _____ the fire alarm at school again. The headmistress is furious!

   3 I've been _____ some money each month for my summer holiday next year.

   4 Simon was doing well at work, but this accident has really _____ his latest project.

   5 Can you _____ your ideas in a proposal and email it to me, Helen?

6 There are many more phrases with *set*, including phrasal verbs. How many can you think of? Check in a dictionary, and make a list or a word web in your notebook.

Listening: multiple matching

1   ⌂ 13.1 PAPER 4, PART 4 **You are going to hear five people talking about communicating with children.**

Task One

For questions **1–5**, choose from the list **A–H** the person who is speaking:

A   a family counsellor

B   a gifted young person

C   a primary school teacher   Speaker 1 [1]

D   a child psychiatrist   Speaker 2 [2]

E   a vet   Speaker 3 [3]

F   a young person with a learning disability   Speaker 4 [4]

G   a working mother   Speaker 5 [5]

H   a parent of a child with special needs

Task Two

For questions **6–10**, choose from the list **A–H** what the person is expressing:

A   support for a system which teaches children to become more responsible/confident.

B   anger over a misunderstanding.

C   relief that early fears were unfounded.   Speaker 1 [6]

Speaker 2 [7]

D   frustration over an inability to communicate.   Speaker 3 [8]

E   appreciation of a small gesture of kindness.   Speaker 4 [9]

Speaker 5 [10]

F   advice on parental approaches to a problem.

G   delight in the effects of a learning strategy.

H   concern that a teaching method won't work.

Grammar (1 & 2): text references and *it/there* as introductory pronouns

1 In the following sentences, circle the word(s) that the underlined word refers back to.

1 In the village, children play football, go cycling, and pick blackberries in the autumn. <u>Such</u> activities are almost impossible in the city.

2 I told him my secret, and he then went and told the whole class. <u>That</u> really annoyed me!

3 Many people have difficulty expressing their feelings. <u>This</u> can result in isolation and loneliness.

4 In the following report, we describe the various ways in which we have tried to communicate with chimpanzees. <u>These</u> attempts have proved successful to a certain degree.

5 I tried phoning her, and then, in desperation, I wrote her a letter. <u>It</u> was no use.

2 Complete the following sentences with *it* or *there*.

1 _____'s funny you should mention that, as I was just about to phone her.

2 Waiter! _____'s something floating in my drink!

3 Karen, _____'s someone at the door!

4 _____ suddenly occurred to me that maybe she intended to leave.

5 _____'s a good idea to check what you write before you hand it in to the teacher.

3 PAPER 3, PART 2 For questions 1–15, read the text below and think of the word which best fits each gap. Use only one word in each gap.

Use of English: gapped sentences

1 PAPER 3, PART 4 For questions 1–5, think of one word only which can be used appropriately in all three sentences.

1 On holiday this year I managed to _____ by with my poor Spanish.

'When giving a presentation, it's vital to _____ your message across without making your audience feel they're being manipulated.'

I told Rob the jam sandwich joke, but he didn't _____ it!

2 'The _____ is that Jim's getting the sack and Dave's up for promotion, but it's not official as yet.'

'Jim, can I have a _____ with you in my office?'

'I give you my _____ that I won't tell anyone about this.'

3 This article was written by our _____ correspondent in Tangier.

'Waiter! There's a _____ body floating about in my soup!'

Clara said she could speak five _____ languages.

4 She did some research, and decided to _____ up her own e-business.

Jane and Colin have finally _____ a date for the wedding.

As his older brother, you should _____ a good example to Callum!

5 'We don't want to wake Mum up, so don't make a _____.'

'I don't like the _____ of this party idea, so you're not going!'

'Peter! That music's too loud! Can you turn the _____ down, please?'

Animal Talk

Animals have various ways of transmitting messages to each other. **(1)** _____ of all, body language is widely used throughout the animal kingdom. **(2)** _____ can be manifested in several ways. A cat, for example, will twitch its tail when agitated or about to attack, **(3)** _____ a dog wags its tail to show a willingness to be friends, or happiness at seeing someone. Some animals use facial expressions or body shapes to send messages to others. Animals **(4)** _____ as the firefly even change colour. **(5)** _____ usually do this to attract a mate, or to ward off enemies.

Sound is another important means **(6)** _____ communication among animals such as whales, **(7)** _____ use sound vibrations to pinpoint prey or attract a mate. **(8)** _____ is known as echolocation, and it is particularly effective under water. On land, crickets ward off enemies **(9)**_____ rubbing their front legs together. **(10)** _____ has also been discovered that apes have a wide range of calling sounds. **(11)** _____ are used to communicate such things as the discovery of food or the threat of imminent danger. Chimpanzees also use touch to form bonds with each other and show affection, much as humans do. **(12)** _____ is known as tactile communication, an example of **(13)** _____ can be seen when one chimp grooms another chimp's body.

Animals also send messages via chemical or hormone secretion. Members of the cat family, **(14)** _____ wild and domestic, will spray certain chemicals to mark out their territory **(15)** _____ others to recognise. A female giraffe urinates to let the male know she is fertile and ready to mate.

Speaking: sustaining interaction

1   Read the dialogue below. Marietta is expressing her views regarding the pictures shown above and responding to her partner's input. Imagine you are her partner, Rahul. Write down the responses her partner makes.

Interlocutor: Now, I'd like you to talk about something together for about three minutes ... Here are some pictures showing various learning aids for language schools.

First, talk to each other about the merits and limitations of using these learning aids. Then, decide which one would be the most useful for your language school to invest in.

All right?

Rahul: *Yes, well, on first sight, I would say that all of these learning aids look useful! Can the school afford to buy all of them? Computers, in particular. Don't you agree, Marietta?*

Marietta: Well, I think they're useful for someone learning alone, but I'm not sure how useful they are in a language classroom. I prefer the ... er ... communication between students and teacher to be direct, and ...

1 _____
   _____

Marietta: Yes, but I think that the language programmes on the computer are good for use at home, for homework, and private study. In the school, where students are together, it's good to use the time for active, direct communication practice.

2 _____
   _____

Marietta: Mm, perhaps you're right. What about the satellite TV idea? Do you think that's useful?

3 _____
   _____

Marietta: No! I'm afraid I disagree with you. I hear that all the time, and perhaps it's true for some kids, but I still think that kids like reading. You can see this with films that have been made out of books. I still hear people say they prefer the book to the film. I don't think that has changed so much.

4 _____
   _____

Marietta: Yes, but only for some students. The whole school wouldn't be able to go!

No, I quite like the idea of these books, and doing group literature in the classroom. Look, there's a DVD of the film, too! That would make you happy! Studying a novel together will encourage discussion, and at the same time students will learn new words. Then, they can see the film and compare it to the book. So, it's ...

Interlocutor: Thank you.

2   ⌒ 13.2 Listen to the dialogue, and compare your responses with what Rahul actually says. Then, turn to the tapescript on page 162, and underline any useful phrases you see for sustaining the conversation.

Writing: contribution to a longer piece

SPOTLIGHT CHECKLIST

PAPER 2, PART 2 Contribution to a longer piece

Remember:

- You're being asked to contribute a section to a larger piece of writing, such as a guide book, or a large feature in a magazine.

- The main purpose of the larger piece will usually be to provide information or offer advice.

- The style of your answer will depend on the longer piece. This will be stated in the question.

Tips

- Identify the style of the longer piece, to determine the style of your answer.

- Organise your answer carefully. You may use headings, if you wish.

1   Read the following question.

> Your student council has decided to produce a booklet giving advice to teenagers. The editor has invited you to contribute a section discussing the problems teenagers sometimes face communicating with their parents, and giving advice on how to deal with them.

Now decide on the following, by circling the option you choose.

1 The intended audience is …?

   a the college governors   b the student body

2 Your style should be …?

   a formal   b informal

3 You will use headings …?

   a yes   b no

2   Read the three opening paragraphs above right. Decide which one would suit the following publications.

1 a teenage magazine

2 a professional psychologist magazine

3 an article giving young people advice

---

a [Heading …]

The following study addresses an issue which often affects teenagers; that of communication with their parents. During this period of emotional and physical transition, it is sometimes difficult for young people and their parents to talk to each other, for various reasons.

b [Heading …]

You're fifteen! You're no longer a child! So, why does Mum keep talking to you as if you were? Why does Dad keep yelling at you to listen to your mother and stop lazing around? Don't they know that important things are happening to you? Don't they realise you're too old for them to be telling you what to do all the time?

c [Heading …]

Your teens represent a period of emotional as well as physical change, and this may cause problems in communication between you and your parents. The terms of such things as rules and discipline need to be adjusted, and this often causes disagreement and misunderstandings.

3   Which of the following points should you include in your answer?

Teenagers

… sometimes have problems with drugs

… are no longer children, but neither are they completely adults

… have to make decisions about their future

… want more freedom

… value their friends more

… have to study, and need advice

Parents

… don't understand them

… find it difficult to accept that their child has grown up.

4   Plan your paragraph structure. Decide whether you need to use headings, and what those headings will be.

Paragraph 1: _____

Paragraph 2: _____

Paragraph 3: _____

Paragraph 4: _____

5   Write your contribution. (220–260 words)

14 Gaia's legacy

EXAM MENU

Reading:	Paper 1, part 3
Listening:	Paper 4, part 2
Speaking:	Paper 5, part 3
Use of English:	Paper 3, parts 3 and 5
Writing:	Paper 2, part 2

Getting started

1 Complete the crossword with the clues provided on the left.

Down

1 One of the group of animals that includes apes, monkeys, baboons and lemurs.

2 One of the group of animals that develop in water but grow lungs to breathe on land.

3 One of the group of animals that gives birth to live young and nourishes them with milk.

4 Snakes, tortoises, and lizards are all a kind of ...

7 An animal with hollow bones and feathers.

Across

2 Human beings are a kind of ...

5 An animal with a three-segmented body and three pairs of legs.

6 An animal that does not have a backbone, such as a jellyfish.

8 An animal that breathes oxygen through gills and lives in water.

2 Unscramble the letters from the grey boxes to find the name of the third spherical orbiting body in sequence from the sun.

_ _ _ _ _   _ _ _ _ _

3 How much do you know about animal species? Match the animals (1–8) with the correct group (a–h) and choose the odd one out in each case.

1 **invertebrate**	a	lizard	snake	crocodile	worm
2 **fish**	b	spider	beetle	cockroach	butterfly
3 **amphibian**	c	snake	salmon	tuna	shark
4 **insect**	d	bat	whale	dog	goose
5 **reptile**	e	gorilla	human being	chimpanzee	spider monkey
6 **bird**	f	worm	jellyfish	tuna	sponge
7 **mammal**	g	ostrich	pterosaur	eagle	penguin
8 **apes**	h	platypus	frog	newt	salamander

Reading: gist and detail

SPOTLIGHT CHECKLIST

PAPER 1, PART 3 Matching gist to detail

Remember:
The correct option and the stem question should have the same meaning as the part of the text it refers to.

Tips
• Always read the text once for gist and again for detail.

• Underline the part of the text which answers the question.

• Beware of qualifying words in the question and the text (*everyone, some, many, a few* etc) as these can alter the meaning.

1 **Read the text on page 107. For questions 1–7, choose the answer (A, B, C or D) which you think fits best according to the text. Underline the answers in the text.**

1 If we wanted to travel to Sirius it would take us
   A almost a million years.
   B twenty-five thousand years.
   C 4.6 light years.
   D almost nine years at the speed of light.

2 If we wanted to reach the centre of our galaxy
   A we would have to travel faster than the speed of light.
   B we would have to go past Sirius.
   C it would take us a billion years.
   D it would take longer than our species' history.

3 The writer mentions alien visitors to Earth in order
   A to show that they also have families like ours.
   B to suggest that they have a sense of humour.
   C to point out that he regards such visits as improbable.
   D to prove that it can be done.

4 In the 1960s Frank Drake tried to calculate
   A the number of stars in the Milky Way.
   B the chances of there existing advanced life in the universe.
   C the number of stars in a selected portion of the universe.
   D the number of planetary systems that could contain life.

5 According to statistical probability,
   A it's highly unlikely that intelligent beings exist anywhere other than Earth.
   B there's a pretty good chance that life exists, but only beyond our galaxy.
   C there could be millions of planets with intelligent life in our galaxy alone.
   D there's only a very slim chance that life exists elsewhere in the universe.

6 If beings from another civilisation were watching us now,
   A they could be seeing light that left Earth 2 centuries ago.
   B they would be studying our history 200 years ago.
   C they would be bemused by our technological progress.
   D they would try to greet us in old-fashioned English.

7 The writer mentions Carl Sagan's observation to show that
   A space is packed with planets.
   B space is mainly empty space.
   C it's hard to find planets at random.
   D planets are worth more than we think.

2 **Scan the text again to find a word or phrase that means the following:**

1 a place with nothing, not even air in it (n) *[para 2]* _____

2 group, collection of something (n) *[para 2]* _____

3 synonym of 2; a group of something all together (n) *[para 2]* _____

4 scare someone to death (exp) *[para 3]* _____

5 huge, enormous (adj) *[para 4]* _____

6 getting smaller and smaller (v) *[para 4]* _____

7 to a very great degree (adv) *[para 5]* _____

8 without any sequence or order (adv) *[para 7]* _____

Lost in the Cosmos

What else is out there, beyond the solar system? Well, nothing and a great deal, depending on how you look at it.

In the short term, it's nothing. The most perfect vacuum ever created by humans is not as empty as the emptiness of interstellar space. And there is a great deal of this nothingness until you get to the next bit of something. Our nearest neighbour in the cosmos, Proxima Centauri, which is part of the three-star cluster known as Alpha Centauri, is 4.3 light years away, a sissy skip in galactic terms, but still a hundred million times further than a trip to the Moon. To reach it by spaceship would take at least 25,000 years, and even if you made the trip you still wouldn't be anywhere except at a lonely clutch of stars in the middle of a vast nowhere. To reach the next landmark of consequence, Sirius, would involve another 4.6 light years of travel. And so it would go if you tried to star-hop your way across the cosmos. Just reaching the centre of our own galaxy would take far longer than we have existed as beings.

Space, let me repeat, is enormous. The average distance between stars out there is over 30 million million kilometres. Even at speeds approaching those of light, these are fantastically challenging distances for any travelling individual. Of course, it is *possible* that alien beings travel billions of miles to amuse themselves by planting crop circles in Wiltshire or frightening the daylights out of some poor guy in a pickup truck on a lonely road in Arizona (they must have teenagers, after all), but it does seem unlikely.

Still, statistically the probability that there are other thinking beings out there is good. Nobody knows how many stars there are in the Milky Way – estimates range from a hundred billion or so to perhaps four hundred billion – and the Milky Way is just one of a hundred and forty billion or so other galaxies, many of them even larger than ours. In the 1960s, a professor at Cornell named Frank Drake, excited by such whopping numbers, worked out a famous equation designed to calculate the chances of advanced life existing in the cosmos, based on a series of diminishing probabilities.

Under Drake's equation you divide the number of stars in a selected portion of the universe by the number of stars that are likely to have planetary systems; divide that by the number of planetary systems that could theoretically support life; divide that by the number on which life, having arisen, advances to a state of intelligence; and so on. At each such division, the number shrinks colossally – yet even with the most conservative inputs the number of advanced civilisations just in the Milky Way always works out to be somewhere in the millions.

What an interesting and exciting thought. We may be only one of millions of advanced civilisations. Unfortunately, space being spacious, the average distance between any two of these civilisations is reckoned to be at least 200 light years, which is a great deal more than merely saying it makes it sound. It means, for a start, that even if these beings know we are here and are somehow able to see us in their telescopes, they're watching light that left Earth 200 years ago. So they're not seeing you and me. They're watching the French Revolution and Thomas Jefferson and people in silk stockings and powdered wigs – people who don't know what an atom is, or a gene, and who make their electricity by rubbing a rod of amber with a piece of fur and think that's quite a trick. Any message we receive from these observers is likely to begin 'Dear Sire', and congratulate us on the handsomeness of our horses and our mastery of whale oil. Two hundred light years is a distance so far beyond us as to be, well, just beyond us.

So even if we are not really alone, in all practical terms we are. Carl Sagan calculated the number of probable planets in the universe at as many as ten billion trillion – a number vastly beyond imagining. But what is equally beyond imagining is the amount of space through which they are lightly scattered. 'If we were randomly inserted into the universe,' Sagan wrote, 'the chances that you would be on or near a planet would be less than one in a billion trillion trillion.' (That's 10^{33}, or 1 followed by 33 zeros.) 'Worlds are precious.'

Language development

1 **Complete the sentences that follow with a suitable expression from the box below.**

clear the air	in deep water
bogged down in	tip of the iceberg
get wind of	out of the woods

1 Jillian thought she'd avoided her father's anger, but when he called her into his study she knew she wasn't _____ yet.

2 The children tried to keep my birthday party a secret, but things being as they are, I managed to _____ it.

3 I told Sarah we really needed to get together and talk if we wanted to _____.

4 I told Bill he'd find himself _____ _____ if he didn't do what his parents had told him.

5 Claude has been in his room for hours – he's always _____ his physics books.

6 We think we've seen the effects of climate change already – but that's just the _____.

2 **Complete the sentences with the correct particle.**

1 We were unaware _____ the damage we were causing.

2 Michelle was disappointed _____ her new CD player.

3 I'm ever so sorry _____ your loss.

4 Richard was angry _____ Peter for giving away his secret.

5 His older brother was always very cruel _____ him.

6 If you are concerned _____ Paul's progress, I suggest you talk to his teacher.

7 Orlando has become fixated _____ classical music.

8 I feel very relaxed _____ the job interview.

9 You were very rude _____ your mother-in-law!

10 It was clever _____ you to suggest going out for dinner.

Key word: *world*

3 **In the coursebook you came across the expression, *to go up/come down in the world*. Look at the expressions that follow (a–j) and match them to the most appropriate situation.**

a make the best of both worlds

b all the time in the world

c dead to the world

d do not have a care in the world

e have the world at [one's] feet

f out of this world

g in another/one's own world

h it's not the end of the world

i on top of the world

j think the world of someone

1 If someone is fast asleep, you may say they are …

2 If someone is distracted or deep in thought you could say they are …

3 If someone has lots of power and can do anything they want you would say they …

4 If someone is upset about something you may try to make them feel better by saying …

5 If someone feels really happy, they may tell you they are …

6 If someone has an amazing experience they may tell you it was …

7 If someone is not in a hurry or under any pressure you could say they have …

8 If you think someone is a wonderful person and you respect them greatly you …

9 If you are caught between two contradictory situations you may have to …

10 If you are free from pressures, worry or strife you might say you …

Grammar: unreal past

1 Choose the best option (a–j) below to complete each of the sentences that follow.

1 I wish they would

2 If only

3 In the morning she regretted

4 We regret

5 I'd rather you

6 You'd better

7 If you'd waited a bit longer

8 It's high time

9 Supposing you inherited a million euro

10 Had I listened to my mother

a hurry up and finish your homework.

b breaking up with John.

c they stopped complaining and did something.

d what would you do?

e I wouldn't have made the same mistake twice.

f to inform you that the show has been cancelled.

g didn't talk while I'm talking.

h stop arguing.

i you would have seen him arrive.

j I hadn't eaten that extra pie.

2 What is the 'real' situation in the following sentences? The first one has been done as an example.

0 If I had owned a car, I would have driven to work.

I didn't own a car, so I took the bus / I walked / I couldn't drive to work.

1 I would have travelled around the world if I'd had more money.

_____

2 I would have read more as a child if I hadn't watched so much TV.

_____

3 I would have gone to Spain if I had studied Spanish instead of French.

_____

4 If Roger had worked harder, he would have passed his course.

_____

3 Complete the text with a word or phrase formed from the words in brackets.

Imagine if I **(1)** _____ (not / go) to California when I did. My life **(2)** _____ (could / be) completely different. I **(3)** (never / meet) George, who took me out in his boat and taught me to sail. Suppose I **(4)** _____ (never / see) those whales or learnt about the threats they faced. I **(5)** _____ (probably / never / get) involved in conservation work to protect them. Had I **(6)** _____ (stay) at home in Coventry, I **(7)** _____ (might / get) a job in advertising. I'm so glad I didn't. Sometimes George talks as if we **(8)** _____ (save) the world. Imagine if we **(9)** _____ (have) more time and money – we would be able to protect even more species of marine mammal. Right, it's time I **(10)** _____ (get) back to work!

4 PAPER 3, PART 5 For questions 1–8, complete the second sentence so that it has a similar meaning to the first sentence, using the word given. Do not change the word given. You must use between three and six words, including the word given.

1 I think you should stop wasting your life!
TIME

It _____ your life!

2 It's a pity you couldn't come to my opening night.
WISH

I _____ to my opening night.

3 He behaves like he's my father!
THOUGH

He acts _____ my father!

4 You should take some sun protection cream with you.
BETTER

You _____ sun protection cream with you.

5 I'd love to know how Sara is doing at college.
KNEW

I _____ doing at college.

6 It would be better if you called me first.
SOONER

I _____ first.

7 I regret not going sky-diving when I had the chance.
ONLY

If _____ when I had the chance.

8 I'd prefer you to help in the kitchen.
RATHER

I _____ in the kitchen.

Listening: sentence completion

SPOTLIGHT CHECKLIST

PAPER 4, PART 2 Focused listening

Remember:

- The word(s) you write should complete the sentence logically and grammatically.

- Correct spelling is expected at this level, although some minor variations are allowed, for example in proper names. Both US and British English spellings are accepted.

1 🎧 **14.1 PAPER 4, PART 2 You will hear a scientist talking about human population growth. For questions 1–8 complete each gap with a word or short phrase.**

1 The Earth's _____ have sustained life for billions of years.

2 Half the species on earth may be _____ in half a century.

3 Apart from some _____ and _____, there are no species on Earth that depend on humans.

4 We would need _____ to support us if we all lived like Americans.

5 There are _____ people on Earth at the moment.

6 Every year the global population increases by another _____ people.

7 We should create global _____ which are ethical and intelligent.

8 Plagues, famine and warfare are some of the _____ which we would inevitably face.

Speaking: evaluating (making choices)

SPOTLIGHT EXAM GUIDANCE

PAPER 5, PART 3 Evaluating

In part 3 you will be provided with a visual stimulus (several photographs or pieces of artwork) to form the basis for a task which you will carry out with your partner. You'll be expected to discuss each visual, expressing and justifying opinions, evaluating and speculating, in order to work towards a negotiated decision towards the end of the task. The decision should only be made after you have explored each of the issues as illustrated by the pictures.

Tips

- Try to discuss each picture in relation to the task before making any decisions.

- Don't try to reach a decision in the first minute or so of the collaborative task. If you begin by saying, 'I think we should choose this one', you leave yourselves with nothing to evaluate or talk about for the remaining time.

1 PAPER 5, PART 3 Turn to page 171 where you will see some pictures showing different natural environments on Earth. Imagine that the interlocutor has asked you to talk with your partner and discuss how these pictures reflect different important environments on Earth, and then to decide which environment it is most important to protect.

2 Think of one reason why each environment is important on Earth. Make notes below.

1 Rainforest: _____

2 Coral reef: _____

3 Rivers and lakes: _____

4 Meadows and grasslands: _____

5 Mountains: _____

6 African savannah: _____

7 The sea: _____

8 The ice caps: _____

3 Now decide which one is the most important. If you think more than one is important then explain your reasons.

_____

_____

Use of English: word formation

1 Add a suffix to each of the words below to form the new word
  as indicated by the brackets.

1 compassion (n) _____ (adj)

2 remark (v) _____ (adv)

3 climate (n) _____ (adj)

4 priority (n) _____ (v)

5 install (v) _____ (n)

6 joy (n) _____ (adj/pos) _____ (adj/neg)

7 consider (v) _____ (adv) _____ (n)

8 remorse (n) _____ (adj/neg) _____ (adj/pos)

9 hesitate (v) _____ (n) _____ (adj)

10 conserve (v) _____ (n) _____ (n, person)

2 PAPER 3, PART 3 For questions 1–10, read the text below. Use the word given in capitals at the end of some of the lines
  to form a word that fits in the gap in the same line.

PLANET EARTH

Planet Earth is an award-winning nature documentary series narrated by David
Attenborough. The first episode illustrates a 'journey' around the globe and reveals the
effect of gradual climatic change and **(1)** _____ transitions en route. During   **(1)** SEASON
Antarctica's winter, emperor penguins endure four months of darkness, with no food, in
temperatures of −70°C. Meanwhile, as spring arrives in the Arctic, polar bear cubs take
their first steps into a world of **(2)** _____ thawing ice. In northern Canada, the   **(2)** RAPID
longest overland **(3)** _____ of any animal – over 2000 miles – is that of three   **(3)** MIGRATE
million caribou, which are hunted by wolves. The forests of eastern Russia are home to the
Amur leopard: with a population of just 40 individuals, it is now the world's rarest cat. This
is **(4)** _____ because of the destruction of its habitat, and Attenborough states that   **(4)** PRIMARY
it 'symbolises the **(5)** _____ of our natural heritage.' However, in the tropics, the   **(5)** FRAGILE
jungle that covers 3 per cent of the planet's surface supports 50 per cent of its animals.

The second instalment focuses on the mountains. All the main ranges are explored
with **(6)** _____ aerial photography. Ethiopia's *Erta Ale* is the longest   **(6)** EXTEND
(7) _____ erupting volcano – for over 100 years. On the nearby highlands,   **(7)** CONTINUE
geladas inhabit precipitous slopes nearly three miles up, in troops
that are 800-strong: the most **(8)** _____ of their kind.   **(8)** NUMERATE
Alongside them live the critically **(9)** _____ walia ibex,   **(9)** DANGER
and both species take turns to act as lookout for
(10) _____ Ethiopian wolves.   **(10)** PREDATOR

Writing: an essay (discussing issues that surround a topic)

PAPER 2, PART 2 Word length

Remember:

- Writing approximately the right number of words is an important part of the task. If you write significantly fewer words, this will show that you haven't answered the task properly. If you write too much, parts of your writing may be repetitive, irrelevant, or poorly organised.

- The expected word length for the part 2 tasks is 220–260 words. You should practise deciding how to allocate this in your plan. Being concise is an advanced level writing skill which you should practise whenever possible.

1 Look at the question below. Then read one student's answer (on the right).

PAPER 2, PART 2

> Your class has been discussing climate change and the issues surrounding this topic. Your teacher has asked you to write an essay about climate change, discussing the effects it will have on the weather, human civilisation, and the natural world and to highlight the severity of the matter.

Climate change

Climate change is a subject we have heard a lot about in the past decade, but we can no longer ignore the severity of the matter and we should be aware of the consequences of climate change on global weather patterns, human civilisations and the natural world.

As far as the weather is concerned, climate change is going to cause <u>rising global temperatures</u>, which will in turn increase the number of <u>hurricanes, storms, and forest fires</u> around the world. There may well be more <u>earthquakes and tsunamis</u> as a result of this. Rising temperatures will also mean that more forests will turn into deserts, thereby <u>destroying more ecosystems</u> and leading to yet more <u>species extinctions</u>. Another very serious consequence of climate change is that the <u>polar ice-caps will melt</u>, causing <u>sea levels to rise</u> by several metres in places.

Nature will continue to suffer. Changing climates can affect many different species of wild animal, for example the <u>polar bear depends on the arctic ice to survive, and may face drowning or starving if the ice melts.</u>

The implications to human society are obvious: tsunamis, storms, earthquakes and fires can all have a devastating effect on our civilisations and <u>cause many deaths and serious injuries</u>. It has been predicted that rising sea levels will <u>destroy many cities and displace millions of people, leading to more food shortages, diseases, and conflicts.</u>

It's clear that the consequences of climate change can no longer be ignored. If we don't do something now to address the problem we will all suffer.

---

2 Using the underlined parts of the essay to help you, complete the spidergram below.

3 Read the essay again and complete the paragraph plan below.

Paragraph 1 (Introduction): climate change and why it is important

Paragraph 2: _____

Paragraph 3: _____

Paragraph 4: _____

Paragraph 5 (Conclusion): we must act now or suffer.

4 Practise drawing spidergrams of your own. Draw a spidergram for the topic below. Think about all the consequences and effects of the topic in question.

> SPECIES EXTINCTIONS

15 Our global village

EXAM MENU

Reading:	Paper 1, part 1
Listening:	Paper 4, part 3
Speaking:	Paper 5, part 1
Use of English:	Paper 3, parts 2 and 4
Writing:	Paper 2, parts 1 and 2

Getting started

1 ⌂ **15.1 PAPER 4, PART 4** You will hear five short extracts in which people talk about different annual traditions.

Task One

For questions **1–5** choose from the list (**A–H**) the tradition that is being described.

A May Day

B Christmas

C Summer Solstice

D St George's Day

E Bonfire night

F Easter

G St Valentine's day

H Hallowe'en

Speaker 1		1
Speaker 2		2
Speaker 3		3
Speaker 4		4
Speaker 5		5

Task Two

For questions **6–10** choose from the list (**A–H**) a reason why each tradition is probably celebrated according to the speaker.

A to commemorate the anniversary of someone's birth.

B to ward off evil spirits or ghosts.

C to remember a crime that was almost committed.

D to bring people together from different backgrounds.

E to educate people about cultural events.

F to prevent people from breaking the law.

G to capitalise on human emotions.

H to celebrate a naturally occurring event.

Speaker 1		6
Speaker 2		7
Speaker 3		8
Speaker 4		9
Speaker 5		10

Valentine's Day

113

Reading: purpose and main idea

1 PAPER 1, PART 1 **The following three extracts are all concerned in some way with different cultures. For questions 1–6, choose the answer (A, B, C or D) which you think fits best according to the text.**

Extract from a travel book

Chapter 1

There are certain idiosyncratic notions that you quietly come to accept when you live for a long time in Britain. One is that British summers used to be longer and sunnier. Another is that the England football team shouldn't have any trouble with Norway. A third is the idea that Britain is a big place. This last is easily the most intractable.

If you mention in the pub that you intend to drive from, say, Surrey to Cornwall, a distance that most
10 Americans would happily go to get a taco, your companions will puff their cheeks, look knowingly at each other, and blow out air as if to say, 'Well, now *that's* a bit of a tall order,' and then they'll launch into a lively and protracted discussion of whether it's better to take the A30 to Stockbridge and then the A303 to Ilchester or the A361 to Glastonbury via Shepton Mallet. Within minutes the conversation will plunge off into a level of detail that leaves you, as a foreigner, swivelling your head in quiet wonderment.

20 'You know that layby outside Warminster, the one with the grit box with the broken handle?' one of them will say. '*You* know, just past the turnoff for Little Puking but before the B6029 mini-roundabout. By the dead sycamore.'

At this point, you find you are the only person in the group not nodding vigorously.

1 What does the phrase 'a tall order' in line 13 mean?
- A a ridiculous idea
- B an expensive choice
- C a difficult undertaking
- D a wise decision

2 The writer mentions Americans in the text to show that ...
- A they often drive from Surrey to Cornwall.
- B that's how far they have to go to get to Mexico.
- C they are foolhardy risk takers.
- D such a distance would not be considered great to them.

PAPER 1, PART 1 Purpose and main idea

Tips

- Look at the headings or titles of the extracts, as well as underlining the key words in the question, which will tell you what the three texts have in common.

- Try to summarise in your mind, the main idea – or gist – of each text.

Extract from a Novel

Lessons about Boys

Mma Ramotswe thought: God put us on this earth. We were all Africans then, in the beginning, because man started in Kenya, as Dr Leakey and his Daddy have proved. So, if one thinks carefully about it, we are all brothers and sisters, and yet everywhere you look, what do you see? Fighting, fighting, fighting. Rich people killing poor people; poor people killing rich people. Everywhere, except Botswana. That is thanks to Sir Seretse Khama, who was a good man, who invented Botswana and made it a good place. She
10 still cried for him sometimes, when she thought of him in his last illness and all those clever doctors in London saying to the Government: 'We're sorry but we cannot cure your President.'

The problem, of course, was that people did not seem to understand the difference between right and wrong. They needed to be reminded about this, because if you left it to them to work out for themselves, they would never bother. They would just find out what was best for them, and then they would call that the right thing. That's how most people thought.

Precious Ramotswe had learnt about good and evil at Sunday 20 School. The cousin had taken her there when she was six, and she had gone there every Sunday without fail until she was eleven. That was enough time for her to learn all about right and wrong, although she had been puzzled and remained so – when it came to certain other aspects of religion. But right and wrong – that was another matter, and she had experienced no difficulty in understanding that it was wrong to lie, and steal, and kill other people.

3 The word 'that' in line 9 refers to
- A the peace that exists in Botswana.
- B the killing that goes on in Botswana.
- C the existence of Botswana as a country.
- D fighting everywhere except Botswana.

4 Mma Ramotswe mentions Sunday School to show that
- A her cousin was very religious when she was younger.
- B she was consistent about attending and liked the routine.
- C she couldn't understand what they were teaching her there.
- D she didn't need religion to show her what was right.

BURYING BONES OF CONTENTION

Indigenous peoples such as Australian Aboriginals have long pressed for the return of ancestors' remains from museum collections around the world. But some museums strongly resist repatriation requests, claiming they hamper archaeological research. Now there's a compromise that could keep everyone happy.

Several handovers have been made from Australia and the UK, but the particular conditions a burial site must have mean it becomes ever harder for communities to find reburial sites, especially as no one wishes to disturb existing graves.

This is where the archaeologists can help. In one of the first 10 collaborations of its kind, Lynley Wallis at Flinders University, Adelaide, and her colleagues teamed up with the Ngarrindjeri Aboriginal community in South Australia to find a site to bury the remains of 374 Ngarrindjeri people, which were returned from the University of Edinburgh in the UK and Museum Victoria in Melbourne in 2006. They used a standard geophysical survey kit that the team say could in future be given to indigenous communities. This in return means the communities could gather useful data for archaeologists.

Last month, the Smithsonian Institution in Washington DC became the first US museum to return human remains to another country, when it sent 33 skeletons to Australia. But it did so only after the discovery of an agreement by the original collector to return most of the samples. 20

5 What does the word 'they' refer to in line 3?

A Indigenous peoples, such as Australian Aboriginals.

B Requests to return human remains to their own people.

C Archaeologists wanting to study Aboriginals.

D Museums that possess human remains.

6 By helping indigenous peoples, archaeologists

A intend to find more graves they can dig up.

B want to find a good place to bury Aboriginal remains.

C hope to gain some useful information in return.

D often make promises they don't intend to keep.

2 **What do the following words mean? Choose the best option in each case (A, B, C or D).**

Extract One

1 idiosyncratic = A normal   B unbelievable
                  C eccentric   D depressing

2 intractable = A annoying   B remarkable
                  C distressing D inflexible

3 protracted   = A lengthy   B boring
                  C confusing   D exciting

Extract Three

4 contention   = A history   B disagreement
                   C civilisation D tradition

5 indigenous   = A foreign   B uncivilised
                   C native   D primitive

6 repatriation = A sending away B giving away
                   C taking back D returning home

7 hamper   = A obstruct   B delay
                   C postpone   D cancel

8 collaboration = A contract   B cooperation
                   C deal   D treaty

Language development:
phrasal verbs and phrases with *pass*

1 Match the sentences below to one of the definitions of *pass* that follows.

1 This beautiful Romanov jewel was passed to my grandfather by his aunt.

2 Fifteen years had passed but she still looked exactly the same.

3 He passed the afternoon quietly reading.

4 He's passing through a stressful time right now.

5 If it passes the 15 metre water mark we will have to evacuate the town.

6 A law was passed banning the ownership of pit-bull terriers.

7 Julian passed to Mikey, who took aim and scored.

8 Martha passed Robert the message that the meeting had been put back to 11.

9 Samantha's hoping she'll finally pass the bar exam this time!

a if you pass information to someone it means you give them information.

b if you pass a ball to someone in a game or match it means you throw or kick or hit it to them.

c if something passes to someone it means they inherit it.

d when a period of time passes, it has finished.

e if you pass a test it means you have reached the required standard.

f if you pass through a stage or phase, you experience it.

g if something passes a level or amount it goes above it.

h if you pass a period of time in a particular way, you spend it that way.

i if a government passes a law they formally agree to it.

2 Complete the sentences below with an expression formed from *pass*.

1 I was going to tell Arnold off for his bad attitude but I decided to _____.

2 Not only did Lucinda pass; she passed with _____!

3 Not a word of what I have seen or heard here tonight shall ever _____.

4 And so, after many years of wandering in the desert, it _____ that the prince finally found himself at the ocean.

5 Scott wouldn't admit that he had finished off the biscuits – in fact he tried to _____ to me by saying it was my idea!

3 Complete the sentences in your own words.

1 Unfortunately her grandfather *passed away* after _____ _____ _____.

2 I can't believe she *passed out* at the sight of _____ _____.

3 Please get me some stamps if you *pass by* the _____ _____.

4 I would never *pass up* the chance to _____ _____.

5 Jim was *passed over* in favour of a more experienced _____.

6 Could you *pass on* the _____.

7 Susan tried to *pass* it *off* as her homework but _____ _____.

8 The stories were *passed down* from _____ _____.

4 Match the meanings below to one of the phrasal verbs in exercise 3.

a to misrepresent something or someone

b to leave or give something to the next generation

c to go near to a place

d to lose consciousness

e to fail to take something (especially an opportunity)

f to communicate something

g to die

h to fail to choose someone

Listening: multiple speakers

1 Ω 15.2 PAPER 4, PART 3 **You will hear part of a radio interview in which the advantages and disadvantages of traditional beliefs are being discussed. For questions 1–6, choose the answer (A, B, C or D) which fits best according to what you hear.**

1 One reason why traditional taboos are important in Tibet is because
 A many people live in villages and the countryside.
 B Tibetan ancestors believed everything in nature had a soul.
 C ordinary people do not have much knowledge of the law.
 D harming nature in any way is considered a crime.

2 According to Professor Cookson, traditional customs and taboos
 A are difficult to enforce.
 B are passed on from parent to child.
 C are enforced in Tibetan society.
 D have brought about the destruction of nature.

3 Cookson says that traditional customs are good because
 A they do not let anyone become rich.
 B they stop everyone from becoming corrupt.
 C they make Tibetan society more advanced.
 D they discourage society's members from developing selfish habits.

4 According to Michael, one reason customs are kept in society is
 A because they have a place in a culture's history.
 B to make sure they change along with society.
 C to remind us that culture is always developing.
 D to keep up with more modern societies.

5 Michael cites the example about his village on Tuesdays because
 A he wants to show that such beliefs can hinder development.
 B he believes it was a significant Ghanaian custom.
 C he thinks the villagers lacked rational powers.
 D he thinks the tradition should be modernised.

6 According to Michael, traditional customs and taboos in Ghana should
 A be banned forever.
 B exist if they can change with the times.
 C allow local people to reject them.
 D only be allowed to exist in certain remote villages.

Speaking: talking about your country, culture, customs and background

1 Ω 15.3 Listen to part one of the Speaking Paper and write down the questions the interlocutor asks each student.

Fernando's questions	Claudia's questions
1	6
2	7
3	8
4	9
5	10

2 Write down your own answers to each of the questions listed above.

1	6
2	7
3	8
4	9
5	10

Grammar: adverbial clauses

1 **Complete each of the sentences below with a suitable adverbial clause.**

1 Heidi took an umbrella with her _____ it rained.
2 _____ had I got into the car, when the storm started.
3 I took my mobile with me _____ I could call Juan from the train.
4 Jen wanted to know _____ he had been.
5 He left his wallet on the table. _____ someone stole it.
6 _____ the fact that I was exhausted, I agreed to host the party.
7 _____ the adverts were on, I dashed to the kitchen to make some tea.
8 _____ being late, Amanda decided to drive to work instead of waiting for the bus.

2 **Read the sentences that follow and underline the adverbial clause in each. Match the clause to the correct type.**

1 Jake had no sooner entered the room than the phone rang. (time / place / manner)
2 It wasn't as expensive as I'd thought it might be. (reason / comparison / concession)
3 It got so late that I started to worry. (manner / condition / result)
4 If I'd thought you'd tell the truth, I would have asked you first. (manner / reason / condition)
5 This is the third time you've turned up late. Nevertheless, I'm prepared to give you another chance. (condition / concession / manner)

3 **Each of the following sentences contains a mistake. Find the mistake and correct it.**

1 Mimi invited me to her house so that to talk about the business.
2 Despite of being the youngest, I was expected to make the speech.
3 For fear to forget her appointment, Salome wrote it on her hand.
4 No matter how much tough it was, Julian was determined to finish the race.
5 We decided to go to London, with a view of going up on the London Eye.
6 Seeing as that you've been to the museum before, why don't we get something to eat instead?
7 Such is the extent of the damage so that he will have to replace the whole wall.
8 You'd better do as you're told or otherwise you'll be sorry!

4 **Read the text. Complete each of the gaps with one suitable adverb or adverbial phrase from the box below.**

although	consequently
due to the fact that	for this reason
in order to	otherwise
so as	this is why
when	with a view to

Marriage Custom: Weeping Marriage

The announcement of a marriage date for girls of the *Tujia* Ethnic Minority is usually welcomed with crying, as is the custom. (1) _____, the new bride should begin to cry up to one month before the wedding ceremony, (2) _____ her suitability and virtue will be poorly judged. (3) _____ be regarded as a good girl, she should begin to learn how to cry for marriage when she is twelve years old. (4) _____ some girls will invite an experienced person to teach them. (5) _____ they are 15 years old, girls will compete to see who cries best and to teach each other.

Some girls sing songs (6) _____ weeping for marriage. These include singing for parents, sisters, brothers, the matchmaker and ancestors. (7) _____, when singing weeping marriage songs, they express their emotions in mournful tones. Some girls sing songs before marriage (8) _____ they are protesting against the arranged marriage system which existed under feudalism and (9) _____ to express sentimental attachment to their relatives. Nowadays, (10) _____ Tujia girls can choose their loves freely, they still cry out of tradition.

Use of English: open cloze text

PAPER 3, PART 2 Open cloze

You'll have to draw on your knowledge of the structure of the language and understanding of the text in order to fill the gaps. The focus of the gapped words will either be grammatical, (eg: articles, auxiliaries, prepositions, pronouns, verb tenses and forms); or lexico-grammatical, (eg: phrasal verbs, linking words or words within fixed phrases).

Practise:

- doing preparation tasks which promote grammatical accuracy. Choose articles from magazines or newspapers and select one word from each sentence to black out. Focus on verb forms, auxiliary and modal verbs, pronouns, prepositions, conjunctions, modifiers and determiners. Then see if you can put them back in again.

1 PAPER 3, PART 2 **For questions 1–15, read the text below and think of the word which best fits each gap. Use only one word in each gap.**

Mexican Day of the Dead – 'Día de los Muertos'

The Day of the Dead is celebrated in Mexico, and other South American countries, on 1 and 2 November. Many people believe that (1) _____ the Day of the Dead, it is easier (2) _____ the souls of the departed to visit the living. People go to cemeteries to communicate with the souls of the departed, and build private altars, (3) _____ they place the favourite foods and beverages, and photos and memorabilia of the departed. The aim is (4) _____ encourage visits by the souls, (5) _____ that the souls will hear the prayers and the comments of the living directed to (6) _____. Celebrations can take a humorous tone, (7) _____ celebrants remember funny events and anecdotes about (8) _____ departed.

A common symbol of the holiday is the skull (colloquially called *calavera*), (9) _____ celebrants represent in masks, called *calacas* (colloquial term for 'skeleton'), and foods (10) _____ as sugar or chocolate skulls, which are inscribed (11) _____ the name of the recipient on the forehead. Sugar skulls are gifts that can be given to (12) _____ the living and the dead. Other holiday foods include *pan de muerto*, a sweet egg bread made in various shapes, (13) _____ plain rounds to skulls and rabbits often decorated with white frosting to look (14) _____ twisted bones. Some people believe that possessing 'Día de los Muertos' items can bring good luck and (15) _____ get tattoos or have dolls of the dead to carry with them.

2 PAPER 3, PART 4 **For questions 1–5, think of one word only which can be used appropriately in all three sentences.**

1 Expecting me to finish all these invitations by tomorrow is a bit of a tall _____!
  The waitress told me it was too late to cancel my _____ of chips.
  The bewildered soldier claimed he hadn't heard the _____ to fall in.

2 It is a religious _____ to make the sign of the cross every time you pass a church.
  Rupert awoke early as was his _____.
  Winifred was working on an advertising campaign to attract more _____.

3 William, could you _____ me that spanner over there please?
  Audrey had made the decision to _____ in her notice.
  I've got to _____ it to you – you really know how to make a cake!

4 What Alison did was stupid beyond _____!
  Contrary to popular _____, there is no monster lurking in these mountains!
  She tried to copy my answers, in the mistaken _____ that I had studied for the test!

5 The city has lost none of its _____ for me over the years.
  Suddenly, as if by _____, Julian turned up at the house.
  Can you please try to work some of your _____ on the baby and make him sleep!

Writing: an article or letter (personal experiences)

1 Read the following article or letter and underline five useful phrases that you could use in any other similar piece of writing. The first one has been done for you.

<u>Last year, while holidaying in Cyprus, I was fortunate enough to</u> be invited to a traditional wedding, as my hosts were friends of the bride's family. It was the most amazing experience – not least because it lasted over three days.

I won't go into too much detail about what went on over those three days; suffice it to say there was a good deal of eating, drinking, and general merrymaking going on. However, the real celebrations started on the day of the wedding itself, and that was a lot of fun, let me tell you.

The most memorable part for me was the money-pinning ceremony. It is not customary in Cyprus to buy presents for the happy couple. Instead guests take turns pinning money on the bride and groom while they dance. In fact, some guests and family members can get quite competitive – each trying to outdo the other as to who can pin the most money on. Many come prepared with bank rolls of notes all stapled together, which they then pin in one go to the newly weds, who are soon literally covered from head to foot in cash.

I was enjoying myself immensely, but when my turn came to pin some money on the bride's dress, you can imagine how embarrassed I was to discover that I only had coins in my pocket!

2 Now look at the exam question below. Using the letter/article as a guide, fill in the empty comment balloons with ideas the writer may have noted down.

A travel magazine has invited readers to send in personal accounts of experiences they have had in another country. Look at the advertisement below.

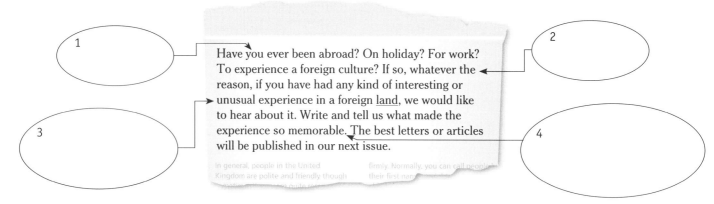

1

2

3

4

Have you ever been abroad? On holiday? For work? To experience a foreign culture? If so, whatever the reason, if you have had any kind of interesting or unusual experience in a foreign <u>land</u>, we would like to hear about it. Write and tell us what made the experience so memorable. The best letters or articles will be published in our next issue.

In general, people in the United Kingdom are polite and friendly though ...

firmly. Normally, you can call people by their first nam...

3 Now complete the paragraph plan that follows.

Paragraph 1 _____
Paragraph 2 _____
Paragraph 3 _____
Paragraph 4 _____

4 Prepare a similar plan with your own ideas for answering the question.

Paragraph 1 _____
Paragraph 2 _____
Paragraph 3 _____
Paragraph 4 _____

5 PAPER 2, PART 1 OR 2 Write your answer to exercise 2 either as an article or letter. See if you can use some of the phrases you underlined in exercise 1. You should write 180–220 words for part one, or 220–260 words for part two.

EXAM MENU

Reading: Paper 1, part 4
Listening: Paper 4, part 1
Use of English: Paper 3, part 1
Speaking: Paper 5, part 2
Writing: Paper 2,
                 parts 1 and 2

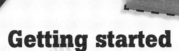

Getting started

1   Circle the correct word in italics to complete the following sentences.

1   The company *activated / discontinued* production of this model in 2001.

2   Gerald Durrell *founded / initiated* The Jersey Wildlife Preservation Trust when still a relatively young man.

3   We can *terminate / finalise* the details of the contract at the meeting on Friday.

4   Greg went to see his solicitor to *settle / conclude* his affairs before leaving the country for good.

5   The firm is *embarking on / launching* a new product this autumn.

6   The Prime Minister has *instigated / extinguished* an investigation into allegations that one of his ministers is a spy.

7   It is believed that a man in his late thirties *inspired / incited* the group of fans to riot.

8   Agent 009 decided to *cease / abort* the mission when he realised there was no hope of rescuing his partner.

9   Her proposal has *generated / conceived* interest among a number of top scientists.

10 Kylie has just *settled / completed* a course in aromatherapy.

Reading: multiple matching texts

1 PAPER 1, PART 4 You are going to read four people's views on changes in our daily lives. For questions 1–15, choose from the extracts below (A–D). The extracts may be chosen more than once.

Which writer(s) …?

- mentions effects on the environment   1 _____
- welcomes the change without reservations   2 _____
- reminisces about the past   3 _____
- suggest the change is inevitable for economic reasons   4 _____ 5 _____
- mentions a moral dilemma   6 _____
- comments on a new application for existing technology   7 _____
- mentions a professional group who won't welcome the change   8 _____
- works as an environmental consultant   9 _____
- refers to a highly-acclaimed technological innovation   10 _____
- cites a view that the technology to help complete the transition doesn't exist yet   11 _____
- admits the new technology is a vast improvement   12 _____
- refer to certain advantages of the old way of doing things   13 _____ 14 _____
- is optimistic about the long term effects of the change   15 _____

PAPER 1, PART 4 Looking for specific information

Remember:

- This part focuses on students' ability to locate specific information, detail, opinion and attitude in a text.
- The text may be continuous, a group of short texts, or divided into four to eight sections.

Tips

- Pay careful attention to the wording of questions, as they lead you to specific information in the text.
- Underline key words in each question, and make sure the information in the text fully answers the question.
- Don't choose an answer based on one word in the text matching a word in the question.

2 Find a word in the text which means the following.

a something which replaces another [text A] _____

b feeling of missing something that you remember with pleasure [text A] _____

c occurring immediately [text A] _____

d following a strict procedure [text A] _____

e very new and revolutionary [text A] _____

f old-fashioned and useless [text A] _____

g be more important than [text B] _____

h destroyed [text B] _____

i feel a sudden moment of intense discomfort [text C] _____

j make oneself feel less guilty [text C] _____

A fond **farewell** to the **old** ...
and a warm **welcome** to the **new** ...?

Four people take a look at the changing face of our daily lives ...

A

Every once in a while we say goodbye to a technology that has been replaced by a demonstrably superior successor, yet we still hold onto a bit of nostalgia for the old way. One of those about to go extinct is Polaroid instant film. Even though I hadn't used it for years, I was sad to hear that the film is going out of production.

Digital photography is our efficient, truly instantaneous modern standard, but there was something magical about a Polaroid picture. The whole process had a satisfying, ritualised nature to it. You composed the photo, clicked the shutter and heard that distinctive whirr. The seemingly blank film shot out. You'd fight to see who got to grab it, shake it and watch as the image teasingly developed before your eyes ...

A few artists had clung to the medium for their work. They are mourning the end of the Polaroid era, saying that for some applications, nothing compares to the look they get from this film.

For me, it is strange to see something I remember as cutting-edge technology as a kid become so thoroughly obsolete.

B

Print newspapers won't go the way of the dinosaur any time soon, predicts Russell Frank. But Frank, an Associate Professor of Communications at Penn State, does think that the print version will become more difficult to find on the news-stand.

'There are people who will always want a print version,' he said, adding that there are places where it's difficult to read a newspaper online, like on a bus or at the beach. But in the end these conveniences simply don't outweigh the costs of printing and distribution.

'The biggest expense after employee salaries is the newsprint,' Frank explains. 'You take that cost, the cost of printing, and the cost of circulation, right down to the kid on the bicycle throwing it onto your front porch. With a wave of the wand, all those costs can be eliminated when papers go online.'

Frank notes that *The Capital Times* in Madison, Wis., recently abandoned its print format and is now exclusively a digital publication. He thinks the reason more newspapers haven't taken that plunge is because no one has developed the perfect hardware for reading electronic newspapers.

C

There are good reasons to cut down on air travel voluntarily: flying not only swells our personal carbon emissions but spews CO_2 and other pollutants into the stratosphere, where they do the most damage. However, the worsening scarcity of the stuff we use for making jet fuel takes the discussion out of the realm of optional moral action and into that of economic necessity and personal adaptation.

I fly to educate both general audiences and policy makers about fossil fuel depletion; in fact, I'm writing this article aboard a plane *en route* from Boston to San Francisco. I wince at my carbon footprint, but console myself with the hope that my message helps thousands of others to change their consumption patterns. This inner conflict is about to be resolved: the decline of affordable air travel is forcing me to rethink my work.

Our species' historically brief fling with flight has been fun, educational and enriching on many levels to those fortunate enough to benefit from it. Saying goodbye will be difficult. But maybe as we do we can say hello to greater involvement in our local communities.

D

... As of today at CES, the Consumer Electronics Show in Las Vegas, videotape is officially dead. Replacing it is something called 'flash memory', which is nothing more than a hard wafer that stores electrical charge easily, quickly, durably and almost indefinitely. Of course, an electrical charge can be read as 'digits', which we see as pictures and video.

You're familiar with flash memory already – you've seen it in those little SD cards that store your camera's pictures, and you've seen it in the so-called 'thumb drives' that slide into your laptop's USB slot and store information.

The great thing about flash is there are no moving parts. Two men won the Nobel prize this past year for their 1988 invention of flash, in part because flash enabled things like the iPod Shuffle and Nano (which store music on a flash memory card) and now video cameras with no spinning hard drive or rolling tape.

123

Language development:

word partners

1 **Choose the correct word in italics to complete the following sentences.**

1 The situation is out of control, and *dramatic / drastic / caustic* action needs to be taken immediately.

2 The government tried hard to *dispel / expel / repel* the rumours surrounding the minister's sudden and extremely mysterious death.

3 She claims that she lives on a *stable / staple / steep* diet of rice and green beans and has done for many years.

4 'He professes to be a *confirmed / confessed / confused* bachelor, but now he's met Kelly, I'm not sure that'll last!'

5 Her leaving shocked him out of his *consistency / constituency / complacency*, and he's now a changed man.

6 'It's raining, so what? I'm not going to let a drop of water *shadow / cloud / shade* my mood on my wedding day!'

7 Simon felt he was *torn / broken / cut* off from the rest of the world when he went to live in that village, and missed the city dreadfully.

8 George went on to *extend / expound / extol* his views at length on the state of the economy, at which point I lost interest and began to play with my hair instead.

2 PAPER 3, PART 4 **For questions 1–4, think of one word only which can be used appropriately in all three sentences.**

1 You can't leave yet! For a _____, we haven't cut the cake!

The play didn't get off to a good _____, as there was a power cut, and the lights went out!

Well, we've only saved €5,000 so far, but it's a _____.

2 John soon realised that he wasn't _____ out to be a lawyer, and became a teacher instead.

We were chatting on the phone when suddenly we were _____ off!

So, anyway, to _____ a long story short, we ended up staying the night in an awful hotel.

3 Although we sorted a lot of things out, this discussion is by no _____ finished yet.

Which _____ of transport do you intend to travel by, bus or train?

Although it's boring, I see revision as a _____ to an end.

4 No sooner had I answered the phone than the person on the other _____ hung up!

Walthamstow! This is the _____ of the line! All passengers must leave the train here!

At the _____ of the day, I think you have to weigh up the pros and cons.

Key word: *end*

3 **Match the beginnings and endings of the following sentences.**

1 I wouldn't like to be on the

2 It was awful! I was at my

3 On my first day at work, I was thrown in at the

4 Come on, love! It's not the

5 I found myself at a

6 In the film, the villain comes to a

7 When we were babysitting for Jane, we had

8 It's no good, Paul, this is the

9 I worry about Nick, as he sits in front of the computer for hours

10 Was the film good? I only saw the

a ... deep end, and had to deal with a complaint from a client!

b ... tail end of it, and couldn't understand what was going on.

c ... loose end last Saturday, so went to see my ex-boyfriend.

d ... end of the road for the company.

e ... on end, playing those games.

f ... receiving end of her temper; she's vicious!

g ... no end of fun, and played games with the kids all evening.

h ... end of the world. He's only gone to university!

i ... sticky end, when his car explodes.

j ... wits' end when Milton disappeared!

Listening: three short extracts

SPOTLIGHT CHECKLIST

PAPER 4, PART 1 **Recognising agreement and disagreement**

Remember:

- In this part, the questions focus on speakers' purpose, attitudes, and opinions, the gist of an argument, and agreement or disagreement between speakers.

- Don't focus on particular words, but rather the overall attitude of the speakers, and the general comment they make.

Tips

- Pay careful attention to whether speakers agree or disagree on certain points.

- Listen to the whole extract before choosing your answers.

1 🎧 16.1 PAPER 4, PART 1 **You will hear three different extracts. For questions 1–6, choose the answer (A, B, or C) which fits best according to what you hear. There are two questions for each extract.**

Extract One

1 The two speakers agree that the ending is
A predictable.
B a letdown.
C convincing.

2 Hayley thinks this book
A is better than the other two.
B reflects certain truths about life.
C leaves too many things unresolved.

Extract Two

3 What is Clive concerned about?
A The destruction of a way of life.
B The threat to a rainforest's survival.
C Both of the above.

4 Clive seems to work for
A a charity organisation.
B the government of Borneo.
C the logging industry.

Extract Three

5 Derek says of his experience that initially he felt
A surreal.
B awkward.
C at ease.

6 Ann and Derek agree that virtual conferences may be the answer to
A the increasing cost of air travel.
B a moral dilemma.
C long, tiring journeys.

Speaking: individual long turn

SPOTLIGHT CHECKLIST

PAPER 5, PART 2 **One minute of talking**

Remember:

- This task asks you to compare and speculate about two pictures from a set of three.

- You are expected to speak for one minute without interruption.

- You need to listen carefully when your partner speaks, so that you can respond with your own comment.

Practise:

- giving presentations on a topic in class;

- using linking words and phrases to connect your ideas.

1 PAPER 5, PART 2 **Read the Interlocutor's question below, and look at the pictures on page 172.**

Then, using the space provided, prepare your answer. Remember, you need to keep talking for one minute.

Interlocutor's instructions: Here are your pictures. They show school leavers making choices about their future.

I'd like you to compare two of the pictures, and say what different options they show, and how the young people might be feeling.

Two pictures chosen: _____

Comments on picture ( ): _____

_____

Comments on picture ( ): _____

_____

Comments on picture ( ): _____

_____

How the people might be feeling:

Picture ( ): _____

_____

Picture ( ): _____

_____

Useful linking words and phrases: _____

_____

Grammar: making and intensifying comparisons

1 **Make comparisons between the following items, using the words in capitals at the end of each line. Make any grammatical changes necessary.**

a The BMW is _____
a Ford Focus. GOOD

b Travelling by train is _____
travelling by bus. FAST

c The film I watched yesterday was _____
the one I saw last week. EXCITING

d Chinese food is _____
Indian food. TASTY

e The book I'm reading now is _____
the last one I read. INTERESTING

f My new Maths teacher is _____
the one I had before. FRIENDLY

g Your haircut _____
the one you had before. SUIT

h This photo of you is _____
that one. ATTRACTIVE

i Digital photography is _____
Polaroid film. EASY

j Online newspapers will be _____
printed ones. EXPENSIVE

2 **Intensify the comparisons in the following sentences in two different ways. Use the words in the box to help you.**

a lot	far
never	not nearly
by far	considerably more/less
much more/less	

1 She works harder at school than she used to.

_____

_____

2 This book isn't as good as the last one he wrote.

_____

_____

3 Dale is fitter than his brother, Simon.

_____

_____

4 They are happier now that they've moved to the country.

_____

_____

5 He's more irritable than he used to be.

_____

_____

6 This is the worst curry I've ever tasted!

_____

_____

3 **Circle the most suitable intensifier in the sentences below.**

a Daisy's room is *by far / much* untidier than Henry's.

b It's becoming *a lot / much more* harder to find this type of fruit in the shops.

c The new Bond film is *a lot / by far* the most exciting one I've seen.

d This summer is *not nearly as / significantly less* warm as the last one.

e We've got *utterly / far* more room in our new house.

4 **Make comparisons between the two pictures below.**

BEFORE

AFTER

Use of English: multiple-choice cloze

1 PAPER 3, PART 1 **For questions 1–12, read the text below and decide which answer (A, B, C or D) on the right best fits each gap.**

BREAKFAST: the end of an era?

It is an undeniable truth of the Western world that the days of 'going to work on an egg' are fast disappearing into the advertisement archives of the 1970s. Busier working lives, eating for energy rather than (1) _____ and more women at work are just a few reasons that might explain the decreasing presence of the breakfast table. And yet, most nutritionists would claim that we should 'breakfast as a king'. A new report on British breakfast habits (2) _____the decreasing popularity of breakfast at home, in favour of the 'deskfast' – a new (3) _____ to describe brekky at the desk.

Apparently, office canteens are the big growth area in the breakfast market as employers are (4) _____ to encourage employees to arrive at work early. In addition, (5) _____ are pushing premium priced on-the-go breakfast options to busy workers and even vending machines will soon be getting in on the (6) _____ as new technology will enable food to be chilled or frozen and then toasted or baked. Children, the report adds, are also being (7) _____ targeted with processed options that satisfy parental convenience and excite children.

For the cash-rich, time-poor consumer, (8) _____ breakfast consumption and 'deskfasts' are fast becoming the chosen option. Manufacturers are moving into this area in order to recover lost (9) _____ from declining at-home consumption, claims the report. It adds that a (10) _____ in social rules with consumers less embarrassed about eating in public places or in front of work colleagues has also contributed to the trend. But it is fair to (11) _____ that this is not a new discovery. For many years the British snacking-on-the-street culture has been well (12) _____, with little or no recognisable shame about eating in public.

PAPER 3, PART 1 Multiple-choice cloze

Remember:
- This part tests your lexical knowledge and comprehension of the text.
- Some items may contain a lexico-grammatical focus, such as words followed by a particular preposition, verb form, etc.
- Some items may test your knowledge of collocations and phrasal verbs.

Tips
- When revising vocabulary for the exam, make sure you revise it in context, paying attention to the grammatical structure it requires.
- Always check through the text when you complete this task, to make sure that your choices make sense!

1 A need	B health
C pleasure	D habit
2 A confirms	B denies
C refutes	D complies
3 A heading	B kind
C title	D term
4 A keen	B enthusiastic
C successful	D frightened
5 A employees	B retailers
C staff	D consumers
6 A wagon	B event
C act	D game
7 A grossly	B heavily
C largely	D extremely
8 A on-the-run	B pay-your-way
C on-the-way	D on-the-go
9 A expenses	B payments
C revenues	D rewards
10 A fall	B breakdown
C abandonment	D drop
11 A say	B tell
C judge	D assess
12 A standardised	B assured
C established	D entrenched

Writing: a letter of reference

1 Read the question below, and underline the key points you need to include in your answer.

> You have been asked to provide a reference for a friend of yours who has applied for a job as a tourist guide for your local town. The person appointed will speak English well, be good at dealing with different people, and will display knowledge of the local area.
>
> You should include information about your friend's character and personal qualities and skills, their previous relevant experience and reasons why they should be considered for this job.

Write your reference.

2 Read the answer below, and use the key points you underlined in the question to complete the plan on the right.

SPOTLIGHT EXAM GUIDANCE

PAPER 2, PARTS 1 AND 2 **Letter**

Part one asks you to write between 180–220 words, whereas part two requires 220–260 words.

Tips

- Underline the key points in the question, and use these to form a plan.

- Organise your points.

- Jot down some relevant words and phrases you would like to use in your answer.

- As you write, be careful not to repeat words too often. Try to use variety.

- Check your answer for relevance, spelling, punctuation and number of words.

Dear Ms Noakes,

RE: Martinique Brun

I have known Martinique for eight years. We studied English together at university, and then spent a year working as volunteers on an environmental project in Britain. For the last three years we have worked together in the administrative office of the local museum.

While participating in the environmental project, we met people from very different cultural backgrounds, and Martinique's warm, friendly character, and her ability to tell entertaining stories made her popular with everyone. Her fluency in both English and Spanish meant that she was particularly good at explaining things whenever there was a misunderstanding. Another quality that made her well liked was her desire to always include everyone in activities. She made sure that no one in the group ever felt left out or ignored.

Martinique is a hard worker, and takes pride in learning all there is to know about a job she is doing. Her work at the museum has involved helping the curator to plan exhibitions of different aspects of local history, and she soon learnt a great deal about historic sites and events in the area. However, she misses meeting people, and having direct contact with the public. For this reason, she would like to leave the office and work as a tourist guide.

Martinique's bright, lively character and knowledge of historical places and events in the area will make her an excellent candidate for this job. I am certain you will find her a valuable asset to your team.

Plan

Opening paragraph ...

_____

_____

Second paragraph ...

_____

_____

Third paragraph ...

_____

_____

Conclusion ...

_____

_____

3 Write a similar plan for an answer to the following question.

PAPER 2, PART 2

> You have been asked to provide a reference for a friend of yours who has applied to take part in a student exchange programme. The person chosen will be a good student and will speak English fluently, so as to understand lectures in the English university they are visiting. They should also be fairly outgoing and independent.
>
> You should include information about your friend's character, and reasons why they should be considered for this opportunity.

4 Write your reference. (220–260 words)

Practice test

Part 1

You are going to read three extracts which are all concerned in some way with dreams. For questions **1–6**, choose the answer (**A**, **B**, **C** or **D**) which you think fits best according to the text.

Extract from a novel

It was the time of year when the river was swollen, fed by the glacier high on the mountain, when it came past rushing with relentless purpose towards the waiting sea. Amongst all the other swirling detritus, Ana noticed a leaf. It stood out with its greenness, and she watched its passage. There it was heading for the bank, then back to the central current, suddenly submerged and then coming up again, spinning onward and onward. It occurred to Ana that the dreams and the river shared a powerful force, and while the river could be touched, the dreams were no less tangible. They had borne her like a leaf through life and the fact that they were not her dreams, but the dreams of her mother, her grandmother, and all the green-eyed first-born women along the matrilineal line before her, made her journey all the more unpredictable. Even before she was born, the dreams had shaped her, announcing her conception, prescribing the dishes that should be consumed and passed to the unborn child, even giving her her name.

For Ana, a life under the direction of dreams was all that she had known. She was aware it was a handicap of sorts, but it was one she was used to, and there was a way around it. By feigning respect for the dreams, Ana was able to offer her own, more favourable interpretations. Had her father been willing to see the sense in this, harmony could have prevailed, but he had been foolish enough to believe he could deal with the dreams by denying them which conversely made them all the more powerful.

1   In the first paragraph, the writer makes a comparison between the leaf and

   A   the unforeseen dangers in Ana's life.
   B   Ana's indifference to events around her.
   C   Ana's lack of control over her life.
   D   the range of possibilities Ana could choose from.

2   How did Ana react to 'a life under the direction of dreams'?

   A   She rebelled against her mother's decisions.
   B   She manipulated her mother's belief in dreams.
   C   She made up her own dreams instead.
   D   She developed a stronger attachment to her mother than father.

Extract from a newspaper article

Recently I have had the same dream during two successive nights. In fact this is a recurring dream that I have had numerous times over the last 30 years, ever since I left high school. There I am, tearing up flights of stairs towards my top floor classroom (with far greater speed than was ever feasible or desired at the time), knowing that if I am late, there will be dire consequences. Once I reach the top floor, the focus of urgency changes; instead I am rummaging through the chaos of my locker [10] for papers and books that I have not but should have read for THE EXAM. Time is marching on, each loud tick shoving me closer to my fate. Other students smugly fold their arms in the knowledge of their weeks of revision. Still I go on with the frantic search – old notes, a highlighted paragraph, anything that could supply the answer and tip the balance in my favour. Then the cold grip of realisation takes hold of me. I look forlornly at the heap of the year's work at my feet. It has all been for nothing.

Now why I should be suffering such dreams after such a [20] length of time, and despite the fact that I *did* go on to go to college, gain a degree, find meaningful (to-a-point) employment and find myself a mate with whom I could guarantee the survival of our genes, I do not truly know. No doubt a psychologist or some other '*ologist*' would say they were a necessary part of brain function, a way of dealing with unresolved issues. But give me a pill that will allow me to censor or fast-forward over those lingering, ever-rewinding ghosts, and I will readily take it. Let me awake in the morning self-assured and bursting [30] with the memories of success. What is the use in going to work with the refreshed knowledge that I never proved myself in maths?

3   The phrase 'the cold grip of realisation' (lines 16–17) refers to the writer's

    A   bitterness regarding the unfair situation.
    B   awareness that they were having a dream.
    C   resignation towards their fate.
    D   embarrassment in front of their classmates.

4   What is the writer emphasising in the second paragraph?

    A   the futility of bad dreams.
    B   the influence of dreams on his choices
    C   the way that dreams help people cope
    D   the fact that bad dreams are more memorable than good ones

Extract from a newspaper article

What are dreams made of? This question has troubled the finest minds ever since people first woke up. Now, the Institute of Contemporary Arts (ICA) in London thinks it can shed some light on the matter. And, in the interests of science, I agreed to help by spending a night in an art gallery, sleeping with 20 people I had never met before. We were part of what the ICA is calling the Dream Director, a sleepover experiment to see if our dreams could be artificially manipulated. The experiment was quite simple: we bedded down in specially designed sleeping pods. I donned an eye mask and before long the sound of children's laughter and far off trains had lulled us to sleep. Our masks contained infra-red sensors that detected when we fell into deep or "dreaming sleep" by measuring rapid eye movement (REM). The readings were logged in a machine: once we were "out", sounds were played through the speakers, each pod having its own theme of sounds. In the morning, we rolled out of bed and wrote down our dreams. Our written recollections were then collected for analysis by scientists. Only afterwards were we told what was played to us.

Frankly, I'd been cynical when I signed up. But I have to admit, my dream was pleasant. I'm prone to sleeping fitfully, plagued by dreams about day-to-day stresses. Sleeping in the pod, my dream took me on an agreeable drive around the countryside in an open-top car, ending at a petrol station in the middle of a forest. In the morning I found out that this was remarkably close to the sounds that played in my pod: a forest and the echoing sounds you would perhaps hear in a canyon. Maybe it was a coincidence: during the day I had been looking at a friend's pictures of Hawaii. Fascinating, perhaps, but it was hard to deduce what purpose it could serve.

5   The purpose of the experiment at ICA is to understand

A   which people suffer more disturbing dreams.
B   how physical comfort influences sleep patterns.
C   whether it is possible to control dreams.
D   the way that people recall dreams when awake.

6   What does the writer say about his experience of the experiment?

A   It left him wondering how useful it would be.
B   It enabled him to remember his dreams with greater accuracy.
C   It helped him recognise the stimulus for different dreams.
D   It resulted in his having more trouble sleeping properly

Part 2

You are going to read an extract from a magazine article. Six paragraphs have been removed from the extract. Choose from the paragraphs **A–G** the one which fits each gap (**7–12**). There is one extra paragraph which you do not need to use.

A pastime to bring peace of mind

Rebecca Front finds a hobby to keep her occupied

I was once told, by someone I have long respected, that the key to being relaxed is to fill your spare time with an absorbing hobby. He did not go as far as to propose anything in particular, but was adamant it would do me the world of good.

| 7 |

That was exactly my response, too. By the time I've taken our son to school, shopped, and done the laundry, it's lunchtime, and I haven't actually started work. I often wonder what happened to the future scientists were always promising us, in which computers and robots would run everything so efficiently that we'd all be free to spend our days lazing in the sun.

| 8 |

To this he gave a firm shake of the head. No, he sighed, that's just relaxation. A hobby is creative, fulfilling, and makes you feel better about yourself. So, finally convinced enough to give it a go, I began my quest for a pastime in which I could lose myself, in the hope that when I found myself again, I wouldn't be quite so neurotic and irritable as I all too frequently am.

| 9 |

My raspberry jam phase had a more promising start. That really did absorb me, and those rows of little fabric-topped pots looked pleasing in a country-kitchen sort of a way. But there are only so many jars of homemade raspberry jam that a household can absorb before everyone becomes repulsed at the thought of any more.

| 10 |

I, however, was smitten. It is like reading a great novel with a plot you have to work out for yourself. You are drawn into the lives of people who are little more than names, eager to follow their changes of fortune, anxious to know what happened to them in times of war, peace, recession. And this, you should understand, is my husband's ancestry, people I know little or nothing about. I haven't even started on my own yet. But for me, the pleasure is in the detail.

| 11 |

For my husband, though, there's another dimension: he's hoping to gain a little more family pride. He discovered years ago that he shares his surname with one of the signatories of the American Declaration of Independence. Since this eminent figure came from Bristol, and my husband's family are from Kent, any connection looked unlikely, but I didn't want to disappoint him. Then, late one night, I stumbled on something: about seven generations ago, an ancestor, asked on a census if he was originally from Kent, replied he was not.

| 12 |

Genealogy is an extremely gratifying hobby. It cannot be dull, any more than life itself can be. Knowing a few facts about people you'll never meet, but whose genetic make-up is imprinted on those you love, is – and I never thought I'd say this – better than a cupboard full of raspberry jam.

A   I had to keep searching, until gratifyingly, at the click of a mouse, there it was: proof that he was indeed born and bred in the same area as the other fellow after all. There may be no connection, and for me, it really doesn't matter. I *do* feel better about myself.

B   The piano seemed to be the obvious choice as I'd had a year of tuition at school. Surely *that* would help extend my creative side? But somehow, when I practised on my son's junior electronic keyboard, the sound I produced failed to make either me or my family feel better about me.

C   An example of this reveals that for generations, his family, like so many others, never moved more than 10 miles from where they had initially settled. The fact that, in those days, not only did you have a job for life, in this case, carpentry, but sons and grandsons would also follow that same path. Something tells me that's not going to happen with IT.

D   I could understand his initial cynicism. What use can information such as this be? I suppose we have become so used to regarding information as something that can provide immediate benefit that we have lost interest in knowledge for knowledge's sake.

E   And then, last week, I stumbled on the answer. We'd been talking to our son about family trees, and I decided to do a bit of rudimentary research to get him involved. He was moderately intrigued; it was a good hour before the allure of poring over a census entry that he could view online with his great-grandfather's name on it was replaced by the Nintendogs.

F   But the 'Man Who Knew' was quietly, and rather annoyingly, insistent. He pointed out that the majority of people who say they have no spare time still seem to find an hour or so to watch one of those 'dreadful reality shows'. Perhaps that's their hobby, I suggested, being careful not to use the first person.

G   Now, almost everyone to whom I have passed this on has retorted that they don't have any spare time. There are barely enough hours in the day to be stressed, without adding to your burden by trying to make models of famous monuments out of matchsticks.

Part 3

You are going to read a magazine article. For questions **13–19**, choose the answer (**A,B,C** or **D**) which you think fits best according to the text.

Man's Best Friend?

Are dogs ideal pets for a suburban lifestyle? Emily Austen isn't convinced

It's 5.30 am and I couldn't be more awake. Had it been the songs of early birds, natural light or soft rainfall that had gently nudged me into life, I would no doubt still be lying here gradually gathering my senses and musing on the order of the morning's rituals. But when you have been forcibly yanked out of your peaceful state and into rude consciousness by a brutal assault on your eardrums, there is no soft transition. And it is still going on – the howling, barking, yelping frenzy over the fence. Yes, my neighbours have returned home from their night shift to be given the canine equivalent of a hero's welcome. And on and on it goes.

It's an early start to the day, but preferable to 2.30 am, another regular time for the masters' return. It is normal, I accept, to wake during the night. But when you are filled with resentment towards all who live next door and with despair at your own helplessness, such emotions tend to stimulate your nerves and a return to sleep becomes unachievable. I am aware that I have unwittingly grown into a bitter person, and my anger at the dogs (rottweiler and XXXXXXXXX) and seems to have heightened my reaction to other irritants that were once mild. I never much minded the sweet little terrier over the road, but now its occasional growls make me bare my own teeth in return … at least through the curtains.

To be fair, I can see why the dogs in question and many others of their kind might be driven to the absurd behaviour of continual barking. I say absurd because it is not the behaviour of normal dogs, but dogs that have been driven to it by the unfair expectations their owners place on them. Admittedly I'm no dog psychologist, let alone an actual pet owner, but a dog, like its ancestor the wolf, is essentially a pack animal. It is a creature which is interdependent on others in its group for protection, hunting and companionship. Deprived of fellowship, it's hardly surprising that their loneliness causes them to seek attention – using the full range of sounds at their command. Not only this, but consider the vast territorial area a dog is supposed to have, and then compare it to the average suburban back yard we confine them to nowadays. Then there is the constant threat of invaders at the gate (delivery men, passers-by etc) so the dog has to be on constant alert.

So why do so many people insist on keeping dogs? Surely they can recognise the cruelty of abandoning an animal for the entire day? I am certain that the exuberant, adoring welcome home at the end of the working day has something to do with it. A faithful, ever-excited-to-see-you, needy 'companion' is something many people desire, and there are few conditions attached when it happens to be a dog. In the small hours, when

I'm staring up at the ceiling, I wonder whether the neighbours realise how far the sound carries and that perhaps they have become immune to it. Then I discount that theory. How could you *not* know? In which case it means that they are completely indifferent to my suffering, and I suspect this is the likeliest scenario. When it comes to the weekend my young son and daughter certainly make their own contribution to the neighbourhood noise level, but they are only allowed out in the garden at a civilised hour in the morning. Therefore I'm ruling out retribution as a factor at least.

I know I am not the only one suffering. The council received over 2000 phone calls regarding the noise levels of neighbouring dogs last year, but only a fraction of the callers took the next step and filed an official complaint. Does this mean the situation was not that serious? I doubt it. Consider the ramifications of making such a complaint: after the council official appears at your neighbour's house, your neighbour is likely to appear at yours. The potential retribution is enough to put most people off. And even if you are willing to confront your neighbour directly and ask them to get 'Jaws', 'Mr Muscle' or 'Assassin' some professional therapy/training, what if nothing is done? You are left with the horrifying option of returning to their door or retreating and accepting defeat.

Thanks to modern technology, more and more people are able to work from home, but this could well be a curse should your home be under siege from incessant barking, booming and growling. It's not just animals that threaten our sanity, though. Who hasn't heard an anecdote about all-night parties where next-door's bass is vibrating the very plaster off the walls, or the teenage son with an absolute passion for the drums and an absolute lack of talent to go with it. I'll go as far as to begrudgingly admit that 'my' dogs don't leave beer bottles strewn over the lawn or invite their mates over for rehearsals.

I wouldn't say I was at breaking point yet but it's got to the point where I'm spending far too much time either enduring it, or anticipating the endurance. Given the current housing market, relocating to another district is off our options list, and of course, there's no guarantee that the new neighbourhood would be a dog-free zone. Likewise, the possibility of sound-proofing our house is well beyond our means. But perhaps fate will shine on us after all. Just yesterday a FOR SALE sign went up next door, much to my household's delight. So perhaps all it will take, as in the case of many siege situations, is time, and in this way, the dreaded confrontation with the neighbour can be postponed indefinitely. By the way, if you are wondering why I have never called the police – my neighbours *are* the police.

13   What does the writer say about waking up at 5.30 am?

   A   They were uncertain as to why they had woken.
   B   They were reluctant to get out of bed.
   C   They were more alert than they wished to be.
   D   There were fortunately accustomed to an early start.

14   The writer refers to the Yorkshire terrier in order to

   A   emphasise how easily annoyed they have become.
   B   highlight how any breed of dog can exhibit poor behaviour.
   C   demonstrate the impact of one dog's behaviour on another.
   D   show how his relationship with other neighbours is deteriorating.

15   The writer believes that some dogs bark excessively because of

   A   certain genes they have inherited.
   B   a need for social interaction.
   C   incorrect training.
   D   their unsuitability as pets.

16   In the fourth paragraph, the writer says their neighbours

   A   are deliberately trying to bother them.
   B   do not care how they feel.
   C   have little idea how bad the noise is.
   D   believe the dog's behaviour is normal.

17   According to the writer, people are reluctant to complain due to

   A   ignorance about potential solutions.
   B   impatience with council procedure.
   C   anxiety over how to bring the subject up.
   D   fear of the neighbour's reaction.

18   What point does the writer make in the sixth paragraph?

   A   There is a growing tendency to be inconsiderate to others.
   B   Working from home can be ineffective.
   C   There are worse situations they could be in.
   D   A bad neighbour can cause problems in diverse ways.

19   In the final paragraph, the writer says they intend to

   A   move to a different place.
   B   do nothing about the problem.
   C   insulate their house from outside noise.
   D   have an honest discussion with the neighbours.

Part 4

You are going to read an article containing reviews of favourite books. For questions **20–34**, choose from the reviews (**A–E**). The reviews may be chosen more than once.

In which review are the following mentioned ...?

the way that the central character seems to be resigned to his fate.	20
the fact that revisions were made in the book's subsequent editions.	21
an explanation of why the reviewer had once felt prevented from writing.	22
the reviewer's admission of having used some of the book's storylines.	23
the fact that the reviewer was once happy to overlook the writer's weaknesses.	24
the reviewer's desire to understand more about the way that writers function.	25
the inner thoughts of the central character not being directly revealed in the book.	26
the reviewer's admiration for the book's blend of comedy and tragedy.	27
the way the writer successfully conveys people's character without long description.	28
the reviewer's appreciation of the type of story that can be adapted as required.	29
a particular reason for the reviewer's empathy towards the central character.	30
the reviewer's claim that the writer has an image which is not deserved.	31
the fact that this book introduced the reviewer to the writer's other work.	32
the way the book helped the reviewer to see something familiar in a new light.	33
the fact that the writer's influence on the reviewer outlasted that of other writers.	34

My Book of A Lifetime

Five writers review their all-time favourite books by other authors.

A

My Uncle Silas, **HE Bates** *reviewed by Steve Augarde*

At art college I fell in love with American writers. Reading them made me want to write but giving yourself permission to try is one thing; finding a way in is another. They had the great cities of New York and San Francisco, the romance of the endless open road. I had rural Somerset. What was there to say? There had been many British writers with English countryside backgrounds but it wasn't until I revisited HE Bates that I finally began to be more inspired by something closer to home. The world as he saw it and the people that he wrote about were very recognisable to me. There was nobody to touch him for evoking atmosphere although he has a reputation for being cosier than is warranted. His tales could be dark, acerbic and strange, as in the Uncle Silas stories. I don't write like Bates, and have never wished that I could be him in the same way I did my old heroes Kerouac or Miller. But his influence was ultimately the stronger. It was he above all others who showed me that I didn't need to be gazing across the Atlantic in search of stories to tell.

B

Fairy Stories, **Jacob and Wilhelm Grimm** *reviewed by Sara Maitland*

I was lucky: from childhood, my parents read fairy stories to us. These have some big advantages for parents because they can be shifted to match the moment's need; there is a fairly even balance of male and female characters and they are mercifully short. Gradually, I learned that the most popular fairy stories had been recorded by two German linguists, brothers called Grimm. They published a first collection in 1812 and the final edition appeared in 1857. During this time, they altered the versions, mainly in response to criticism. For instance, Cinderella's stepsisters were not originally 'ugly' but 'fair of face, but black of heart'. But the shape of the stories does not change; the structure is sturdy and the plot lines wonderfully clear. When I grew up and became a writer I went back to these sources and have been using them ever since, working on the principle that a tale which has been around for centuries is highly likely to be a better story than one that I made up yesterday.

C

A Writer's Diary, **Virginia Woolf** *reviewed by Susan Hill*

I had never heard of Virginia Woolf when at 16, and starting my first book, I chanced upon *A Writer's Diary*. I was hungry for anything which would not only teach me how to write novels but would tell me about how to be a writer, whatever that meant. Something that would reveal the secrets of the writing life. It is hard to convey the excitement with which I read the book. I learned how each of her novels germinated and grew, how she worked, sometimes quickly, before careful revision, and wove life around her writing, how anxious she became about it. The diary introduced me to the woman, and led me to her books, which came as a revelation, as they did to her audience then. The shock of discovering her style has never really left me. I pick up *A Writer's Diary* every day, at random. It has so many moods, contains so much intelligence, and gossip. It is a record of the times through which she was living while writing. Many of her contemporaries are here, in swift intimate pen sketches which reveal them to us as well as many a lengthy biography.

D

The Enigma of Arrival, **VS Naipaul** *reviewed by Andrew Miller*

The Enigma is the story of a writer from Trinidad who goes to live, as Naipaul did, in a secluded valley in Wiltshire. What excited me about this book was the way a landscape I knew very well was shown to me in a new, meticulous and entirely convincing way. The narrator walks, he has the occasional conversation, he listens, he misses little but he is never able to overcome his 'stranger's nerves'. About the private life of the narrator we learn very little in a direct sense. The book's 'characters' are the neighbours he sees on his circuits. There are little scandals, people leave, new people come. Everyone, even the valley itself, is subject to the same immutable law of decay. The narrator, however, is not in opposition to this; indeed, it perfectly suits his sensibility which is the book's true target. And so he patrols his exile's refuge with a fatalistic love of the place, a quiet sense of his good fortune in finding it at all.

E

David Copperfield, **Charles Dickens** *reviewed by Gaynor Arnold*

David Copperfield was the first book that bridged the gap between my childhood and adult reading. It was not the first of his books I had read but it was an adult story with a child hero. My own father had recently died, and although I was by no means friendless and poor, I still identified with the orphan David as he negotiated his way through loss and deprivation. How I sympathised with David's twin emotions of grief and self-importance as he walked alone in the playground, conscious of the sympathetic attention of the other boys. Of course, I appreciated the tremendous humour alongside the pathos: David's first attempt at a dinner party, and first experience of getting drunk, made me laugh out loud. As an adult, I can see that Dickens has many faults: too insipidly sentimental in places, too conventional in his treatment of women – but none of that bothered me then. On the contrary, Dickens had me gripped.

Part 1

You must answer this question. Write your answer in **180–220** words in an appropriate style.

You are a student at an international college. The social committee recently planned an end-of-year visit to a local tourist attraction and has asked you to write a report.

Read the advertisement for the tourist attraction below, and the comments that you have made on it after you received other students' feedback. Then, **using the information appropriately,** write your report for the committee, describing the visit and making recommendations for improvements for a future visit to the same attraction.

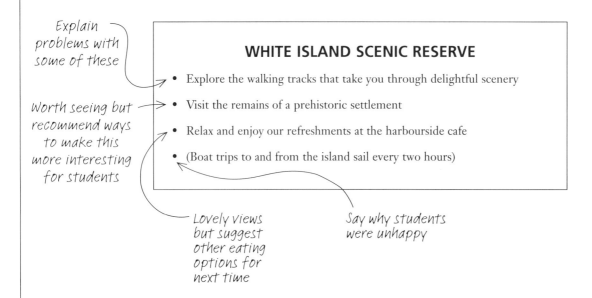

Explain problems with some of these

Worth seeing but recommend ways to make this more interesting for students

WHITE ISLAND SCENIC RESERVE

- Explore the walking tracks that take you through delightful scenery
- Visit the remains of a prehistoric settlement
- Relax and enjoy our refreshments at the harbourside cafe
- (Boat trips to and from the island sail every two hours)

Lovely views but suggest other eating options for next time

Say why students were unhappy

Write your **report**. You should use your own words as far as possible.

Part 2

Write an answer to one of the following questions **2–5** in this part. Write your answer in **220–260** words in an appropriate style.

2   You see the following announcement in an international environmental issues magazine.

> ## ENVIRONMENTALLY-FRIENDLY COMMUNITY COMPETITION
>
> We are writing a series of articles on how individual communities can make a difference to the environment. Nominate your community for inclusion in the series by:
>
> • describing the ways in which it already helps preserve the environment
>
> • proposing ways in which a $40,000 grant could be spent on local environmental improvements

Write your **competition entry**.

3   An international guidebook called *Small World* has recently asked readers to submit contributions on the subject of old traditional stories or legends. You have decided to write a contribution to the guidebook. Your contribution should:

• describe one particular story or legend from your country

• say in what way the story or legend still has an impact on modern life

• suggest how visitors to your country can learn more about this story or legend

Write your **contribution to the guidebook**.

4   Last year you went on a trip which was organised by a company called *New Horizons*. A friend of yours has written to you saying that he is considering whether to book a trip with the same company and asking you for your opinion.

Write a letter to your friend, explaining in what ways the trip was a positive and negative experience, and saying to what extent you think a trip with *New Horizons* would suit your friend's needs.

Write your **letter**.

5   Answer **one** of the following two questions based on **one** of the set texts.

   (a) You have recently had a class discussion about the supporting characters in (the set text). Your teacher has now asked you to write an essay saying which supporting character is most vital to the development of the story. You should describe this character and say how he or she contributes to the story's development.

Write your **essay**.

   (b) You have been asked to write a review of (the set text) for your college website. In your review, give a brief outline of the plot, explain what you think are the central themes of the story, and say whether or not you would recommend the story to other students.

Write your **review**.

Part 1

For questions **1–12**, read the text below and decide which answer (**A**, **B**, **C** or **D**) best fits each gap. There is an example at the beginning.

Example:

0 **A** appear   **B** arrive   **C** turn   **D** come

0   A B C **D**

Underground coal fires

When we think of fire which is out of control, it is usually forest fires that first **(0)** ...... to mind. However, underground coal fires have also become a serious issue and are making a significant **(1)** ...... to the rise in global temperature. They exist across the world, with **(2)** ...... ones occurring in China and India, and one of the oldest in Australia where 'Burning Mountain' is **(3)** ...... to have been on fire for over 6000 years. One of the most famous **(4)** ......, however, can be found in Pennsylvania, USA. The town of Centralia was built around a coal mine and at its **(5)** ......, the township boasted a population of around 2000. Then, when the coal became too hard to extract, the mining operation was **(6)** ...... and the entrance to the mine was **(7)** ...... up. Some time later, in 1962, it became evident that the mine was burning and fire was raging below **(8)** .... There are several theories about how this happened but the popular **(9)** ...... of the story was that some rubbish had been **(10)** ...... on fire and this in turn had ignited a coal seam lying just below it. The town's inhabitants began to suffer from carbon monoxide poisoning and were forced to **(11)** ...... as the land began to **(12)** ...... beneath their houses. The remaining population currently stands at four.

1	**A** contribution	**B** problem	**C** development	**D** involvement
2	**A** prime	**B** lead	**C** major	**D** strong
3	**A** rated	**B** estimated	**C** measured	**D** evaluated
4	**A** circumstances	**B** scenarios	**C** samples	**D** cases
5	**A** limit	**B** height	**C** point	**D** maximum
6	**A** discarded	**B** rejected	**C** abandoned	**D** withdrawn
7	**A** drawn	**B** sealed	**C** finished	**D** fixed
8	**A** earth	**B** surface	**C** cover	**D** ground
9	**A** variety	**B** alternative	**C** version	**D** aspect
10	**A** put	**B** set	**C** lit	**D** struck
11	**A** evacuate	**B** transfer	**C** evade	**D** divert
12	**A** sink	**B** decline	**C** revert	**D** shrink

Part 2

For questions **13–27**, read the text below and think of the word which best fits each gap. Use only one word in each gap. There is an example at the beginning (**0**).

Example: 0 of

The origins of Stonehenge

The ancient monument **(0)** .... Stonehenge in South East England is world famous. A circular group of standing stones, **(13)** .... draws thousands of fascinated observers every year, **(14)** .... intrigued by the mystery that has remained **(15)** .... the present day. It is accepted as fact by most archaeologists, **(16)** .... that the monument was built in three stages over a period of approximately 800 years. **(17)** .... to their research, the first stage was a circle of timbers surrounded by a ditch and bank, **(18)** .... the next stage beginning about 2500 BC, when enormous bluestones were brought from the Prescelli Mountains. **(19)** .... makes this a remarkable feat of engineering was that the stones were transported over 245 miles **(20)** .... their average weight of five tons each. The final phase occurred about 2300 BC, during **(21)** .... time the bluestones were dug up and re-arranged and even bigger stones were used. These new giant sandstones were hammered into shape so that they **(22)** .... sit on top of each other.

Recently archaeologists have become aware of the number of people buried nearby who were **(23)** .... native to the local area or even to England and **(24)** .... corpses displayed signs of serious physical injury or illness. These two factors suggest they were coming to Stonehenge in the hope of **(25)** .... cured, possibly **(26)** .... some kind of healing powers that the bluestones **(27)** .... said to possess.

Part 3

For questions **28–37**, read the text below. Use the word given in capitals at the end of some of the lines to form a word that fits in the gap in the same line. There is an example at the beginning (**0**).

Example: 0 SELECTION

Vitamin Pills

In the fight to stay healthy, the vitamin pill is seen by many as a great ally.
Whereas once upon a time a small **(0)** .... of vitamin bottles, mostly   **SELECT**
containing C, B, and A, could be found reaching their expiry dates in the dusty
corner of a chemist's shelf, the market is now a hugely **(28)** .... one   **PROFIT**
for the pharmaceutical industry. Interestingly enough, as world obesity rates
rise, so does our **(29)** .... of these dietary supplements as more and   **CONSUME**
more shoppers regard them as an absolutely **(30)** .... part of their   **VALUE**
daily **(31)** .... intake. The vast range of vitamins means that they are   **NUTRIENT**
used for **(32)** .... reasons; common ones being for the   **NUMBER**
(33) .... of skin cells, as natural aids to digestion, cures for   **GENERATE**
(34) .... and for stress-related symptoms such as headaches,   **SLEEP**
(35) .... and depression. However, vitamin manufacturers are   **IRRITATE**
(36) .... coming under attack for making unrealistic claims about their   **INCREASE**
products. Can the right mix of vitamins really help you **(37)** .... your   **LIVE**
contemporaries and reach great old age? There is no scientific evidence to
support this.

Part 4

For questions **38–42**, think of one word only which can be used appropriately in all three sentences. Here is an example (**0**).

Example:

0 Jessica loves to .... attention to herself in social situations.

The nurse asked me if I wanted her to .... the curtain.

To my surprise, I watched the limousine .... up outside my house.

Example: 0 DRAW

---

38   The scenery on that road is lovely but you ought to take the more .... route.

        Tests have shown a .... link between the pill and the headaches patients suffered.

        Her manner is very .... which some employees actually appreciate.

39   It's rare for Andy to have any .... with his children nowadays.

        The disease is thought to spread through .... with infected people.

        I have a .... in the publishing industry who might be able to help you find work.

40   A diet of such .... food cannot be particularly health.

        The island is .... in natural resources.

        He may be an entrepreneur, but his company has hardly made him ....

41   The event was .... in an old castle by the sea.

        Many of the team were .... up by a last-minute flight cancellation.

        After I finished playing, she told me that I hadn't .... the instrument correctly.

42   Nothing would ever .... Emma to accept money from her elderly parents.

        Government soldiers are now attempting to .... the rebels out of the jungle.

        He seems to lack .... and ambition, both of which are crucial in this job.

Part 5

For questions **43–50**, complete the second sentence so that it has a similar meaning to the first sentence, using the word given. Do not change the word given. You must use between three and six words, including the word given. Here is an example (**0**).

Example: 0 Everyone welcomed the idea apart from Anna.

EXCEPTION

Everyone welcomed the idea .... Anna.

The gap can be filled with the words 'with the exception of', so you write:

Example:

0 WITH THE EXCEPTION OF

---

43 Simon was quick to accept the offer of work in Australia.

HESITATION

Simon .... the offer of work in Australia.

44 I don't like the way that Jane gets angry so often with other staff.

WOULD

I wish .... temper so often with other staff.

45 The critic said that the group had certainly never performed as well as they did that night.

DOUBT

The critic said that it was .... ever on that night.

46 We were just about to leave the restaurant when the waitress finally brought our food.

POINT

We were .... the restaurant when the waitress finally brought our food.

47 Although I had imagined my parachute jump would terrify me, it was actually quite exciting.

BEING

Far .... experience I had imagined, my parachute jump was actually quite exciting.

48 They've made a decision about the new site for the supermarket.

REGARD

A decision .... the new site for the supermarket.

49 Winning the lottery meant we no longer had to work at the factory.

GIVE

Winning the lottery enabled .... working at the factory.

50 The guide said we should take umbrellas to be prepared for any rain.

CASE

The guide recommended that .... rained.

Part 1

You will hear three different extracts. For questions **1–6**, choose the answer (**A**, **B** or **C**) which fits best according to what you hear. There are two questions for each extract.

Extract One

You hear part of an interview with a successful comedian called Andy Evans.

1   How does Andy compare live comedy to film work.

    A   He appreciates the chance to edit mistakes.

    B   He prefers working within a tight schedule.

    C   He feels uncomfortable following a script.

2   Andy reacts to inaccurate media reports about him by

    A   refusing to read them.

    B   protesting to editors.

    C   complaining during his performances.

Extract Two

You hear an actress talking about a film in which she was asked to ride a horse.

3   Why did the actress tell the director she could ride horses?

    A   She genuinely believed she had the ability.

    B   She was hoping to impress her co-star.

    C   She desperately wanted some acting work.

4   How did the actress feel during the riding scene?

    A   She was embarrassed by her lack of skill.

    B   She was annoyed by the behaviour of the horse.

    C   She was fearful that the horse would go too fast.

Extract Three

You hear part of a radio discussion in which two mountaineers, Donald and Fiona, are talking about their experiences.

5   How did Donald feel before the final ascent of the mountain?

    A   He doubted that he would be able to finish the climb.

    B   He was proud to have beaten other mountaineers he knew.

    C   He regretted not being able to share the experience.

6   Fiona and Donald agree that many younger mountaineers

    A   lack sufficient respect for mountains.

    B   underestimate the level of fitness required.

    C   have the wrong motivation for climbing.

Part 2

You will hear a landscape designer called Tom Pearce talking about his work. For questions **7–14**, complete the sentences.

Landscape Designer

Tom's landscape design company is known as ………….. **(7)**

He was attracted to landscape design because of the combination of **(8)** ………….. and discipline.

As well as being able to communicate well with people, a landscape designer should have good ………….. **(9)**

Tom specialises in creating designs for ………….. **(10)**

One of the first things he checks after interviewing clients is the type of ………….. **(11)**

Tom says that some of his clients forget about ………….. **(12)** when they are thinking of ideas.

Many of the plants that Tom chooses for clients have a ………….. **(13)**

The one drawback of his work are the ………….. **(14)** Tom gets.

Part 3

You will hear part of an interview with a chef and restaurateur called Stephen Rees. For questions **15–20**, choose the answer (**A**, **B**, **C** or **D**) which fits best according to what you hear.

15   According to Stephen, why did he become a chef?

    A   He was determined to prove a point.

    B   He felt under pressure to please his mother.

    C   He wished to fulfil a dream.

    D   He was anxious to find temporary employment.

16   What is Stephen's advice to people wishing to set up a restaurant?

    A   They should take a chance rather than wait until they feel ready.

    B   They should gain a lot of experience in the industry beforehand.

    C   They should be cautious about involving too many business partners.

    D   They should make a careful study of an established successful restaurant.

17   How does Stephen feel about the young chefs he mentions?

    A   He admires their originality in creating dishes.

    B   He doubts their commitment to the job.

    C   He is concerned about their lack of basic knowledge.

    D   He disapproves of their egoistic attitude.

18   According to Stephen, why do his employees prefer to stay at his restaurant?

    A   They appreciate their involvement in the decision-making process.

    B   They are nervous about setting up their own ventures.

    C   They are aware that other restaurants have low morale.

    D   They recognise that they are working towards the same goal.

19   For Stephen, what is a disadvantage of working in the kitchen?

    A   He intimidates other chefs.

    B   He is unable to manage staff.

    C   He has less contact with customers.

    D   He has insufficient time for financial planning.

20   Which aspect of Stephen's work does he find most fulfilling?

    A   writing cookery books.

    B   updating the menus.

    C   opening new restaurants.

    D   travelling abroad.

Part 4

You will hear five short extracts in which people are talking about their use of mobile phones.

Task One

For questions **21–25**, choose from the list (**A–H**) the main reason why each speaker uses their mobile phone.

Task Two

For questions **26–30**, choose from the list (**A–H**) the attitude the speaker has towards their mobile phone.

When you listen you must complete both tasks.

A for making social arrangements

B for recording images

Speaker 1 [21] [ ]

C for communicating with business contacts

Speaker 1 [22] [ ]

D for staying in touch with family members

Speaker 1 [23] [ ]

E for finding employment

Speaker 1 [24] [ ]

F for emergency use only

Speaker 1 [25] [ ]

G for amusement

H for reasons of safety

A I resent its impact on my life.

B It cheers me up

Speaker 1 [26] [ ]

C I find it reassuring

Speaker 1 [27] [ ]

D I'm addicted to it

Speaker 1 [28] [ ]

E I'd be lost without it.

F I'm unsure how to use it.

Speaker 1 [29] [ ]

G I like showing it off

Speaker 1 [30] [ ]

H I rarely think about it.

Part 1

3 minutes (or 5 minutes for groups of 3)

select one or two questions and answer as appropriate.

- Where are you from?
- What do you do?
- How long have you been studying English?
- What do you enjoy most about studying English?
- What are the advantages and disadvantages of studying in another country?
- What sport or hobby would you like to take up? Why?
- How do you think your life may change in the future?
- What has been one of your proudest achievements so far?

Part 2

4 minutes (6 minutes for groups of three)

1 Travel

For both candidates:
Here are some pictures showing people who are travelling abroad for their holiday.

Candidate A:
Compare two of these pictures and say what aspect of travel they show and how the people might be feeling. (*1 minute*)

Candidate B:
Which of these people might have the most interesting experience? (*approximately 30 seconds*)

2 Food

For both candidates:
Here are some pictures of people and food which has been prepared.

Candidate B:
Compare two of the pictures and say why these people might have come together and how big a role food might play in their lives. (*1 minute*)

Candidate A:
Which of these people do you think appreciate the food the most? (*30 seconds*)

Travel

- What aspect of travel do these pictures show and how might the people be feeling?

- Which of these people might have the most interesting experience?

Food

- Why might these people have come together and how big a role does food play in their lives?

- Which of these people do you think appreciate the food the most?

Part 3

8 minutes (12 minutes for groups of three)

Climate

For both candidates

Here are some pictures showing different ways in which climate affects our lives.

First talk to each other about how these pictures show the impact of climate on our lives. Then decide which picture best reflects the greatest impact.

Part 4

Further discussion

For both candidates

*   How far do you agree with the idea that climate affects national character?

*   To what extent does climate influence your choice of holiday destination?

*   In your opinion, what might be the advantages or disadvantages of living in a country with a very variable climate?

*   What effects of climate change most concern you? Why?

*   How are people tackling climate change in your country?

Tapescript

Listening 1.1

Extract One

Woman: Well that's my earliest memory. How about you?

Man: I'm not really sure but I remember ... I think I must have been about three or four, and I remember losing my teddy – don't laugh, it was my favourite possession and I took it everywhere with me – and one day, my parents had taken me out somewhere, to a park I think. I remember lots of other children playing all over the place and feeling a bit intimidated ...

Woman: What, because they were bigger than you?

Man: Yeah, mainly, and also because this was probably one of my first experiences of other children in such large numbers. Anyway, I think eventually I must have found the courage to venture forth into a large Wendy house I think it was, where all these other kids were playing, and pretty soon forgot my inhibitions and had a great time.

Woman: And the teddy?

Man: Oh yeah, that was the sad part. On our way home I asked Mummy where teddy was and she said she didn't have him – I must have left him in the Wendy house. I just bawled all the way home.

Extract Two

Interviewer: Kathy Brent left school at 16 to focus on her song writing ambitions and was lucky enough to begin recording almost immediaely. Within two years she had recorded her first album and had had a number one hit. Kathy, tell us about that time.

Kathy: Well, it meant everything to record an album, I felt like, this is amazing. And to actually be doing it was fantastic – unbelievable really.

Interviewer: And the reviews were just so positive – people said that as a first album it was already so mature – so polished in fact, and it clearly had such a sense of identity unlike so many first albums. How did you feel about your sudden success? Did it go to your head?

Kathy: Well it was an incredible surprise but at the time I just felt that this is what I had to do, like I had a mission to make an album, and that was all. I didn't want to be famous, I didn't want to make lots of money, I just wanted to make an album that people would like, and so all my energy went into that.

Extract Three

Interviewer: So, what made you decide to set up your own baby slings business?

Woman: Well, people saw me carrying my own daughters in these South American pouch slings, and asked me about them, so I knew there was definitely some interest.

Interviewer: But there are so many different types of baby carrier on the market. What is it about your pouch slings that makes them so popular?

Woman: The majority of baby carriers are made with metal frames, or with adjustable straps, belts or buckles. Mine are just made from a large piece of colourful cotton threaded through a couple of metal rings and worn over the shoulder.

Interviewer: And are they easy to use?

Woman: Definitely! Newborns can be safely carried close to your breast in the most secure and comfortable position, while older kids can sit on your hip. I carried both my daughters until they were three and never felt they were too heavy. Dads find them practical too and we even have designs that are more suitable for men.

Interviewer: And what I love about them is there's just no end to the choice of fabric available ...

Listening 2.1

Man: One of the greatest challenges teachers face today is that of persuading their students to read. How can the written word hope to compete with the more visually stimulating video games that are so widely available? The answer, ladies and gentleman, is a simple one. Comics! Children have been reading comics since the 1930s, and recent years have seen a rise in the number of comic, or graphic books available, inspired by the impressive Japanese manga artwork. So, why not present children with the novels of Charles Dickens, or Jules Verne, in comic format? The advantages are obvious, since the visual nature of each page could be used to target new vocabulary and develop children's communicative skills. Similarly, pictures would help stimulate weaker readers to understand and respond effectively to what they are reading.

How many of us struggle to teach children to read Shakespeare, let alone love him? Now, several publishing houses are working hard to reproduce some of his plays in comic format. 'Self Made Hero' comics have published *Romeo and Juliet* in manga-style cartoons, setting the story on the gang-filled streets of Tokyo. The language has had to be abridged, and certain cuts have been unavoidable, so that some of the poetry is lost. No doubt some of the purists among you will protest against this outrage, but while I sympathise with your view, surely, we have to look realistically at what we can hope to achieve in the long term. By creating Romeo and Juliet as cartoon figures, we enable a wider number of children to relate to them in today's social context, and stimulate their interest in the story. The aim is to use the comic format as a stepping stone, to make the sophisticated language of Shakespeare accessible to children, and lead them towards eventually reading the play in its original form with relative ease.

'Classical Comics' have taken this idea a step further, by producing three full-colour comic versions of *Henry V* and *Macbeth*. They present the play in the original text, in the 'plain text' of today, and in a simplified 'quick text' version, aimed at slow readers. They suggest that students of mixed abilities will be able to read the play together, using the version that suits their ability. The company chose to produce these particular plays first, because they believe boys will be attracted to the battle scenes and the conflict within the stories, enhanced by intricate artwork.

Personally, I'm not sure that presenting students in the same class with different texts is practical from a teaching point of view, but the idea of rendering Shakespearean language in visual form is certainly appealing, and gains my support. I'd be delighted to hear your views on the subject, so …

Listening 3.1

Speaker 1: Without a shadow of doubt, it was the most exhilarating moment of my life and something that I have unfortunately not had the opportunity to attempt again since.

Speaker 2: It irked me that I couldn't remember the name of the person who'd helped me.

Speaker 3: I remained unconvinced by his story and was reluctant to offer him yet more money.

Listening 3.2

Extract One

Interviewer: So Gillian, how did you feel about jumping out of an aeroplane when you actually did it?

Gillian: Without a shadow of doubt, it was the most exhilarating moment of my life and something that I have unfortunately not had the opportunity to attempt again since.

Interviewer: So you would do it again if the chance came along?

Gillian: Absolutely! Although, I'm quite a bit older now than I was then, so I suppose I'd have to be a bit more careful.

Interviewer: Careful, in what way?

Gillian: Well, I'd have to make sure I was fit enough to do something like that again. Unfortunately my body doesn't bend quite as easily as it used to!

Interviewer: And if your seventeen-year-old daughter told you she wanted to do the same thing, what would you say?

Gillian: Ah well, yes. That's a bit different isn't it? I mean, it's not that it isn't safe – I know all about the stringent safety measures – but I know I'd be worried if she said she wanted to do something like that.

Extract Two

Interviewer: Peter, what do you remember as being the strongest emotion you felt after the incident?

Peter: It irked me that I couldn't remember the name of the person who'd helped me.

Interviewer: You mean the man who had chased away your attackers and called the ambulance?

Peter: Yes, that's right. I was still conscious when the ambulance came and that man had stayed with me and tried to make sure I was OK. He talked to me and told me his name. If it hadn't been for him, I'm sure I wouldn't be here today. I wanted to get in touch with him, of course, so that I could thank him in some way. After all, he had put his own life at risk.

Interviewer: And what about your attackers?

Peter: Yes, well, unfortunately they're still out there, aren't they? I mean the coppers did their best and all, but there are just too many hooligans and yobbos on the streets to keep track of.

Interviewer: And what is your advice then to anyone who has to walk home in the early hours through the back streets of Glasgow.

Peter: 'Best not to mate', that's what I'd say. 'Get a cab.'

Extract Three

Interviewer: Angela, you've been the victim of fraud, haven't you? Can you tell us what happened?

Angela: Yes, we had a lodger staying with us. Pleasant young man, well-spoken, very polite. In the beginning he was very prompt with his payments.

Interviewer: And then everything changed?

Angela: That's right. One day he came to me and said his father had been the victim of a robbery and was waiting for the insurance to pay up. Until then he needed three thousand pounds to keep the debtors at bay. He'd be willing to repay me with interest of course. He was so convincing that I gave him the money, but at the time, I confess that I did have my doubts. Several months went by and there was still no sign of any cash. Then he had the audacity to ask for another loan, saying the insurance people were being difficult.

Interviewer: And did you give it to him?

Angela: I remained unconvinced by his story and was reluctant to offer him yet more money.

Interviewer: What happened then?

Angela: He disappeared next day without a trace. The police told us he'd used a false identity and was probably the man they'd been looking for.

Listening 4.1

Speaker One

H. G. Wells' *Invisible Man* used to fascinate me. Once I became professionally involved in the subject, however, I realised that Wells' idea of a chemical cocktail bringing about invisibility was highly improbable. To make something invisible, you have to address the problem of light in relation to the space around an object. Chemicals can't do that. So, while fiction may occasionally inspire scientific thought, it lacks the practical details necessary to make that thought reality. Our group is currently researching into the possibility of creating an electromagnetic material that could distort space in relation to the paths of light around an object, thus rendering that object invisible …

Speaker Two

Yeah, I mean it was incredible! Our company was in the process of developing tablet PCs, display boards and computerised wall screens, and I was responsible for promoting them … So you can imagine my surprise when, lo and behold, examples of all three concepts appeared in the new series of *Star Trek*! We couldn't believe it. We were sure there had been no leakage of information from us, so how the producers got the ideas, I don't know. But certainly, the wall screen concept had been knocking around for a while, and scientific journals had speculated the prospect of display boards and tablet PCs. Mindblowing, though. A real case of fiction reflecting fact!

Speaker Three

I think science fiction's got a lot to answer for, actually, in terms of how it's inspired 'big brother' type electronic identification systems.

Take films like *Gattaca*, for instance, where individuals can be instantly recognised by DNA analysis, and *The Bourne Identity*, where automated palm-print identification is used. Countries like Britain and the States are already discussing the value of a DNA databank for convicted criminals, and palm-print identification is becoming increasingly popular in various places in the public sector. It's the responsibility of me and my colleagues to examine the possible effects on society of such systems being widely used and, I can tell you, they may not be as desirable as we might hope. The trouble is, science fiction films often present them in a positive light, without considering the broader consequences of having such systems in place.

Speaker Four

Oh, I love exploring the connections between science fiction and fact. There is no doubt that many young sci-fi enthusiasts grow up to become scientists, inspired by futuristic ideas they've read about. And this is something I actively encourage in the classroom, by setting projects based on ideas from a novel. A particular favourite is getting students to set up a moon base. They have to work out a programme for survival on the moon, and decide how they would need to adapt in order to survive. Even kids who are not particularly interested in scientific theory, enjoy doing this, and this can lead to a kindling of enthusiasm for other aspects of science ...

Speaker Five

Personally, I think the connection can be mutually beneficial. Several well-known science fiction novels have inspired scientific research. We'd be naïve to ignore the contributions of Jules Verne and Isaac Asimov, for example! My last book was based on time I'd spent in a lab observing the experts at work. And I also find science journals are an excellent source of material. Don't forget that many successful writers of science fiction are research scientists themselves, who, frustrated by the limitations of relying on experiments to prove their theories, escape to the realm of fiction to allow their scientific imaginations to run free ...

Listening 5.1

Prison warden: The job of a prison-based Probation Officer is a challenging one, and not for the faint-hearted. Like any job which involves dealing with people, it requires social skills, and an ability to 'connect' with people. Broadly speaking, as a probation officer, your areas of responsibility are as follows:

You have to liaise with prison officers and with probation officers on the outside. You're involved in the ongoing process of assessing an individual's progress during his or her sentence, and assessing them in terms of the risk they present to harm others, themselves, the prison staff, and generally the risk of them re-offending. In the Women's prison where I work, I form part of a multi-disciplinary team. When making my assessments, I have access to a special Offender Management website, which enables me to obtain professional advice from health care staff, psychologists, drugs specialists and housing and employment staff. I also sit on Parole Assessment Panels. All of this means writing reports on a daily basis and, due to rising numbers in the prison population, there is increasing pressure on probation officers to do this, which often encroaches on the time spent in direct contact with the individuals themselves!

This is the most challenging, but also the most rewarding aspect of the job. Having regular contact with an inmate is vital for you to build up a rapport, and try to divert them from getting into trouble again. We aim to help them find a new direction, new channels, offer them structured programmes to help them think differently. It can be great to feel that you're genuinely contributing to someone's rehabilitation. The key is to remember that offenders are people. Yes, very troubled people, and in some cases, dangerous. But if you're going to get anywhere with them, you have to treat them with dignity. Do so, and you'll be amazed at how many respond.

Recently, the profession has come in for a lot of unfair criticism, but we should remember that it's only the failures that make the headlines! The successes go unnoticed, largely due to the fact that there is no further crime committed! In reality, the Probation Service does a pretty good job in diverting people from crime, and a very small number commit a further serious offence while under supervision.

If you're considering this as a career then, my advice to you is this: Expect the unexpected on any given day, and be able to think on your feet. Situations need to be dealt with quickly and effectively. Training takes two years, and the course involves both academic and on-the-job training.

Listening 5.2

Student: Mmm, what do I like about Volos? Well, first, it's not too big! It has all the advantages a town has to offer, such as attractive shops, cafeterias, bars, restaurants, and also cinemas, and a theatre, without the chaos of the big city. You can't get lost here very easily! Then there's the sea front, which is a great place to go and relax and drink coffee after school or work. There is always conversation and laughter, without the noise of the traffic! But ... I think the best thing about the town is that it is easy to escape! Volos is situated at the foot of Pelion, one of the most beautiful mountains in Greece. Within twenty minutes, it is possible to leave behind the noisy town and find yourself wandering through trees, by the side of a stream.

Listening 6.1

Speaker One: Essential oils can be very effective in boosting one's immune system, fighting infections or just making you feel relaxed or positive. They can be applied by a gentle massage to the skin where they're quickly absorbed, or the powerful properties of the oils can be inhaled, either by heating them over a candle in some water, or just by putting a few drops on a tissue and holding it to your nose. Lavender is the most versatile and gentle of the oils. I use it just about every day and the children love it.

Speaker Two: The name comes from the Greek words 'Homoio', which means 'similar' and 'pathos' meaning 'disease' or 'suffering'. Treatments are very small doses of compounds derived from plants or minerals which stimulate the patient's natural defence system into action. The medicines are specially selected for their ability to cause similar symptoms to those the sick person is experiencing. It's not entirely clear how it works, but it's thought that because symptoms are actually the body's attempts to re-establish a balance, a substance that causes similar symptoms to those the patient is experiencing would put the body into an even more effective form of defence.

Speaker Three: The Chinese have been doing it for over 3000 years. The first needles were actually made of stone. Today the needles are surgical steel, but everything else is essentially the same. The basic principle behind the treatment says that 'chi' flows through meridian pathways in the body. Illness is caused when, for whatever reason, one or more of these meridians is blocked. By gently inserting needles into specific points in the body, the practitioner can release the blockage and allow 'chi' to flow smoothly again.

Listening 6.2

Interviewer: With me today is Dr Gordon Bennett, who has just published a book about the history of early medicine. Dr Bennett, it seems amazing to think that medicine is almost as old as human civilisation.

Dr Bennett: Yes, although there is no actual record of when people started trying to cure illnesses, cave paintings discovered in the Lascaux caves in France, do show that plants were used for medicinal purposes even as far back as 27 000 years ago.

Interviewer: But wasn't it in ancient India that the earliest form of medical practices, very similar to our own system of medicine, appears to have begun?

Dr Bennett: That's right. Archaeological evidence of teeth having been drilled, dating back nine thousand years, has been found in modern day Pakistan, while 'Ayurveda' which means 'the science of living', possibly the oldest system of medicine to be acquired through study and examination, originated over 2000 years ago in southern Asia. Ancient texts belonging to that period define the purpose of medicine as being to cure the diseases of the sick, protect the healthy, and to prolong life. They also describe procedures on various forms of surgery, including the earliest form of cosmetic surgery. Students were taught anatomy, surgery, as well as knowledge of physiology and pathology. The normal length of the student's training appears to have been seven years, at the end of which, the student was to pass a test in order to graduate.

Interviewer: How interesting! Although in your chapter on the ancient Egyptians, you say it was they who were actually the first to perform surgery and have established doctors.

Dr Bennett: Yes, incredibly, the earliest known physician is credited to ancient Egypt in 2700 BC! The earliest known woman physician is also credited to Ancient Egypt, though she practiced some time later, during the fourth dynasty. However, actual medical records in Egypt only date back 5000 years, showing the earliest surgery to have been performed around 250 years later. A document written in the third dynasty is an ancient textbook on surgery that describes in detail the examination, diagnosis, treatment and prognosis of numerous ailments.

Interviewer: But it was the Persians who invented the teaching hospital, wasn't it?

Dr Bennett: Yes, indeed. In fact the first generation of Persian physicians was trained in a special academy, but the Persians had a great deal more to offer modern medicine too. The philosopher and doctor Ibn Sina (also known as Avicenna in the western world) wrote *The Canon of Medicine*, sometimes considered the most famous book in the history of medicine, and this remained a standard text in Europe up until its Age of Enlightenment.

Interviewer: But you don't focus purely on the roots of modern western medicine. I mean, several chapters of your book focus on the earliest forms of alternative and complementary medicines. One chapter is just about traditional Chinese medicine.

Dr Bennett: Well of course! China's use of needles to help the flow of 'chi' around the body is at least 5000 years old. The Chinese developed a huge body of traditional medicine, most of which remains unchanged today. Acupuncture is a very important form of treatment, even now in the West, with many modern doctors advocating its use, or using it in conjunction with other techniques.

Interviewer: Naturally no book on ancient medicine would be complete without a chapter dedicated to the ancient Greeks, in particular, Hippocrates, who we all know as the Father of Medicine …

Dr Bennett: That's very true. Hippocrates and his students were first to describe many diseases and medical conditions. Hippocrates began to categorise illnesses and give them classifications such as acute, chronic, endemic and epidemic, and use terms such as exacerbation, relapse, crisis, paroxysm, and convalescence. His teachings remain relevant to many present day medical students. Hippocrates highlighted the healing properties of many plants and flowers – which is of course where many of our modern medications come from.

Interviewer: Dr Bennett, for anyone with an interest in early medicine, this book is certainly a source of knowledge. Thank you for telling us about your book …

Listening 6.3

Student: These pictures both show people who are doctors. They help people in some ways to get better from illnesses. The main difference between the two pictures is that one picture shows a western doctor, like we see in a modern hospital, while the other picture shows a doctor from a country like Africa. The first doctor uses modern technology and medicines to make people better, but this one uses a kind of magic to make people better. I think maybe this doctor is trying to help this woman because she has a pain in her stomach, or maybe she just ate something she didn't like. The other doctor is listening to her patient's back – maybe to see if he has a problem with his breathing. Both doctors seem to be concentrating hard on what they are doing. I think they are enjoying what they do.

Listening 7.1

Speaker One

My sister and I thought that this kind of thing was for old age pensioners or tight-fisted couples who don't want to spend money, so we had visions of being bored stuck in someone else's house with nothing to do. Mum and Dad chose to swap with some people in Sydney, Australia, however, and things started looking up. We really changed our minds when this information pack arrived from our exchange family, containing photos and guides on all the things to do and see in the city. The opportunity of a lifetime began to unfold, and we realised that saving money on accommodation would give us the means to do and see more. The holiday was unforgettable, and for our next exchange we're off to Copenhagen!

Speaker Two

We find our members really appreciate receiving our directory through the post. The information on each location and type of accommodation is fairly thorough, and this makes people feel more comfortable about making that initial contact. Also, we offer advice and clear guidelines about building up a relationship with the people you're swapping with before the exchange, and laying down some ground rules for both parties to follow. Generally, direct home exchange between two parties is preferable to random exchange, as it tends to instil a sense of mutual respect for each other's property and makes it easier to agree on things such as breakages, potential maintenance bills and car exchange.

Speaker Three

Well, it sounded ideal, and a great way to save money! Didn't think it through properly, though. We found ourselves in this small flat in New York with the kids, looking after the owners' Jack Russell. Three days into the holiday, the dog bit our three-year-old daughter. So, we had to keep them separate for the rest of our stay. The owners' computer crashed on the first day, so we couldn't access any of the information they'd left us! The icing on the cake was the washing machine breaking down. The trouble we had finding someone to fix it, and waiting for them to arrive meant the kids were stuck in and bored for two days. You don't have to put up with any of this when you go to a hotel!

Speaker Four

Oh, it's wonderful! Of course, you worry about things getting broken. I was anxious about what the other couple would think when they saw all my clutter the first time I exchanged, so spent a couple of days filling bin bags with old, unwanted clothes mainly! Then, I made sure I locked away a few valuables and things I definitely didn't want to get broken, and that made me more relaxed about the whole thing. The real beauty of exchanging for us though, is the saving we make. Now we're retired, we have a lot of free time, but not much money. So, home exchange allows us the luxury of being able to travel three or four times a year!

Speaker Five

Well, generally speaking, we are in favour of such a project. Our company policy is that it's preferable for clients' homes to be occupied while they're away. This renders break-ins much less likely. But it's important that clients inform us when they are intending to exchange, as we usually draw up a special policy providing cover against damages incurred in the home while they are away. Some insurance companies are unwilling to offer such cover at all. So, it's advisable to check things like this before agreeing to exchange homes. I always advise clients to draw up a written agreement with their exchange partners regarding the cost of potential damages.

Listening 7.2

Girl: Well, I think that package tour operators had the greatest impact on tourism, because ... er, you know ... suddenly, people from lower social classes could travel abroad. No longer was it reserved just for the rich ... Don't you agree?

Boy: Absolutely! It became easier for everyone to afford a holiday, and, of course, this led to more hotels and guest houses being built, and generated business in coastal areas that ... where previously, fishing and farming had been the main industries. Of course, the downside of this has been that these areas became very spoilt by overcrowding and pollution.

Girl: Yes, the effects of tourism on the environment have generally not been good, and package tour operators tend to flood an area with visitors for a few years, then leave and take them somewhere else, leaving a lot of waste behind them.

Boy: You're right, and now, with the Internet, they provide an even wider range of choices, and what was fashionable last year has been replaced this year by another destination.

Girl: Do you think only the Internet is responsible for that?

Boy: To a large extent, yes, because websites promote particular kinds of holidays, and reach more people, since it is a lot easier to sit at home and surf the net looking for a holiday than it is to go to a tourist office and look through brochures.

Girl: Mmm ... and another thing I think is ...

Listening 8.1

Speaker One: But nothing is permanent – we should aim to take pleasure out of the process – the present moment – rather than from the future result or past action.

Speaker Two: Actually, she's been painting since she was two. A brush was placed in her trunk, she was given a canvas and three pots of primary colours and left to her own devices. You could tell right away that she loved it.

Speaker Three: Some people may think it's ugly, but I feel much safer knowing that no one can get in without my inviting them, or knowing about it.

Listening 8.2

Extract One

Interviewer: The question I've been wanting to ask is, how come you don't get frustrated by the transience of your work?

James: Well, the truth is, it's the momentary satisfaction that I get that makes it so much stronger. True, I may spend hours working on a drawing, only to see it wash away before my eyes an hour later when it starts to rain. But nothing is permanent – we should aim to take pleasure out of the process – the present moment – rather than from the future result or past action.

Interviewer: Even if that means that no one else gets to see it, or appreciate it as much as they could?

James: If I've enjoyed creating it, then it doesn't matter if no one else sees it. That's what's so beautiful about what I do. When someone spends three hours cooking a beautiful meal for others to eat in a moment, is it worth any less? We should learn to appreciate the effort that goes into every thing we do, not just the finished result.

Extract Two

Man: Wow – this is quite a remarkable painting! Did Emma do this too? How long has she been painting?

Woman: Actually, she's been painting since she was two. A brush was placed in her trunk, she was given a canvas and three pots of primary colours and left to her own devices. You could tell right away that she loved it.

Man: Surely she wasn't painting like this from the beginning?

Woman: At first I suppose you could say her pictures looked like abstract splotches – kind of what you'd expect from any two-year-old, but gradually it became apparent that she had a flair for painting, and it started to become part of her daily routine. Then one day I noticed that what she'd painted resembled the tall fir tree overlooking the enclosure. She'd been looking in that direction while she'd been painting and had chosen the colours carefully.

Man: Can she paint other things?

Woman: She always paints something different – it's hard to tell exactly what she's painting, but every now and then it looks like something recognisable. Look at this one – doesn't it remind you of a giraffe? She gets a good view of them from here.

Extract Three

Woman: I think the house is lovely, and obviously the architect has put a lot of thought into it, but I can't understand why you would want to conceal it behind this great stone wall!

Man: Some people may think it's ugly, but I feel much safer knowing that no one can get in without my inviting them, or knowing about it. It's often said that an Englishman's home is his castle, and that's very true with me. I don't like the idea of being exposed to the whole world, and that's the reason I built this around my property. I'm a very private person I suppose you could say.

Woman: But don't you think it puts people off? I mean, a structure like this seems to say: 'Stay away!'

Man: If anyone wants to come in they have to come to the main gate and ring the buzzer. I have a security camera on the gate so I can see who's there and buzz them in if I want to. The broken glass on the top of the wall is for security but I think it looks quite nice too. I was going to build a two metre wall originally but decided on three in the end so nobody can see in from adjacent buildings.

Listening 9.1

Interviewer: ... Right! The next topic on the programme this morning is web design. Many of you have sent in requests for advice on either choosing a good web designer to design your business site, or on creating your own. So, my next guest is here to do just that. She is an expert in teaching web design, and is also a successful designer in her own right. Alex Bookman, welcome!

Alex: Thank you, Tim. It's a pleasure to be here.

Interviewer: Alex, can you tell us some of the things we should, and shouldn't look for, in designing an effective website?

Alex: Well, people's views differ slightly, but I have my own list of dos and don'ts when it comes to web design. A basic thing you need when designing a website is to make sure you have a search facility that is easy to use. So, make sure your pages have simple, clear titles and headlines that make sense. The trick is to think of the elderly user, who often finds searching online confusing. How would he or she search for specific information? Remember that the average user is browsing, so they won't be interested in reading any long texts. Generally, online texts of over one hundred and fifty words can be both tiring to read and off-putting visually. People browsing want to see something eye-catching, with clear, well-documented information that they can understand at a glance. Useful tricks such as subheadings, bullet-pointed lists and highlighted keywords are effective in achieving this. Also, make sure your company name and logo appears on every page of the site, to keep the user focussed on your company. People browsing for a particular product may have seen several sites before reaching yours, so you need to constantly remind them who you are!

Interviewer: ... And of course, there are always PDFs for detailed information ...

Alex: In my experience, the average user is not always aware of how to open a PDF file, and so feels intimidated by it. If a person browsing comes across a PDF, he's likely to give up, and you've lost his custom. PDFs are great for manuals and large documents like this, which may need printing, but general product information for browsers should be restricted to real web pages.

Interviewer: What about photos and artwork? Aren't they effective tools?

Alex: Product photos are always useful, but you want to avoid placing too many on a single page, as that way, they lose their effectiveness. Zoomable photos are great if you want to be able to show specific details of the product. Another big no-no is not anticipating users' questions. Web users are looking for specific information, and experienced ones tend to ask specific questions. Predict what kind of questions potential customers will ask you about your product, and have the answers ready for them on your site. The worst possible mistake companies make is not mentioning their prices. This is a key question for any user, as someone seriously considering buying the product, nine times out of ten, will want to compare your prices with those of other companies ... Don't give them the price, and you've lost the sale!

Interviewer: I must admit, I often get confused when attempting to go to useful links. Very often, they turn out not to be useful!

Alex: Yes, the thing to consider here is using clear link titles so that users can understand what the links offer them. I think on the whole, the golden rule is the 'follow the sheep' principle ... Look at what other websites are doing, and do the same. That way, users will know what to expect from your website, 'cause they've seen this kind of thing before. So, it makes them feel at home, and you're half way to making a sale!

Interviewer: Great! Right, we're going to take a break now, and then listeners can call to ask Alex their questions, and ...

Listening 9.2

Interlocutor: Now, I'd like you to talk about something together for about three minutes. I'd like you to imagine that the gallery you work for wants to hold an exhibition that will attract young people. Here are some of the styles of art that have been suggested. First, talk to each other about how each style might attract young people. Then, decide which two would be the most successful. Alright?

Enrique: Well, Jasmine, I think we have some very interesting suggestions here ... Don't you agree?

Jasmine: We certainly do! What about this idea of advertising posters from the 1960s? Look at this one of the housewife with a Hoover. That wouldn't be approved of now.

Enrique: No! Now there'd be a man in the advertisement instead! Do you think young people would be interested in this?

Jasmine: Well, not everyone, maybe, but I think a lot of young people are attracted by the style of the 60s, and so would want to see some of the artwork the decade inspired. Also, some youngsters are interested in adverts, generally, don't you think?

Enrique: I'm not so sure that many will be interested enough to go and see an exhibition of them, though! If it was 60s fashion, maybe! No, I like this idea of cartoon drawings for animation. Lots of kids I know love drawing their favourite characters from Disney, and Pokémon, Bugs Bunny etc. So, they would be delighted to have the chance to see the original drawings up close.

Jasmine: Yes, but isn't that really for smaller kids? I can't imagine 15-year-olds wanting to go.

Enrique: I'm afraid I can't agree with you there. I think 15-year-olds would be fascinated to see just how many drawings have to be made for a single scene of a cartoon. They are at an age where they want to find out how things are done.

Jasmine: I suppose you're right. Perhaps it's just that I'm not interested in that kind of art. How about this design for the environment idea? This is a subject of common interest nowadays.

Enrique: Yes, but often too much. 'Think Green' is everywhere, and I think young people want something to look at that doesn't make them feel guilty. Do you think the graffiti idea is any good?

Jasmine: Actually, yes! I really like this idea, partly because so much graffiti is created by young people. So, it relates to styles they like, colour they like, and ... represents the beliefs that young people express. What do you think of it, Enrique?

Enrique: I totally agree with you. Graffiti definitely represents the interests of young people, and some of it is very impressive! I wonder if it might attract more boys than girls, though?

Jasmine: Do you really think so? I have to say, a lot of my friends – boys and girls – do graffiti-style drawings on their school books, and I think they'd all like to see such an exhibition. It would inspire them!

Enrique: ... Their teachers wouldn't like it much, though! So, which ones do you think would make the most successful exhibitions?

Jasmine: Well, personally, I like the 60s adverts and the graffiti, but I'm sure you won't agree with me!

Enrique: Well, I'm with you on the graffiti option! But the adverts don't appeal to me. I prefer the cartoon drawings, and believe they would attract more youngsters than the 60s adverts ...

Listening 10.1

Speaker One

Lydia and I met in Thailand after the tsunami disaster. We'd both gone as volunteers and both with the same goal: to help those in dire need. Like most of the doctors and nurses who went we had become disillusioned with the medical 'industry' back home. Doctors ostensibly choose their vocation to help others, yet at the same time they get sucked up in the commercial aspect of medicine, which tries to make money first and foremost, and treats only those who can pay. In Thailand we helped, and all we got out of it was a complete lifestyle change, and the satisfaction of knowing that we were actually saving lives.

Speaker Two

I'd been a high-powered businesswoman with my own company; Jeremy a successful salesman; our children were doing well in school – but when our Alice got ill it changed our lives. The doctors told us to get out of the city for a while – we decided to get out of the city for good. I sold the business, Jeremy quit his job, and we bought a smallholding in the country. Within a year we were selling our produce to local traders and self-schooling our children at home. Five years on I can honestly say that none of us regrets it. We may not have the luxuries, but we're all healthy and have something to look forward to each day.

Speaker Three

One evening, Colin and I were watching TV when this programme came on about intensive animal farming. We were both shocked! Couldn't believe the way those poor animals were being kept, and

even worse, the way they were killed! Colin put his hamburger down half-eaten and said: 'I ain't having none of that no more.' I felt even more strongly and couldn't eat anything from animals – eggs, milk, butter ... At first I didn't know how I was going to survive, but then a friend of Colin's lent him a book about giving up animal produce and we were surprised to find how easy it was. We haven't missed it at all!

Speaker Four

Scientists have been warning us of the dangers of climate change caused by our overuse of fossil fuels. We know that if we don't do something drastic today, it'll be too late for our children to do anything about it tomorrow, and that, although the technology for alternative energy exists, the politics that controls who makes money out of fuels doesn't allow for it to be developed. I was sick of all this so I decided to take matters into my own hands. I built a wind turbine in the garden and covered my roof in photovoltaic cells. Now, I get to sell my excess energy to the grid which helps others reduce their use of fossil fuels.

Speaker Five

Once my children had left home I found myself at a bit of a loose end. I'd given up the past 20-odd years of my life and, suddenly, I didn't know what to do with myself. Then a friend mentioned volunteering and, seeing as I didn't really have any need of money, I thought why not? The one thing I knew how to do was look after children so it wasn't hard to take care of children that couldn't look after themselves. In fact, it was so much more rewarding. Most of them are so affectionate that you just can't help wanting to be with them – it's just so spiritually fulfilling.

Listening 10.2

Interlocutor: In this part of the test, I'm going to give each of you three pictures. I'd like you to talk about them on your own for about a minute, and also to answer a question briefly about your partner's pictures. Elisabeth, it's your turn first. Here are your pictures. They show people working in different situations. I'd like you to compare two of the pictures, and say why the people might be working in these situations, and what the advantages and disadvantages of it might be. All right?

Elisabeth: Yes, alright. Both of these pictures show people who are working but not in a normal place. In this picture I can see a man – he must be a business man I think because he is wearing a suit and he is talking on a mobile telephone. Also he has a lap-top computer open in front of him, but he is not in an office. It looks like he is on a train – um, yes, a train. He is probably travelling to his work – commuting to his work. The second picture is a bit different because a woman is trying to work at home but it is not easy for her I think because she has small children. She is trying to work at her desk but there is a baby on the floor with toys and another child standing at the door. She has a computer and telephone on her desk but she is looking at the toddler, so I don't think she is getting much work done. In both of these situations it must be very difficult I think to work, because you are not in your proper working environment and there are too many distractions. However, if you ask me, one good thing about both pictures is that you can work when you are not in your office, which gives you more flexibility.

Interlocutor: Thank you. Giovanni, which of these environments do you think it would be most difficult to work in?

Giovanni: Oh definitely at home if you have children, because children are very demanding and need so much attention. I know because I have a younger brother and my mother is always saying she can do nothing all day long with him! Sometimes I work on a train and it is OK. I do not mind it.

Interlocutor: Thank you. Can I have the booklet, please? Now, Giovanni, here are your pictures. They show different places where people live. I'd like you to compare two of the pictures, and say what it might be like to live in each place and how the people seem to feel about living there. All right?

Giovanni: Well, they are all pictures of remote locations. This one shows a snow-covered mountain. There is a little wooden house and someone is coming out of the door dressed in skiing clothes. I guess it is Switzerland – the Alps maybe. He must be very excited to have all this snow, but if you live there every day, I suppose you would get a little bit fed up with it. The snow and trees makes it very beautiful. Very peaceful I think it must be. On the other hand this picture shows a completely different environment. It is the desert and here we can see a tent where people live. I think we call them Bedouin? This man with the black clothes … must live here. This is a camel and this is the place where they drink – an oasis? It must be very tough living here – you don't know where to find water all the time, and of course it is very hot, and dry. I think this man likes it though – he looks very happy.

Interlocutor: Thank you. Elisabeth, which of these places would you rather live in?

Elisabeth: Oh, definitely not the desert. I like hot places but only if it is next to the sea. So, I would have to say the mountains, even though I don't like the cold very much either, but it's OK if you have a nice warm place to live, and a hot fire, and a nice cup of hot chocolate.

Interlocutor: Thank you.

Listening 11.1

Woman: … so how can families get the most out of their money, and make ends meet?

Your plan should aim to achieve six things:

- avoid living beyond your means – buy things when you can afford them
- give your needs priority over your wants
- set money aside for both planned expenses and unforeseen emergencies
- save for things that you want, rather than simply using the credit card!
- reduce family arguments over money
- be able to realise your dreams

To make this happen, there are five major steps to take. Firstly, sit down as a family and work out what each member wants to achieve now and in the near future that requires money. Get each family member to write down three or four goals. Add all of the goals together, and discuss which are the most important to the family as a whole. Once you've done this, draw up and complete a chart of things to accomplish this month, within one year, within three years etc.

The next step is to look closely at your family's income. If possible, try and work out each person's income over the year, and estimate the average amount they receive each month. Create another chart, this time for disposable income – that is, the amount of money you have after taxes have been deducted.

Step number three, then! Work out your family expenses … Now, these should fall into the following four main categories:

- Fixed expenses, such as housing, bills, children's activities – clubs, lessons etc.
- Periodic expenses. For instance, licences, subscriptions, insurance payments and Christmas. You should set money aside for these things on a regular basis.
- Miscellaneous expenses – these vary from month to month, and include such things as clothes, entertainment etc.
- Unforeseen expenses - in which you should consider possible car repairs, medical care etc.

The fourth step is to train all family members to get into the following good habits: organise the payment of bills, by making one person responsible for this. Prepare a monthly budget – list all the things the family needs to buy this month, and calculate how much money will be needed to achieve that. Allocate expenses for specific things to a particular family member.

Finally, step number five is to actually make your plan work. So, there you have it! The perfect recipe for making ends meet!

Listening 11.2

Interlocutor: In your opinion, is the work ethic dead?

Raul: Yes, most definitely. I think the problem is that young people no longer see the value in doing something well. They just want to get the job done as quickly as possible, get paid and go home … There is no respect any more, you see. A job is simply a way to earn money, and no-one is interested in anything else. You see it when you go into shops. The shop assistants are often rude, or indifferent. Sometimes, they even talk on the phone while serving you! They don't care. People don't feel pride in their work any more …

Listening 12.1

Extract One

Interviewer: … but why, Claudia, did you suddenly decide to write a musical?

Claudia: Every rock band or rock star has a secret wish to have a musical based on their music. Where else can you combine your words and music into a visual story?

Interviewer: I see. So what can you tell us about the story?

Claudia: It tells the tale of a black teenage girl, disillusioned with her lot in life, who runs away from her New York home to travel to Europe with a guitar. There she falls in and out with an assortment of lively characters, each of whom has a story to tell, and in some way also helps her to find her way in life.

Interviewer: But what's your message exactly?

Claudia: There are hundreds of films documenting white American males, and films about teen angst go back to the earliest days of moviemaking, but there's very little about black people or women that doesn't make a statement about poverty, racism, abuse or inequality. I wanted to show that you can be black, female and young, and still have the same problems and worries that your average white male has in our society.

Extract Two

Woman: It wasn't at all what I expected.

Man: No, it wasn't, but I still enjoyed it. It seemed to have so many different layers to it.

Woman: Yes, the characters were certainly interesting. I would never have expected to see Brad Pitt in a role like that. Or George Clooney, come to think of it.

Man: It did make me laugh though.

Woman: Yeah, but did you notice how we were the only ones laughing through most of it?

Man: I suppose the humour was mainly cultural. If we'd been watching this with an English speaking audience I think everyone would have been laughing. I expect they just didn't get it.

Woman: Not that there were any puns as such ...

Man: No, but the humour wasn't so much about what they said or did. It was more to do with the fact that they did things they shouldn't have done, and that we could see that they were behaving in bizarre and idiotic ways, but they themselves couldn't.

Woman: It was a comedy of errors really wasn't it, in true Shakespearean fashion.

Man: Yes, I suppose you could say that!

Extract Three

Director: No, you see what I want is to give the feeling of size, I mean, I want everything to be super large, so that the actors will look as if they are lost in these huge, imposing dark mountains ...

Set designer: I hear what you're saying, but this ain't a film set and the trouble with a stage production is that you have to build a set that's easy to manipulate. I mean, it's all right for Act Two when they're in the mountains, ain't it, but what about Acts One and Three?

Director: Yes, well Act One takes place mainly indoors doesn't it, so we just have a closed set for that – a nice living room, say, then between acts we pull up the backdrop and reveal the mountains. Then in Act Three when they arrive in the city, we could just bring down another backdrop with a painted skyline or something ...

Set designer: That's all very well, but it ain't very inspiring is it? I mean, I was kind of hoping I'd be given free reign with this project 'cause I've got quite a few ideas and we could do something really exciting with the theatre we've got.

Listening 12.2

Interlocutor: Now, I'd like you to talk about something together for about three minutes. Here are some pictures showing different ways in which people spend their free time. First, talk to each other about how these pictures show the different forms of entertainment nowadays. Then decide which picture best reflects the most common form of entertainment of modern times. All right?

Marcel: Well the first picture shows ...

Roberta: It shows people at the theatre ... no wait – I think it's the opera because I can see here that she seems to be singing and this man has binoculars. Also the costumes look more like the costumes people wear in the opera. But this picture shows someone reading a book. I don't think people read books so much any more as a form of entertainment, do they? No, really they read newspapers and books for studies but I wouldn't say it is really entertainment. On the other hand, this picture is showing people at the cinema. And this one shows young people at a big concert. Lots of people go to the cinema and concerts and I think they are both quite important forms of entertainment, but not as many people as stay at home and watch TV. In this picture that they are watching TV. Surely that is the most common form of entertainment of modern times?

Marcel: ... but in this picture they are playing computer games. That is also very common for ...

Roberta: Common for young people yes, but TV is watched by every person of every age so I think that one is the most common.

Marcel: I agree with Roberta.

Interlocutor: Thank you. Can I have the booklet, please?

Listening 13.1

Speaker One

I just don't know what else to do. I mean, I love Joe to bits, and he can be adorable, but a lot of the time, I seem to be yelling at him. He's so naughty, and there are times when he just won't listen! His reaction to criticism can be so intense, and he gets horribly upset over the silliest things. If he's angry about something and I try talking to him, he often just screams at me, or may even throw things. And I'm so busy at the moment, I just haven't got the time or the patience to deal with this kind of behaviour ...

Speaker Two

I find that the benefits of allowing young children to form bonds with a pet are many. Pre-school children can learn social awareness and confidence. Research has shown that the shared responsibility in caring for a pet enhances communication and understanding between family members, and encourages children to respond to and display affection. This can clearly be seen in the care they show when bringing a sick cat to me for treatment. Allowing children to be actively involved in the daily care of the pet teaches them to be responsible and raises their self-esteem.

Speaker Three

In the families that I see, parents often find it difficult to adapt the level of vocabulary they use to one that's suitable for their child to understand. Take the word, 'embarrassed', for instance. Ask your four-year-old child why he's embarrassed, and he probably won't know what you mean. It's better to use words like 'feel funny', or 'shy'. Similarly, using positive language is more effective in getting your child to cooperate. I tend to advise parents to include more 'do's' than 'don'ts' in their instructions to their children. In my experience, 'Nick, take your plate out to the kitchen' is a lot more successful than 'Nick, don't leave your plate on the table'.

Speaker Four

When I was small, my parents thought there was something wrong with me! So, they took me to see this psychologist, and, fortunately, she realised that, in fact, the opposite was true. My intellect was developing faster than my social skills, and I couldn't express myself like a normal seven-year-old. My disruptive behaviour and temper tantrums were the result of frustration at not being able to play with girls of my own age, because they were interested in dolls when I was already playing Mozart on the piano.

Speaker Five

The Shared Reading Project really worked wonders for us, because it required active interaction between my hearing older son, John, and Ellie, who's deaf. Evening story time has become our time together as a family, when John and I use a mixture of pictures, mime and sign language to tell Ellie the story, and she responds in a similar fashion. It's brought them closer together, by increasing John's interest in communicating with her, and has given us parents the means to develop conversation topics with both our children. Ellie's ability to express herself is improving all the time, and we tend to find that John understands her now better than anyone!

Listening 13.2

Interlocutor: Now, I'd like you to talk about something together for about three minutes ... Here are some pictures showing various learning aids for language schools. First, talk to each other about the merits and limitations of using these learning aids. Then, decide which one would be the most useful for your language school to invest in. All right?

Rahul: Yes, well, on first sight, I would say that all of these learning aids look useful! Can the school afford to buy all of them? Computers, in particular. Don't you agree, Marietta?

Marietta: Well, I think they're useful for someone learning alone, but I'm not sure how useful they are in a language classroom. I prefer the ... erm ... communication between students and teacher to be direct, and ...

Rahul: Yes, but the students can learn a lot of things from the computer, and there are interactive programmes as well and ...

Marietta: Yes, but I think that the language programmes on the computer are good for use at home, for homework, and private study. In the school, where students are together, it's good to use the time for active, direct communication practice.

Rahul: I see your point, but I think it's useful for students to have access to computers, and particularly the Internet, at school, because they can use them to find out information, and the teachers can show their students clips etc, which, you know, can start a discussion in class ...

Marietta: Mm, perhaps you're right. What about the satellite TV idea? Do you think that's useful?

Raul: Yes, I do. For the same reason as the computers. Satellite TV means that students can watch such channels as BBC World. I have this at home, and it's really good, because you can learn things. Again, teachers can use it to give students listening practice, and for discussion. Today, I think students find it easier to respond to pictures, you know – computers, TV – than they do to something they read ...

Marietta: No! I'm afraid I disagree with you. I hear that all the time, and perhaps it's true for some kids, but I still think that kids like reading. You can see this with films that have been made out of books. I still hear people say they prefer the book to the film. I don't think that has changed so much.

Rahul: OK, maybe you're right, but in the language classroom, pictures help students understand certain things, and I think are easier to respond to. For that reason, I think the computers and the TV are useful tools. What about the group trip to England? That would be fun, wouldn't it?

Marietta: Yes, but only for some students. The whole school wouldn't be able to go! No, I quite like the idea of these books, and doing group literature in the classroom. Look, there's a DVD of the film, too! That would make you happy! Studying a novel together will encourage discussion, and at the same time students will learn new words. Then, they can see the film and compare it to the book. So, it's ...

Interlocutor: Thank you.

Listening 14.1

Scientist: We conveniently tend to forget that the Earth is the only planet in the universe known to be teeming with millions of different life forms, each of which has evolved to interact with other species to survive, thereby creating Earth's varied and intricate ecosystems. For billions of years these ecosystems have maintained the equilibrium needed to sustain all life on Earth. Yet, as a result of greed, ignorance, and a very rapid expansion in human population, we have brought about the destruction of the Earth's living resources. Thousands of species are now threatened, endangered, or extinct. At the current rate of destruction, 50% of species on earth will be wiped out within the next 50 years. What we should remember, however, is that we depend on many of these species for our existence; even though there are very few species (namely viruses and parasites) that depend on us for theirs. If we do not find a way to reduce human population growth globally, we may eventually force ourselves to extinction.

It's been calculated that if everyone on earth consumed as many of the earth's resources as the average American, we would need approximately five planets to live on. Planet Earth is a finite entity, with finite resources, yet we live on it as if we could just move on to the next when this one is exhausted. The human population already far exceeds ecologically sustainable levels. The total world human population, now at 6.5 billion, at the moment is inexorably climbing by almost 90 million a year (that's 10,000 new people an hour, 240,000 a day) but this amount is about to rise exponentially from 6.5 billion to 9 billion in less than a century. This is a faster rate of growth than at any time in our history. With the environmental changes brought about by global warming, the planet will soon only be able to support around half a billion people anyway, so what will happen to everyone else?

We can only imagine the consequences of allowing the human population to continue to increase as it is at the moment. It's imperative that we begin to implement measures aimed at curbing the growth in the human population. This can be done using ethical and intelligent policies globally or we must be prepared to face the inevitable side-effects of our consumerism, including plagues, extreme weather conditions, famines, and warfare. We've all witnessed these factors increasing in modern times and we know they are linked to the rising human population.

Listening 15.1

Speaker One

'Remember, remember the 5th of November!' I always used to love this night. It's especially fun for the kids with all the impressive firework displays we have these days. When I was a kid we usually just used to throw together a great big heap of wood, and branches and other stuff to burn, and we'd wave sparklers around. Of course most people forget the real reason for celebrating: it was when Guy Fawkes almost succeeded in blowing up the King and Parliament. He didn't get away with it though, which is why we throw a stuffed dummy of the poor bloke on top of the pyre and watch him go up in flames!

Speaker Two

Silvia and I are at least agreed on one thing: this is not the night to go out looking for a table for two if you haven't booked anywhere. Not that we mind. The best way to celebrate is to stay in and cook a romantic meal. I hate the commercialism and all the paraphernalia associated with it. It's not one of our old classic traditions or anything – but someone worked out there was money to be made from it and exploited it, so now, for months before, all the shops are selling these enormous ugly stuffed red hearts and cuddly toys with lovey-dovey messages on – urgh!

Speaker Three

We always go to the Glastonbury Tor to celebrate the longest day of the year, as it's a place that's shrouded in myth and magic. It's a pagan tradition that harks back to pre-Christian times when things like changes in the season were important. June twenty first is the day when the sun reaches it's furthest point in it's journey north, and begins to return south again and the days begin to get shorter. Sitting on top of the hill, like, singing songs and watching the sun rise and set on the longest day is an amazing experience.

Speaker Four

It's not my favourite time of year, I must say, not any more. I think the over-commercialism of the season has killed it for me. Now we have to endure it from early October till the end of January, and that's just too much. Once upon a time there was a magical quality to it, when the message was more about giving than it was about getting. Nowadays, I don't think religion even plays such a big role anymore – to some people it does of course – but how many consumers actually remember it's supposed to be about the birth of a certain person when they're ripping open their presents?

Speaker Five

This has really been growing in popularity in recent years, mainly I think due to the publicity and attention it gets in the United States. It really is quite a big event over there, even though it originated here in Ireland. Nowadays all the kids dress up and go out 'trick or treating' whereas when I was a kid, we rarely were so bold. It's an old pagan tradition and the basic belief was that on this night – 'All Hallow's Eve' – the night before 'All Saints Day', ghosts and spirits, witches and warlocks, were abroad in the land of the living, and if they came to your door, you gave them something nice to make them go away, or you faced the consequences!

Listening 15.2

Interviewer: Today we will be discussing the role of superstitions and taboos in society. With me in the studio I have Professor Thomas Cookson, who is here to talk to us about Tibetan customs and beliefs. My second guest is Michael Appiah, who has very different views about the role of taboos in his own Ghanaian society.

Professor Cookson, why are certain beliefs and taboos important in Tibetan society?

Cookson: In Tibet, especially in many villages or pastoral areas, the people lack legal knowledge, so the traditional taboos play an important role in controlling how people behave in society. Tibetan ancestors taught that everything has a soul and that therefore everything in nature must be worshipped and even holy mountains and lakes must be venerated.

Interviewer: And why is this such a good thing?

Cookson: Today in western society we are forever trying to pass laws to protect nature. It is difficult to enforce these laws, or to educate people about them. With traditional customs and taboos each law is passed on to the next generation by word of mouth; everyone knows about them and upholds them. It's such taboos that encourage people to love the land, which nurtures them, and to appreciate the beauty and harmony of everything around them.

Interviewer: So what you are saying is that certain taboos in Tibetan society are necessary to keep that society alive?

Cookson: These traditional ethnic customs offer no material gain and they do not encourage such bad social phenomena as money worship, corruption, moral degeneration, greed and so many more of the negative social aspects that so-called 'progressive' societies are victims to.

Interviewer: Thank you Professor. Michael, what is your view about traditions and customs in Ghanaian society?

Michael: I have the greatest respect for our Ghanaian traditional institutions, but I must argue that some of our customs and traditions have no place in modern-day society. In other cultures, as progress is made and societies develop, their customs change too, and over time they either disappear altogether, or they're kept to honour a traditional heritage. Culture is not stagnant – it must change with the times, or it will hinder the development of that society.

Interviewer: Can you give us an example of a taboo that holds back development?

Michael: In my village, I remember that on Tuesdays residents were forbidden to go to the farm or the main river that encircled the town because it was believed that the gods and spirits of the river performed their rituals to bless the land, its people and their crops on this day of the week. No-one was allowed to cross that river on Tuesdays except those with special permission. Anyone without permission who dared to cross the river would be visited by some bad fortune. Everyone in the village adhered strictly to this custom even if this meant they could not continue their daily business because of this.

Interviewer: And this kind of thing goes on all over Ghana?

Michael: Ghana has many colourful and exciting customs and traditions which have shaped the lives of its people over the years. Some of these cultures have adapted to the changing times but there are some ethnic groups who cling to certain regressive aspects of their culture. Many of the chiefs and elders of these ethnic groups still live in medieval times, oblivious to the fast-paced changes that are shaping the development of modern society.

Interviewer: So, unlike Professor Cookson, what you are saying is that these superstitions and taboos are actually bad for society …

Listening 15.3

Interlocutor: Good afternoon. My name is Simon and this is my colleague Rebecca. And your names are?

Fernando: Fernando

Claudia: My name is Claudia.

Interlocutor: That's lovely. Can I have your mark sheets, please? Thank you. First of all, we'd like to know something about you. Fernando, where are you from?

Fernando: I am from Madrid in Spain. It is the capital city of Spain.

Interlocutor: How would you describe your home city to someone who has never been there?

Fernando: I would say that Madrid is a very beautiful and lively city. There are museums and art galleries to visit, and there is a lot to do.

Interlocutor: What can young people do in your country?

Fernando: There are good shops and at night many restaurants, clubs and bars.

Interlocutor: Thank you. How about you Claudia – where do you live?

Claudia: I live in Vienna. It is the most beautiful city in the world.

Interlocutor: Really? What do you like about it?

Claudia: Well Vienna has such beautiful architecture and there are many parks and we keep our city very clean.

Interlocutor: What are the advantages and disadvantages of living abroad for a short time?

Claudia: Well it depends where you would live. For me, one disadvantage of course would be that I miss my home, family and friends. But of course it would be good to see another culture and learn about other people in other countries.

Interlocutor: Fernando, if you could live in another country, where would you choose?

Fernando: I would like to live in South America – maybe Brazil or Argentina.

Interlocutor: Why?

Fernando: Well because it would be very different from what I am used to, and they are such amazing countries and the people are so happy and I think, so friendly.

Interlocutor: Claudia, what are the most popular sports in your country?

Claudia: Well, skiing of course is very popular. In the mountains we have a lot of snow in the winter, and of course ice-skating and other winter sports are quite popular too.

Interlocutor: What do you do to keep fit and healthy?

Claudia: Actually I don't do much sport really. I'm not very competitive, but I walk my dog everyday in the park, and I ride my bicycle everywhere.

Interlocutor: OK, thank you. Now, we're going to move on to part two of the test …

Listening 16.1

Extract One

Mike: So, did you finish it then?

Hayley: I cried at the end! It was so sad! I kind of assumed that we'd see a traditional 'happily ever after' ending. So, you can imagine how …

Mike: But weren't you a little disappointed?

Hayley: What? With the ending? No. Although it was really sad, it was moving. The feelings were so intense... It was beautiful. It was somehow more believable, don't you think?

Mike: Yeah, fair enough. But I found this book a bit of a letdown, after the other two. This one seemed to ramble. The question of right and wrong, good and evil kind of took over, and the plot got lost … Some threads just seemed to be left hanging, and I felt that many

of the questions went unanswered, you know? I didn't always know what was going on.

Hayley: But I don't think we're meant to. Like in real life – we can't expect to understand everything that happens to us, but must accept certain things and make the best of the situations we find ourselves in. At least, that's the message I got.

Mike: Mm … I hadn't thought of it like that! Perhaps I'll read it again …

Extract Two

Interviewer: So, Clive, you're a man with a mission! Tell us all about it!

Clive: On the island of Borneo, the days of the Sarawak rainforest are numbered. Loggers are felling trees at an alarming rate, and the forest is rapidly disappearing. But it's not just the rainforest that's threatened. The lives of 10000 people will also inevitably be affected. The Penan tribe live and hunt in the forest. They move through it with the same ease as the abundant wildlife which also lives there. They are part of the forest landscape. This destruction of the rainforest will devastate them.

Interviewer: Mmm … What are the Penan like, Clive?

Clive: The Penan are an inherently gentle people. Unlike other tribes in the area, they despise violence. There's something touchingly innocent about the tender regard they have for the forest. They see themselves as its children and are mourning the fact that it is dying before their eyes. They protest against the loggers by setting up blockades, but are increasingly powerless to stop them. So, they came to our group for help. Can we simply stand by and let yet another rainforest be ruthlessly destroyed, and see another way of life come to an end?

Extract Three

Ann: … So, Derek, what did you think of it? Are virtual education conferences here to stay?

Derek: You know, Ann, it's an interesting concept. I won't lie. It felt weird to be sitting in front of a computer screen, interacting via avatar with 40 other academics. There was something surreal about it, and at first, I found it hard to take it seriously. But the talks were certainly serious, from university lecturers – a lot more experienced and at ease with the medium than I – who put forward some very thought-provoking proposals on how to use the virtual world as an educational tool.

Ann: And if you think about it on a broader scale, Derek, it may be a viable solution to the environmental threat presented actually travelling to international conferences!

Derek: Mm, admittedly there were about forty of us from all over Europe and the US gathered together, without having created a single carbon footprint. So, who knows? Maybe this will set the precedent for things to come! Personally, though, I'll miss the camaraderie of face-to-face interaction …

Practice test
Part One

Extract One

Interviewer: Now you've finished the film, will you be returning to the stage and going live again?

Andy: Absolutely. It's the only way to find out if you're really still funny. When you're doing film, the material is mostly written for you and the director has already approved it. But in front of a live audience – if they don't like you – you just won't get the laughs. It's a reality check. That's not to say I don't like doing TV. You see when I'm researching material for a live tour, I'm rather prone to laziness and end up panicking at the last moment. But you're working to someone else's deadlines on a film set, and I rather welcome that sort of discipline.

Interviewer: The films have given you a higher profile, haven't they? And with that comes more media attention.

Andy: Yes. I suppose you're referring to particular stories that have appeared in the press about me. I expect to receive criticism for my shows, but when the media invent stuff just to sell a few more copies, I won't tolerate it. I suppose I could choose to ignore it, but I have friends ringing me up – outraged on my behalf and I get to hear the details whether I like it or not. I usually send off an angry letter to the editor. The responsibility ultimately lies with them if their writers can't be bothered to check their facts. I've been tempted to launch my own personal attacks during my shows – but that would come across as bitter and that's not what people are coming for.

Extract Two

Interviewer: Is there any truth to the rumour that you refuse to work with animals?

Actress: Not quite. It's just horses that I'm wary of. You see, when I was just starting to make a name for myself, I managed to secure a part in a film that was the 'next big step'. And I was to do it with another actor that I particularly admired at the time. But the reason the director agreed to hire me was that I had said I had ridden horses. And at the time, I didn't think it was an outright lie – I just omitted to say that I hadn't been on a horse's back since I was about four or five. But I was thinking to myself, how hard can it be. Have confidence, show the horse who's boss and it'll all work out.

Interviewer: And I'm guessing that's not the way it turned out?

Actress: Unfortunately not. In one scene, my character Charlotte was supposed to be out on the moor when she sees smoke and flames pouring from her house. Her elderly grandmother and young sister are inside and she jumps up on her horse and races back to save them. Well, I did a pretty good job of leaping into the saddle but then I simply couldn't get the horse to move. It wouldn't budge. I was mortified. I had just exposed myself as a complete fraud and it was all rather shameful. I could hardly blame the horse.

Extract Three

Fiona: Donald, what were your thoughts before you began the final ascent?

Donald: I was thinking about friends who hadn't made it – people I'd shared part of my life with and who ... over the years ... had lost their lives on that mountain. I was wishing they were still alive ... still climbing ... that we could have stood there together. But, well, it wasn't to be. And I was at my own physical limit, too, but the final steps are comparatively easy and of course you have the sheer adrenalin to push you on.

Fiona: On the subject of physical fitness, I can't help thinking that certain younger climbers believe that's all that's required, whereas actually what they need to understand is the potential danger of a climb.

Donald: Mmm, you often hear it said amongst older climbers that the younger generation are attempting climbs just for fun, but

personally I don't see anything wrong with that. But yes, you can still have fun while appreciating the risks. You need reverence for the mountain you intend to climb. You should be scared. Apart from anything else, your mistake can cost other people their lives.

Part Two

Well, I've been in this business for a good many years now. I started off, naturally, working for someone else – for a company called Greenfingers, which you may well have heard of. But after gaining what I thought was a lot of experience – I took a risk and branched out on my own. I was going to call my company Blue Sky Design – but someone had beaten me to it – so I settled on Exotic Earth ... and I think that hopefully conveys the right image for the company. I think one of the things that clearly separates a gardener from a designer is their sense of vision. Landscape designers are able to see a site's full potential. And in fact, I suppose what got me into landscape design in the first place was the way that it involves both an understanding of rules, I mean the rules and principles of design, and also creativity. Gardeners are happy to put in whatever individual plants they find appealing – landscape designers look at how everything works as a whole. That's not to say you should ignore what your clients want. There must be a mutual respect – both parties must listen to one another and you must explain your ideas clearly. You should also provide them with very detailed sketches – or concept plans – so they can really have a sense of what their garden will look like. To do this, your drawing skills will need to be fairly impressive. When you're starting out as a freelance designer, you'll take whatever work you can get to build up your reputation ... and of course, to pay your bills. It can be a struggle for a while. But I'm in a position now where I can pick and choose, and so I've dedicated myself to designing urban gardens. It's a challenge to design something to work well in a 5 by 5 metre square space – but I've managed to do something quite unique every time. After you've done your interview, and carried out your site survey, you have to investigate what kind – or kinds of soil – you'll be working with. It can vary within the same area you'll be working on, and of course, certain plants will thrive in it, and others will wither and die pretty quickly. The other thing that clients sometimes overlook when they're fantasising about the kind of landscape they want is the climate. Again – you have to make sure the plants you choose are suitable. Interestingly enough, and I suppose it's thanks to design programmes on the TV, many clients are moving away from flowers and an ornamental look and they want plants with a more practical purpose, so that's what I select for them – as long as the conditions are right. So, yes, edible plants, plants which provide shade or a natural sun screen, plants which require little maintenance – that's what they're going for. The best part about the job is when I've managed to design something which exceeds the client's expectations. The downside ... well back injuries I know how to avoid – but I do get headaches from doing the designs on the computer. As for stress, it's something that's not bothered me so far – so I'm pretty lucky to be doing something I love.

Part Three

Interviewer: We have with us today well-known chef and restaurateur Stephen Rees, who has taken time out of an extremely busy schedule to be here this morning. So – may I start by asking how did you begin your career?

Stephen: Well, first of all I should dispel the myth that it was all to do with my mother. I've read several articles citing my mother as an influence, and while she was certainly an amazing cook, I had little interest in cooking while I was growing up. Actually a friend of mine announced his intention to go to culinary school and train as a chef and I thought it sounded like an easy option and that there was bound to be a job waiting afterwards. So I enrolled at culinary school but I'm afraid to say it wasn't a good experience – I felt quite discouraged by a particular tutor who made it clear he thought I had no natural talent. So I dropped out, but with no intention of giving up. I wanted to prove him wrong. I waited tables for a while and worked my way up into the kitchen itself, all the time thinking I can do this.

Interviewer: Interesting! When did you open your first restaurant? And how did you know you were ready to own a restaurant and not just work for someone else?

Stephen: I opened my first restaurant – The Red Mill – in 1992. Some chefs work under one mentor – one top chef for years and years – but I had the idea to work in as many kitchens as possible – thinking that the diversity of experience would allow me to make an informed decision – that I would know what kind of restaurant I wanted to open. If you're thinking of going into the restaurant business, that's what you have to do. Too many people go in with their eyes closed – and especially in regards to the financial aspects of running this kind of business. They think there's no point waiting – they should just take the plunge and give it a go, but I've seen too many places fail that way. Even with the best of ideas, it's such a high risk industry, and you should never allow yourself to forget that.

Interviewer: What is your approach to food? I mean, what are the secrets of a successful dish?

Stephen: To my mind, it has to be something simple which is done perfectly. What you see today – well, I suppose it's always been like this – is young chefs taking an idea and then adding and adding to it, and in fact, what they're doing actually works against the dish. They find it hard to accept criticism. They believe they can become a master chef, without putting the hard work in. Sure, they are dedicated and they have passion, but you cannot ignore the way that ingredients and flavours complement or detract from one another. What it comes down to is egotism and for me this doesn't work in a kitchen.

Interviewer: Your restaurants have a reputation for retaining the same employees for a long time, something which is not that common in this industry. How do you achieve this?

Stephen: Well, as you say, this is an industry which is known for its high turnover of staff – chefs, waiters, head of service. Of course they talk to each other – and if it gets out that there's a general level of dissatisfaction in a restaurant, that restaurant will find it increasingly difficult to take on good people. But for me, for my staff, I believe everybody knows it's a team thing and that we all share the same purpose – creating the best possible dining experience for our customers. Whatever I decide to do – whether it's to do with menus or staff rotation or even the decor, I make sure the staff understand why. In this way, you avoid misunderstandings and doubt. We also pass our success on to our employees through bonuses and other incentives. And when our chefs want to leave and branch out on their own, they know I'll back them.

Interviewer: How do you divide your time? I mean, how much are you a chef and how much a restaurateur?

Stephen: I'd probably give you a different answer on any different day of the week. I go where I'm needed most. My partner, Colin Donnelly, has really taken over most of the budgeting, so I'm happy to leave that to him and we meet twice a week to go over the figures. Right now I'm more involved in the kitchen as one of our chefs is away sick, and anyway, it's my duty to lead by example – to inspire. All the same, being in the kitchen means you are not amongst the diners. Whether they approach you with praise, or with a concern, it's all valid feedback. I'm not one of those chefs who shouts at patrons for daring to send a dish back to the kitchen. Not that they do!

Interviewer: And what does the future hold for you? Will we be seeing another restaurant, perhaps?

Stephen: That's always a possibility but to do so, you need exactly the right people. You need someone who shares your vision and has the same work ethic, but who can also bring something fresh to the table. No pun intended. And I'm working on a new book at the moment – which is a pleasure in some ways to write because it's another way to express yourself and share your love of food – but it's also another thing that's taking me away from my family, and that's something I have to resolve. And in the very short term, I'm looking forward to sitting down with the other chefs and working on the new season's menu. We change it eight times a year and that's what gives me the greatest reward – being able to present something new so that our diners are always stimulated and surprised. Never let yourself or your restaurant become stale.

Part Four

Speaker One

It's funny, if you're under twenty five, you've probably never known a life without mobile phones. Young people have been brought up with them – they're just a part of their lives the same way television was for our generation. The difference is that you can leave the TV at home – you're not tied to it 24 hours a day. But many of our top clients are overseas, and when they want to get hold of you, they will, regardless of the hour. I suppose it's part of the job description, but I feel quite bitter about it at times ... the unpredictability of when a call is going to come – how much sleep you're going to lose. And you have to sound as though you don't mind at all – otherwise you risk putting a potential contract in jeopardy.

Speaker Two

My kids are on theirs all the time. Too much, I think. The youngest uses his for games whenever we're out in the car – keeps him from being bored, I suppose. I bought one for myself when my daughter got a bit older and started going out with her mates and going off to clubs and stuff. You know what they're like. They tell you they're getting a lift home with a friend and then that friend suddenly changes their mind and your kid's left stranded. You don't want to be waiting around for taxis at that time of night – too dangerous. I'd rather get a call saying 'Mum, can you pick me up?' than lie awake in bed fretting about it. Having the phone means I can call her back while I'm on the way and know she's alright. It puts my mind at ease.

Speaker Three

I work hard – it's a very demanding job, so at the end of the day, I want to go out and have a good time ... unwind. Sometimes it's work colleagues – or other times I want to catch up with friends – I'm pretty outgoing I guess – and I know a lot of different people. I suppose I'm the one that organises things – we'll be going to this venue, at this time – see you there. Actually, it's probably a bit of a risk having all their numbers on the phone – but no-one uses address books anymore – I mean the actual book ones. If I left it somewhere, or it got stolen, I don't know what I'd do. I'm completely reliant on it, I guess. Yeah, maybe I should rethink that.

Speaker Four

Um, I suppose I only bought a phone 'cause I got this flat tyre once, miles from anywhere, in the dark, and in the middle of a storm, and I know it sounds feeble, but I had no idea how to change it. That was fun, that was. I never want to be in that position again. To be honest, most of the time, I forget about the phone entirely, until it starts making that beeping noise and you know it needs recharging. I suppose I ought to be more responsible and not let the battery run so low, but I usually only do local trips so I'm not so worried about breaking down. That's the only reason I'd probably use it – I mean if I were stuck somewhere and I had to call for help.

Speaker Five

I'm away for up to a week at a time and I miss out on what the kids are doing and I'm not there to help my wife out when she needs me. The phone at least allows me to know what's going on at home and if there was any trouble, I'd turn the lorry around and head straight back, no matter whether I'd done the delivery or not. But mainly it's there for me to speak to the kids every day – usually a quick hello before they're off to school and a catch-up in the evening before they go to bed. The lifestyle does get me down but I only need to hear my kids' voices and it puts me in a good mood.

Information Files

Answers to Quiz: How environmentally conscious are you?

Add up your scores to questions 1–6:
1 a = 1, b = 5, c = 3
2 a = 3, b = 1, c = 5
3 a = 1, b = 5, c = 3
4 a = 5, b = 1, c = 3
5 a = 1, b = 3, c = 5
6 a = 5, b = 1, c = 3

Analysis:

If you scored 12 points or under:
Shame on you! You really don't care at all about the impact you have on your environment. You have never considered recycling, reusing or cutting down on waste. Your comfort and convenience is the most important thing to you. It's time to make some changes!

If you scored between 12–22 points:
You're trying hard: you're making an effort to cut down on the waste and pollution caused by consumerism, as long as it doesn't inconvenience you too much. You could do more so keep at it.

If you scored over 23 points:
You really are an eco-warrior! In fact you go so far that most people think you're a bit eccentric! Good for you!

Explanations:

1 We don't often think about the plastic bags we use when we go shopping, but we should. Somewhere between 500 billion and a trillion plastic bags are consumed worldwide each year. Of those, millions end up as litter. Once in the environment, it takes months to hundreds of years for plastic bags to breakdown. As they decompose, tiny toxic bits seep into soils, lakes, rivers, and the oceans.

2 Not only are fresh, organically grown fruit or vegetables better for your health, they are also better for the planet. The greater the distance food has to travel from the grower, to the packer, to the supermarket, to your home, the more food miles it collects, thereby contributing to the carbon footprint it leaves. The fewer stages food has to go through before it reaches your mouth, the better.

3 Collecting rainwater may soon be the only way to go. Many parts of the earth are facing an increasing threat of water shortages. We all need to take care how much water we use, especially in the home. The usual advice is to have showers instead of baths, but in fact this is not always the best advice. A standard shower uses 35 litres every 5 minutes while an average depth bath uses 80 litres. One alternative is to simply turn off the water while you are soaping and shampooing.

4 Most people leave their TVs, DVD players and other appliances on standby when they are not in use, but this wastes a lot of electricity, thereby adding to the amount of carbon dioxide in the atmosphere. In fact 8–10% of the total electricity used in your home is due to appliances left on standby – creating an extra 4 million tonnes of excess carbon dioxide each year.

5 Washing everything by hand would save on water and on electricity, but in our modern lifestyles it is not the easiest choice. Washing machines use a lot of water and electricity but some are more eco-friendly than others, so it is worth spending a bit more on an environmentally friendly machine.

6 The technology exists to meet all of the earth's power needs with renewable energy several times over. A large, 10-megawatt wind turbine could produce 10,000 megawatt hours of energy in a year, enough to meet the needs of 1000 average homes.

Speaking reference files

Unit 3

- How dangerous are these sports?
- Which sport would you most like to learn with a qualified instructor?

Unit 6

- Is exercise good for everyone?
- How might these people be feeling?

Unit 14

- How are these different environments important for our planet?
- Which should we make more of an effort to protect?

Answer key

Unit 1

Getting started p1

1 **Across** 1 inaugurate   **Down** 1 initiate
   5 prompts   2 embark
   6 trigger   3 provoke
   8 kick off   4 establish
   10 produce   7 generate
   11 launch   9 found
   12 stimulate

Reading pp 2–3

1 a Text 3   b Text 2   c Text 1
2 1 C   2 B   3 D   4 C   5 C   6 D
3 1 The 'zeroists' were adamant that the new century started
      when 1899 gave way to 1900 …
   2 Others made their way to church or chapel, keeping the
      tradition of the night-watch service and listening in
      solemn silence for the first stroke of the midnight hour.
   3 But a mouse cannot transmute into a cat. A fox cannot
      transmute into a penguin. A monkey cannot transmute
      into a human.
   4 To ascertain by experimentation how fast each species
      learns from danger – then, perhaps, to take specimens on
      board, and see if their offspring really can receive their
      parents' newly acquired knowledge at birth.
   5 … undertaking environmental sampling, monitoring and
      assessment. Accountable for the data generated from your
      survey sampling and analysis
   6 … experience in the operation and maintenance of
      mechanical or electronic instrumentation being an
      advantage.
4 make up [one's] mind; make [one's] way; make a special study of

Language development p4

1 1 start from scratch, go back to the drawing board, start
      from square one
   2 make a fresh start, turn over a new leaf, wipe the slate
      clean
2 1 f   2 g   3 i   4 a   5 e   6 b
   7 h   8 j   9 c   10 d
3 1 made off   4 made up
   2 make it up to you   5 made off with
   3 make out   6 make up for

Grammar p5

1 1 had ever seen   5 didn't call
   2 had been walking   6 takes
   3 was listening   7 is going/is going to go
   4 have never been   8 have been sitting
2 1 have eaten   5 chopped
   2 was walking   6 haven't read
   3 has been working   7 is having
   4 broke   8 have you been doing

4 1 haven't forgotten   11 marched
   2 had expected   12 tossed
   3 had been training   13 blew
   4 woke   14 passed
   5 was shining   15 cheered
   6 put   16 were putting
   7 waited   17 was beginning
   8 arrived   18 saw
   9 were already doing   19 kicked
   10 have been training   20 was

Listening p6

1 1 B   2 C   3 B   4 A   5 B   6 A

Use of English p7

1 1 I had had enough pie   5 to make the most of
   2 have known each other for 6 was three years before
   3 (been) ages since we   I heard
   4 has been under   7 not as easy to get
      construction for   8 make ends meet

Unit 2

Getting started p9

1 1 march   5 clamber
   2 bound   6 wrestle
   3 heave   7 wander
   4 wade   8 tiptoe
   The word 'movement' is spelt out.

Reading pp10–11

1 a Three people are mentioned.
   b Two people speak.
   c Joseph Hooper and his son, Edmund.
2 a **After gap 2:** 'But I came through … He felt exonerated.'
      After gap 5: 'Though he remembered … the high windows.'
      Paragraph A: 'Looking up now … his own son was pale.'
      Paragraph B: 'Mr Hooper coughed … his own father.'
   b the son
   c A book he is reading, and a boy called Kingshaw, who
      bothers him.
3 1 D   2 B   3 G   4 F   5 E   6 A

Language development p12

1 1 down in the mouth   5 is a pain in the neck
   2 did not/didn't bat an eyelid 6 have never seen eye to eye
   3 (just) gave me the cold   7 had a (brilliant) brainwave
      shoulder   8 too wet behind the ears.
   4 was all fingers and thumbs
2 1 take your pick   5 pick you up
   2 pick your brains   6 pick up the pieces
   3 picked it up   7 picked holes in
   4 picked her way   8 picked up on

173

3
1 office
2 risk
3 story
4 counter
5 engine

Grammar p13
1 1 b   2 a   3 a   4 b   5 b
2 1a ... nine-year-old James Edwards is very talented.
b ... very talented.
2a ... is/has been rumoured that Mrs Reed is leaving the school.
b ... is rumoured to be leaving the school.
3a ... was thought/felt/believed that the new sports programme had benefited the school.
b ... was believed to have benefited from the new sports programme.
4a ... has been suggested that graphic novels could encourage children to read.
b ... have been made that graphic novels could encourage children to read.
5a ... is often assumed that an only child will be selfish.
b ... are often made that an only child will be selfish.
3 (Possible answers) 1 had her camera
2 is having/getting his washing machine
3 get/have her hair
4 had/got our sitting room window
5 his hand

Listening p14
1 1 visually stimulating
2 novels
3 Tokyo/Japan
4 poetry
5 stepping stone
6 three
7 mixed abilities
8 practical

Use of English p15
1 1 perception
2 unconscious
3 imbued
4 instincts
5 method
6 entrusting
7 findings
8 incentive
2 1 D   2 C   3 A   4 B   5 C   6 B
7 B   8 C   9 A   10 B   11 D   12 A

Writing p16
1 Underline: 'describing the services it provides'; 'stating whether all the added services are really useful'; and 'saying who you would recommend your choice of mobile phone to and why'.
2 Example b is the best (Example a threatens to be irrelevant by becoming a report and examining 'different types of mobile phone' when the question asks for one; Example c is too informal and vague in style).
3 The sample conclusion is unsuitable because it fails to follow the instructions in the question rubric.

Unit 3

Getting started p17
1 a white water rafting; b yacht racing; c snowboarding; d triathlon; e mountain climbing

Reading p18–19
1 1 B   2 D   3 C   4 A   5 D   6 D   7 C

Language development p20
1 a down   c down
b up   d up
e up   g down
f up   h up
2 a takes after   e taken [you] for
b take over   f take apart
c take back   g took to
d take on   h taken up
3 a lying down   e the wind out of my/his/her sails
b it or leave it   f with a pinch of salt
c the bull by the horns   g it out of you
d hat off to her   h it from me

4 game

Grammar p21
1 1 B   2 C   3 D   4 A
2 1 e   2 f   3 a   4 b   5 h
6 i   7 j   8 d   9 g   10 c
3 a 1   b 2, 4, 5   c 3   d 6, 7, 10   e 8, 9
4 1 a   2 b

Listening p22
1 **certainty:** definite, confident, secure, unambiguous
uncertainty: doubtful, unconvinced, hesitant, cynical
positive feelings: exuberant, delighted, elated, thrilled
negative feelings: frustrated, annoyed, irked, exasperated
2 1 A   2 C   3 B
3 1 A   2 B   3 D

Use of English p23
1 1 against
2 than
3 for
4 with
5 same
6 each
7 under/within
8 be
9 could/might
10 which/that
11 after/during
12 instead
13 receive/win
14 final
15 such

Unit 4

Getting started p25
1 A Cretaceous, evolution, erosion, fossils, geology, Jurassic, tyrannosaurus rex
B artificial intelligence artificial life, cells, DNA, genetics, laboratory, microchip, nanotechnology, $E=MC^2$, forensic
C sci-fi, androids, robotic implants, virtual reality
D cortex, grey matter, neurology
E black hole, dark matter, extraterrestrial, supernova
2 a palaeontology   f psychology
b android   g cortex
c nanotechnology   h dark matter;
d extra terrestrial   i artificial intelligence
e DNA   j grey matter

Reading p26
1 1 B   2 C   3 A   4 B   5 C   6 D
7 D   8 A   9 B   10 D   11 A   12 C
13 B   14 D   15 A

Language development p28

1
a target   b cognitive   c suppressing
d accomplice   e communal   f conducive
g hamper   h con   i testimonial
j calibrated

2
1	began to tell	5	I told you so
2	tell them apart	6	only time will tell
3	tell on	7	never can tell
4	as far as I can tell	8	telltale

3
a	blue	i	black
b	red	j	green
c	green	k	blue
d	red	l	greener
e	blue	m	blue
f	black	n	black
g	red	o	red
h	red	p	blue

4 **red**: in the red; see red; be caught red-handed; red tape; red herring
blue: out of the blue; (talk) till you're blue in the face; feel blue; once in a blue moon; like a bolt from the blue
black: black mark; black humour; be on a black list;
green: green fingers; green with envy; the grass looks greener on the other side

Grammar p29

1 1 a 2 b 3 a 4 b 5 b 6 b 7 a

2
a in ten minutes   d as soon as
b in three weeks' time   e until then
c by then

3
1 are you going to do about
2 is bound to pass
3 what the future will hold
4 will have been doing/in business
5 'll/will be waiting (for you) outside
6 are on the point of discovering
7 is/will be coming to help us
8 is going to

Listening p30

1
1	E	2	F	3	H	4	B	5	A	6	H
7	C	8	A	9	F	10	G				

Use of English p31

1 Gaps 2 and 4

2
1	inevitably	6	living
2	unhealthy	7	typically
3	epidemiologists	8	ceaseless
4	unexpected	9	overreact
5	findings	10	implications

Writing p32

1 Underline: 'Read the extract below and comments from members of the public, and write an article for the magazine, referring to the points raised and describing your own view of the future of shopping'; 'Read them, and send us your views in an article entitled, 'Is high street shopping a thing of the past?'; 'It's so much easier to order my books online'; 'You can find things reasonably priced, and you save time'; 'Shopping is one of my favourite activities, and I love to browse'; 'Online shopping means avoiding parking fees, and crowds'; 'Going shopping gives me the chance to meet up with friends.'

2 (Possible answers) Paragraph 1: Introduction, referring to the survey conducted.

Paragraph 2: refer to comments made in favour of online shopping, and my response.
Paragraph 3: refer to comments made in favour of high street shopping, and my response.
Paragraph 4: Conclusion. My overall view of the future of high street shopping.

Unit 5

Getting started p33

1
1	fraud	9	virus
2	arson	10	convict
3	crimeware	11	implicate
4	sentence	12	murder
5	hacking	13	kidnapping
6	confess	14	victim
7	incriminate	15	charge
8	acquit		

The phrase in the central column is 'forensic science'.

Reading pp34–35

1 1 F 2 C 3 A 4 E 5 B 6 G

Language development p36

1
1 b	2 a	3 a	4 b	5 b	6 b
7 d	8 c	9 a	10 d		

2
1 T	2 F	3 T	4 T	5 F	6 T
7 F	8 F				

3
1	enforce	3	break
2	obey	4	lay down

4 1 b 2 a 3 c

Grammar p37

1
1	racing	9	to kill
2	to drop	10	seeing
3	to do	11	to find
4	to ram	12	to steal
5	to board	13	chasing
6	to knock	14	to head
7	to tie	15	to continue
8	to defend		

Listening p38

1 1 d 2 b 3 f 4 e 5 a 6 c

2
1	the risk	5	dignity
2	website	6	(unfair) criticism
3	probation officers	7	small
4	regular contact	8	the unexpected

Use of English p39

1
1	instruments	4	conviction
2	law	5	turned
3	profile		

Speaking p39

1 (Possible answers): The facilities: attractive shops, cafeterias, bars, restaurants, and also cinemas, and a theatre, without the chaos of a big city.
The atmosphere: constant buzz of conversation and laughter, without the intrusive noise of the traffic!
Access to other places: it is easy to escape the town to the country.

Writing p40

1 (Possible answers): The notes are irrelevant for this question and too knowledge specific, and there is no organisation of ideas. The student has misunderstood part of the input material, has failed to use it effectively, and has not created headings for each paragraph.

2 (Possible answers): Paragraph 1: Introduction (purpose of the report).
Paragraph 2: Use of mobile phones (approximately 75% of students have a mobile phone; They must switch them off in the classroom).
Paragraph 3: Potential dangers (unknown, but possible brain damage, and increased risk of disease from long-term exposure).
Paragraph 4: Recommendations (teachers give talks advising students on the dangers of using phones too much; students switch off phones as soon as they arrive at school, and only switch them on again when the final bell rings).

Unit 6

Getting started p41

1 a acupuncture   b aromatherapy
   c herbalism   d homeopathy
   e reflexology   f meditation
2 1 herbalism   4 homeopathy
   2 acupuncture   5 reflexology
   3 aromatherapy   6 meditation
3 1 aromatherapy
   2 homeopathy
   3 acupuncture

Reading p42–43

1 Text 1: reflexology;   Text 2: Ayurveda;
Text 3: maggot debridement therapy
2 1 D   2 A   3 A   4 B   5 C   6 B
3 1 complementary   4 potential
   2 consultant   5 infested
   3 superficial   6 yuck factor

Language development p44

1 1 b   2 b   3 a   4 a   5 b   6 b
2 1 lifelong friends   7 a lifetime's ambition
   2 lay down their lives   8 a matter of life and death
   3 life-threatening illness   9 life-jackets
   4 fact of life   10 a new lease of life
   5 have the time of their lives
   6 the life and soul of the
     party

Grammar p45

1 1 If you were to go to America ...
   2 Should you see Garry in town ...
   3 As long as you eat all your green vegetables ...
   4 If you happen to find ...
   5 But for Julian's intervention ...
   6 Had you been invited ...
   7 Even if you had been on time/hadn't been late ...
2 1 had remembered/wouldn't have run out
   2 had/would be able to
   3 walks/will be
   4 hadn't driven/could have got
   5 had taken/would be
   6 comes/will have
   7 was/didn't he fill
   8 runs out/stops

Listening p45

1 1 C   2 B   3 C   4 D   5 A   6 B

Speaking p46

1 These pictures both show ...; ... while the other picture ...; The main similarity/difference between the two pictures is that ...

Use of English p47

1 1 D   2 B   3 B   4 D   5 A   6 A
   7 B   8 C   9 D   10 A   11 B   12 B

Unit 7

Getting started p49

1 1 trip   6 package holiday
   2 safari   7 voyage
   3 excursions   8 flight
   4 ride   9 travel
   5 cruise   10 journey
2 a 2   b 5   c 4   d 8

Reading p50

1 1 C   2 A/D   3 A/D   4 B   5 A   6 C
   7 D   8 A/C   9 A/C   10 B   11 A/D   12 A/D
   13 B   14 A/C   15 A/C

Language development p52

1 1 C   2 B   3 C   4 A
2 1 like the look of it   5 looked him in the eye
   2 much to look at   6 overlook
   3 get a look-in   7 look ahead
   4 look the other way   8 by the looks of it
3 a roadhouse   b road rage   c road test   d roadside
   e road hog   f road map   g road works   h road block
   i road sign   j road show

Grammar p53

1 a the rope would never   b was she aware   c than
   d should you leave   e he had left   f have we seen
   g failed   h had they arrived   i am I to be
   j had finished
2 1 Only later were the details of the scandal made known ...
   2 No sooner had we arrived than ...
   3 Barely had the concert started ...
   4 Seldom do you see ...
   5 On no account must you ...
   6 Never have I seen ...
   7 Scarcely had Gina walked ...
   8 Not only is he a musician, but also ...
3 1 had just come out when
   2 have checked your passport will you
   3 had the plane taken off when
   4 time did Tom apologise
   5 the bus driver stopped did he

Listening p54

1 1 E   2 G   3 B   4 F   5 H   6 C
   7 A   8 F   9 D   10 G

Use of English p55

1 1 not   6 obtaining/gaining/
   2 this/it   acquiring/getting
   3 However/Nevertheless   7 had
   4 eventually/finally   8 one
   5 would   9 although/while

10	but	13	this
11	rather/fairly/particularly	14	never/previously
12	let	15	which/that

Speaking p55

1 (Possible answers): **Package tour operators:** 'suddenly, people from lower social classes could travel abroad. No longer was it reserved just for the rich'; 'this led to more hotels and guest houses being built, and generated business in coastal areas. Of course, the downside of this has been that these areas became very spoilt by overcrowding and pollution'; 'package tour operators tend to flood an area with visitors ...'

The Internet: 'an even wider range of choices, and what was fashionable last year has been replaced this year by another destination'; 'websites promote particular kinds of holidays, and reach more people, since it is a lot easier to sit at home and surf the net looking for a holiday ...'

Writing p56

1 Underline: 'Then, using the information carefully, write a proposal, suggesting the best ways to update the company website'; 'colourful home page with photos from holidays, comprehensive drag down contents list'; 'Holidays separated into 3 main categories – Family Adventure, Extreme Adventure, Expeditions – click on photo for each'; 'Features section, and Last Minute Offers'

2 (Possible answers): **Proposal to update website**

1 Colourful Homepage: photos from holidays (visually stimulating/appealing comprehensive drag down contents list; give easy access to inexperienced computer users)

2 Three main holiday categories: Family Adventure, Extreme Adventure, Expeditions (click on relevant photo to go to category page; clear instructions for easy access, so that user knows what to expect)

3 Special Features and Last Minute Offers section: This section will allow company to focus on particular promotions, or last minute offers on holiday places that need to be sold.

Unit 8

Getting started p57

1
1 The Great Sphinx of Giza
2 Stonehenge
3 The Parthenon
4 The Eiffel Tower
5 The Statue of Liberty

2 A4   B3   C1   D5   E2

Reading pp58–59

1 1 C   2 B   3 C   4 B   5 D   6 A   7 B

Language development p60

1
1 brought home to me
2 brought him to his knees
3 bring your characters to life
4 brought back to me
5 bring me to eat
6 has brought triplets into the world

2
1	bring down	4	bring off
	[the government]		[running a business]
2	correct	5	bring out [the best]
3	bring in [enough money]		

3 11 times; a 2   b 5   c 2   d 0   e 2

4 7 times

Grammar p60

1
1 by which time
2 whose cat
3 correct
4 neither of whom
5 who/that you were ...
6 correct
7 where I was born/in which/that I was born in
8 correct

2 1 ND   2 ND   3 D   4 ND   5 D

3
1	point	5	neither
2	case	6	both
3	time	7	which
4	result	8	whom

Listening p61

1 a Speaker 3   b Speaker 2   c Speaker 1

2 1 B   2 C   3 A   4 C   5 C   6 A

Use of English p63

1
1	ventilation	6	survival
2	organism	7	diligence
3	inhabitants	8	construction
4	colony	9	utilisation
5	harshness	10	estimation

Writing p64

1
1 a brochure for tourists
2 semi-formal/neutral
3 a description of a national historical monument in your country and why they are interesting for tourists to visit
4 Suggestions could include the name of the monument, the area, the history etc.

2
1	amphitheatre	7	mythology
2	architecture	8	entertainment
3	construction	9	earthquakes
4	spectators	10	symbol
5	spectacles	11	attractions
6	contests	12	procession

3 elliptical, largest, greatest, ruined, iconic, popular

4 The Colosseum, History, Present condition
Other headings: Function, Design, Builders

Unit 9

Getting started p65

1
a	2	b	1	c	5	d	not used	e	6
f	4	g	not used	h	3				

Reading p66–67

1 1 C   2 B   3 C   4 A   5 D   6 B

Language development p68

1
1	c	2	f	3	h	4	b	5	d	6	a
7	g	8	e								

2
1	d	2	a	3	j	4	b	5	h	6	i
7	f	8	c	9	g	10	e				

3
a	pay me a compliment	d	pay my respects
b	paid through the nose	e	paid tribute to
c	pay [you] back		

4
1	pay you back	4	paying out on
2	pay out	5	paid him off
3	pay this cheque into		

Listening p69

1 (Possible answers): 1 pages with simple, clear titles and headings
2 long texts
3 information in bullet-pointed lists and use sub-headings etc
4 using PDFs for general product information
5 photos of product/prices of product

2 1 D 2 B 3 C 4 A 5 B 6 B

Grammar p70

1 (Possible answer): 'When we are obliged to read, because of computers, we expect the words to be arranged in helpful modules, with plenty of graphics.'

2 1 a2 b1
2 a1 b2
3 a1 b2

3 1 How he manages to run six miles after a full day's work
2 Easy though the job may seem
3 What you should do is buy
4 (It's quite simple.) All you need to do is (to)
5 Where he gets his bad temper from

4 a What did Sarah do? b What did Sarah steal (from the boutique on the corner)? c Where did Sarah steal a dress from? d Who stole a dress from the boutique on the corner? E Who saw Sarah steal a dress? F Where did Sarah hide the dress?

Use of English p71

1 1 all you do is tell him
2 paid a tribute to
3 Mandy, it was Peter (not Harry)
4 though she may be
5 what I like most (of all)
6 but for Mr. Smith's
7 never before have I been
8 has not/hasn't spoken to her grandfather

Speaking p71

1 First, talk to each other about how each style might attract young people. Then, decide which two would be the most successful.

2 'Don't you agree?'; 'What about this idea of advertising posters from the 1960s?'; 'Do you think young people would be interested in this?'; 'Yes, but isn't that really for smaller kids?'; 'How about this design for the environment idea?'; 'Do you think the Graffiti idea any good?'; 'What do *you* think of it, Enrique?'; 'So, which ones do you think would make the most successful exhibitions?'

3 'I'm not so sure that many will be interested'; 'Yes, but isn't that really for smaller kids? I can't imagine'; 'I'm afraid I can't agree with you there'; 'Yes, but often too much. Think Green is everywhere'; 'I wonder if it might attract more boys than girls, though?'; 'Do you really think so? I have to say ...'; 'but I'm sure you won't agree with me!'; 'But the adverts don't appeal to me'.

Writing p72

1 (Possible answers): Reason 1: Graphic novels increasingly popular. Justification: More serious graphic novels for adults show that interest in the genre is growing.
Reason 2: Graphic illustrators have developed exciting styles, and Kishimoto's work is considered among the best. Justification: He has developed his own distinctive style.
Reason 3: The popularity of his graphic books. Justification: The number of websites covering his work stand testimony to his popularity, and many young artists try to emulate his style of manga drawing.

Unit 10

Getting started p73

1 a material wealth b Good health c Social standing d A good job/career e A happy family f Personal success

Reading pp74–75

1 1 F 2 C 3 B 4 G 5 E 6 A

Language development p76

1 1 strains 4 line
2 alarm 5 toll
3 up

2 a to pull out (of) b to pull on/at c to pull off
d to pull down e to pull over f to pull away/out
g to pull (something) together h to pull through i to pull back
j to pull (something) apart

Listening p76

1 1 E 2 A 3 D 4 G 5 B 6 C
7 H 8 F 9 A 10 E

Grammar p77

1 1 Jenny told Ed that she wished they could go on holiday the following week.
2 Michael asked if/whether he could have a salad for lunch.
3 Mum wanted to know if/whether I/we had any homework to do.
4 Philip said it was the best meal he had eaten this/that year.

2 1 [It] wasn't me who broke the porcelain vase!
2 I'm paying for lunch. [Anyway,] it's my birthday.
3 [You] spoiled the surprise party we had planned for Dad!

3 1 begged Sara not to leave
2 threatened to tell Mum
3 advised Jim to get his arm seen (to)
4 admitted to having [had]/that he had had
5 mother encouraged her to take
6 blamed Tony for the fact that
7 complained that his beer was warm

4 1 decided to wear/put on
2 dismay that he was
3 Feeling slightly hurt
4 he liked
5 couldn't see what
6 that she had already decided to wear
7 that they couldn't go
8 annoyed
9 she had a number of dresses
10 him he was being ridiculous
11 that if he was going to wear
12 wouldn't go

Speaking p78

1 **Student 1** Contrast: The second picture is a bit different because ...
Express an opinion: I don't think she is getting much work done ...; However, if you ask me ...
Student 2 Compare: They are all pictures of ...
Describe: This one shows ...; Here we can see ...
Speculate: I guess it is Switzerland ...; He must be very excited ...; I suppose you would get ...

2 a 2 woman working at home, sitting at a desk with a computer and phone. Behind her the door is open and a child is standing at the door. Toys are strewn across the carpet and a baby is crawling towards her. She is looking at the toddler. b 1 an alpine lodge, mountains covered with snow, fir-trees scattered around, someone in ski-suit; 2 a [Bedouin] tent in the desert, camels in the background, perhaps an oasis

Use of English p79

1 (Possible answers): She decided to play the songs in alphabetical order; Martin received an order from his Captain; Jesse ordered chicken but was served veal.
The students were presented with the award for Best Dressed Class; I presented my ticket to the guard but he wouldn't let me onto the platform; May I present Lady Smythe, my Lord.

2 1 inch   3 mental   5 range
   2 luck   4 pull   6 shook

Writing p80

1 a explain/give advice/   b local residents
    make recommendations
   c formal/semi-formal

4 a take showers rather than baths, turn off the water while soaping ourselves, use the washing machine less, use washing machines and dishwashers that have good water economy, recycle water used for washing hands; b avoid using a hose in hot weather, avoid watering during the day, avoid washing the car or yard unless essential and use a bucket when doing so, collect rainfall water; c pass the leaflet on to help others save water.

Unit 11

Getting started p81

1 a workaholic   b consumer   c debt
   d identity theft   e expenditure   f transaction
   g accountant   h credit card fraud   i finance
   j invest

Reading pp82–83

1 1 C   2 B   3 B   4 D   5 B   6 C   7 C
2 a sequence   b spin   c fortune   d inane   e mechanically
   f ostensibly   g random   h implication   i adept
   j incredulous   k close shave   l composure

Language development p84

1 a your mind   b place   c money   d the blue   e luck
2 1 put out   4 hand out
   2 find out   5 sort out
   3 work out
3 a Nouns: outback, outbuilding, outboard, outburst, outcome, outcry, outfall, outfit, outfitters, outflow, outgrowth, outgoings, outhouse, outing, outlay, outlet, outline, outlook etc.
   b Verbs: outclass, outflank, outfox, outgrow, outguess, outgun, outlast, outlaw, outline, outlive, outmanoeuvre, outnumber, outpace, outshine, outwit etc.
   c Adjectives: outgoing, outlandish, outmoded, outnumbered, out of touch, out of date, outlying, outrageous, outright, outstanding, outstretched, outspoken etc.
   d (Possible answers): The school has a large outdoor swimming pool in its grounds; It's such a lovely day that you should be outdoors playing football, not sitting in front of the computer.
4 a raise money   b not made of money
   c pumped money into   d save money
   e money is no object   f put your money where your mouth is

   g have money to burn   h Money talks
   i got our money's worth   j throw money

Listening p85

1 1 means   5 income
   2 unforeseen emergencies   6 four
   3 five   7 habits
   4 chart   8 budget

Grammar p86

1 1 resignation   6 criticism
   2 prediction   7 resignation
   3 criticism   8 annoyance
   4 annoyance   9 plan
   5 plan   10 prediction
2 1 might have/could have   4 could
   2 wouldn't be   5 will
   3 would
3 1 will be/is going to be
   2 will buy/get
   3 will (all) have
   4 might have killed/run over/hit
   5 will keep
   6 may/might as well

Use of English p87

1 1 D   2 B   3 A   4 C   5 B   6 D
   7 C   8 C   9 B   10 C   11 A   12 D

Speaking p87

1 (Possible answers): a 'I agree with you to a certain extent, but …'; 'I think you've got a point, but …'; 'To a point, you're right, but I have to say …'; b 'I'm afraid I can't agree with you there'; 'Personally, I don't feel that way'; 'I think there's another way of looking at it'; 'Perhaps, but I think there's another way of looking at it'; 'I don't think that's true for everyone …'

Writing p88

2 (suggested answer) **Introduction**
The aim of this report is to examine the issues surrounding the workers' complaints, and to make some recommendations for improving the current situation.

Exposure to chemicals in a poorly ventilated environment

It was discovered that due to production demands and recent cutbacks in the workforce, workers are now working for more than three hours at a time without a break, and are constantly exposed to fumes from the paint chemicals. As the ventilation filters are damaged, air is not circulating effectively on the factory floor. We need to ensure that workers have a fifteen-minute break every one and a half hours, during which they should leave the factory floor. The air filters should be replaced, and checked more regularly.

Protective clothing

Furthermore, the clothing currently provided to the workers for their protection is sadly inadequate. The overalls are faded and worn, and the facial masks fail to give workers sufficient protection from the hazardous fumes. Providing workers with new overalls, and masks with air filters would ensure they are not affected by chemical fumes while working.

Conclusion

As can be seen from the points raised above, there are several problems facing workers at present. However, with the implementation of the improvements suggested, the situation will soon improve, to the satisfaction of workforce and management alike.

Unit 12

Getting started p89

1
1	blockbuster	8	plot
2	musical	9	photography
3	screenplay	10	director
4	setting	11	trailer
5	documentary	12	script
6	cast	13	thriller
7	actor	14	lyrics

The word 'cinematography' is spelt out.

Reading pp90–91

1 a irony (n); ironic (adj); ironically (adv)
   b sarcasm (n); sarcastic (adj); sarcastically (adv)

2 1 C   2 B   3 D   4 C   5 A/D 6 D/A
   7 B   8 A   9 C   10 A   11 B   12 D
   13 A   14 C   15 D

3 1 take the reins
   2 pin (something) down
   3 a means to an end
   4 to bridge the gap (between)
   5 to climb through the ranks

4
1	period-piece	4	genre
2	dot-com	5	apprentice
3	digital		

Language development p92

1 (Possible answers): 1 painful 2 beautiful 3 slow
   4 dull/boring 5 devoted 6 natural

2 1 d   2 e   3 a   4 c   5 b

3 1 perplexingly named
   2 especially under-powered
   3 coolly ruthless agent
   4 coldly suppressed rage
   5 crash-bang Bond
   6 deafening episodes
   7 similarly powerful vehicle
   8 baffling decision
   9 thrilling music
   10 short, sharp, bone-cracking bursts
   11 cool, cruel presence
   12 perpetually semi-pursed
   13 some new nastiness
   14 smart elegance
   15 conventional action
   16 indefinably difficult task

Listening p93

1 1 C   2 B   3 B   4 A   5 C   6 B

Speaking p93

1 Picture 1: people at the opera
   Picture 2: someone reading a book
   Picture 3: people at the cinema
   Picture 4: young people at a concert
   Picture 5: people watching TV
   Picture 6: people playing computer games

Grammar pp94–95

1 1 e   2 f   3 a   4 c   5 g   6 h
   7 d   8 b

2 1 b   2 c   3 a   4 b   5 a   6 d
   7 c   8 b   9 a   10 c   11 d   12 c
   13 b   14 a

3 1 Cynthia and I, both fans of …
   2 The film, directed by Woody Allen had received … /
     Directed by Woody Allen, the film had received …
   3 Having been given …
   4 Crossing the road …
   5 Dick and Isabella, good friends of Cynthia's, who we
     invited
   6 Arriving at the cinema
   7 Not wanting to go …
   8 Having already seen the film she
   9 Not wanting to see
   10 nearby restaurant run by an Italian couple

Use of English p95

1 They admire it as an icon.

2 1 preposition of time
   2 adjective before noun
   3 preposition
   4 auxiliary verb
   5 conjunction (particle expressing comparison)
   6 adjective (preceded by a possessive)
   7 particle after noun
   8 verb (simple present, third person plural)
   9 adjective after noun
   10 adverb
   11 particle before noun
   12 particle (forming phrasal verb)
   13 modal auxiliary
   14 adjective (defining adjective before noun)
   15 relative pronoun

3
1	after	6	own	11	in
2	such	7	of	12	together
3	without	8	is	13	must/should
4	have	9	else	14	other
5	than	10	more/again	15	which/that

Writing p96

3 Points mentioned: an outline of the story, a description of the
   characters, what you liked about it, background information,
   the writer, director or actors, how successful it was

4 1 d   2 e   3 c   4 a   5 b

5 1 e   2 a   3 c   4 f   5 d   6 b

Unit 13

Getting started p97

2 publicise

Reading pp98–99

1 1 D   2 B   3 G   4 A   5 E   6 C

Language development p100

1 a to; b for; c of; d of; e into

2
1	of	5	of
2	to	6	with
3	to	7	of
4	to	8	over

3 1 be settled in certain habits and find it difficult to change
   2 don't approve of
   3 is due to
   4 a fixed choice of food
   5 is determined to

4 1 f   2 b   3 j   4 d   5 a
   6 e   7 g   8 c   9 h   10 i

5
1	set in		4	set back
2	set off		5	set down
3	setting aside			

Listening p101

1 1 G 2 E 3 A 4 B 5 H 6 D
7 A 8 F 9 C 10 G

Grammar p102

1 1 playing football, cycling and picking blackberries
2 the fact that he told the class
3 the difficulty people have (in expressing their feelings)
4 the various ways
5 writing a letter and phoning

2
1	It		4	It
2	There		5	It
3	there			

3
1	First		9	by
2	This		10	It
3	whereas		11	These
4	such		12	This
5	They		13	which
6	of		14	both
7	which		15	for
8	This			

Use of English p102

1
1	get		4	set
2	word		5	sound
3	foreign			

Speaking p103

1–2 (Rahul's actual answers):
1 Yes, but the students can learn a lot of things from the computer, and there are interactive programmes as well ...
2 I see your point, but I think it's useful for students to have access to computers, and particularly the internet, at school, because they can use them to find out information, and the teachers can show their students clips, etcetera, which can start a discussion in class ...
3 Yes, I do. For the same reason as the computers. Satellite TV means that students can watch such channels as BBC World. I have this at home, and it's really good, because you can learn things. Again, teachers can use it to give students listening practice, and for discussion. Today, I think students find it easier to respond to pictures – you know? computers, TV – than they do to something they read ...
4 OK, maybe you're right, but in the language classroom, pictures help students understand certain things, and I think they are easier to respond to. For that reason, I think the computers and the TV are useful tools. What about the group trip to England? That would be fun, wouldn't it?

Writing p104

1 1 b 2 b 3 a
2 1 b 2 a 3 c
3 Teenagers are no longer children, but neither are they completely adults; they have to make decisions about their future; they want more freedom; they have to study, and need advice; parents don't understand them; parents find it difficult to accept that their child has grown up
4 (Possible answers):
Paragraph 1: Introduction/No Longer Children
Paragraph 2: Problems Communicating
Paragraph 3: Practical Solutions/Solutions that Work
Paragraph 4: Conclusion/A Final Word

Unit 14

Getting started p105

1
Down 1 primate	**Across** 2 ape
2 amphibian	5 insect
3 mammal	6 invertebrate
4 reptile	8 fish
7 bird	

2 Planet Earth
3
1	f tuna		5	a worm
2	c snake		6	g pterosaur
3	h platypus		7	d goose
4	b spider		8	e spider monkey

Reading pp106–107

1 1 D 2 D 3 C 4 B 5 C 6 A 7 B
2
1	vacuum		5	whopping
2	cluster		6	diminishing
3	clutch		7	colossally
4	frighten the daylights out of someone		8	randomly

Language development p108

1
1	out of the woods		4	in deep water
2	get wind of		5	bogged down in
3	clear the air		6	the tip of the iceberg

2
1	of		6	about
2	with		7	with
3	for		8	about
4	with		9	to
5	to		10	of

3 1 c 2 g 3 e 4 h 5 i 6 f
7 b 8 j 9 a 10 d

Grammar p109

1 1 h 2 j 3 b 4 f 5 g 6 a
7 i 8 c 9 d 10 e
2
1 I didn't have much money, so I didn't travel around the world.
2 I did watch a lot of TV, so I didn't read very much.
3 I studied French instead of Spanish so I went to France/didn't go to Spain.
4 He didn't work hard enough so he didn't pass his course.
3
1	hadn't gone		6	stayed
2	could have been		7	might have got
3	might/would never have met		8	could save
4	had never seen		9	had
5	would probably never have got		10	got

4
1 is (high/about) time you stopped wasting
2 wish you had come/could have come
3 as though he were
4 had better take some
5 wish I knew how Sara was
6 would sooner you called me
7 only I had gone sky-diving
8 would rather you helped

Listening p110

1
1	ecosystems		5	6.5 billion
2	wiped out		6	90 million
3	viruses [and] parasites		7	policies
4	five planets		8	side-effects

Use of English p111

1
1	compassionate	6	joyful/joyless
2	remarkably	7	considerably/consideration
3	climatic	8	remorseless/remorseful
4	prioritise	9	hesitation/hesitant
5	installation	10	conservation/
			conservationist

2
1	seasonal	6	extensive
2	rapidly	7	continuously
3	migration	8	numerous
4	primarily	9	endangered
5	fragility	10	predatory

Writing p112

2 (Answers are clockwise from top centre): earthquakes/ tsunamis; species extinctions; desertification/dying forests/ threatened ecosystems; rising global temperatures; cities destroyed/millions displaced/famine/disease/conflict; melting ice caps = rising sea levels; polar bears face drowning/ starving; hurricanes/storms/forest fires; human deaths/injuries

3 Paragraph 2: how the weather will change
Paragraph 3: how nature will suffer
Paragraph 4: how human civilisation will suffer

Unit 15

Getting started p113

1
1 E	2 G	3 C	4 B	5 H	6 C
7 G	8 H	9 A	10 B		

Reading pp114–115

1
1 C	2 D	3 A	4 D	5 B	6 C

2
1 C	2 D	3 A	4 B	5 C	6 D
7 A	8 B				

Language development p116

1
1 c	2 d	3 h	4 f	5 g	6 i
7 b	8 a	9 e			

2
1	let it pass	4	came to pass
2	flying colours	5	pass the buck
3	pass my lips		

3 (Possible answers): 1 a long illness. 2 a drop of blood. 3 post office. 4 travel around the world. 5 employee etc. 6 message that dinner will be at 8. 7 it was clearly her brother's work. 8 mother to child.

4 a pass off as; b pass down; c pass by; d pass out; e pass up; f pass on; g pass away; h pass over

Listening p117

1
1 C	2 B	3 D	4 A	5 A	6 B

Speaking p117

1
1 Fernando, where are you from?
2 How would you describe your home city to someone who has never been there?
3 What can young people do in your country?
4 Claudia, where do you live now?
5 What do you like about it?
6 What are the advantages/disadvantages of living abroad (for a short time)?
7 Fernando, if you could live in another country, where would you choose?

8 Why?
9 Claudia, what are the most popular sports in your country?
10 What do you do to keep fit and healthy?

Grammar p118

1
1	in case	6	In spite of/Despite/
2	Hardly/Barely		Notwithstanding
3	so that	7	While/When
4	where	8	For fear of
5	Consequently/As a result/		
	Therefore		

2
1	no sooner ... than (time)	4	if (condition)
2	as ... as (comparison)	5	Nevertheless (concession)
3	so ... that (result)		

3
1	to her house to talk ...	5	with a view to going ...
2	Despite being/In spite	6	Seeing as you've ...
	of being	7	Such is the extent of the
3	For fear of forgetting ...		damage that ...
4	No matter how tough	8	do as you're told or else/
	it was ...		otherwise ...

4
1	For this reason	6	with a view to
2	otherwise	7	Consequently
3	In order to	8	due to the fact that
4	This is why	9	so as
5	When	10	although

Use of English p119

1
1	during/on	9	which
2	for	10	such
3	where	11	with
4	to	12	both
5	so	13	from
6	them	14	like
7	as/when	15	so/consequently/therefore
8	the		

2
1	order	4	belief
2	custom	5	magic
3	hand		

Writing p120

1 It was the most amazing experience; I won't go into too much detail about; suffice it to say there was; The most memorable part for me was; I was enjoying myself immensely ...

2 (Possible answers): 1 Yes, to Cyprus on holiday.
2 Yes, a wedding that went on for three days!
3 Lots of eating and drinking plus the money pinning ceremony.
4 I only had coins in my pocket.

3 Paragraph 1: Where I went (introduction to the experience)
Paragraph 2: General summary of the experience
Paragraph 3: Details of what made it special/memorable
Paragraph 4: What happened at the end.

Unit 16

Getting started p121

1
1	discontinued	6	instigated
2	founded	7	incited
3	finalise	8	abort
4	settle	9	generated
5	launching	10	completed

Reading pp122–123

1
1 C	2 D	3 A	4 B/C	5 B/C	6 C
7 D	8 A	9 C	10 D	11 B	12 A
13 A/B	14 A/B	15 C			

2 a successor　　　　b nostalgia　　　c instantaneous
　　d ritualised　　　　e cutting-edge　　f obsolete
　　g outweigh　　　　h eliminated　　　i wince (at)
　　j console (myself)

Language development p124

1　1　drastic　　　　　　5　complacency
　　2　dispel　　　　　　 6　cloud
　　3　staple　　　　　　 7　cut
　　4　confirmed　　　　　8　expound
2　1　start　　　　　　　3　means
　　2　cut　　　　　　　　4　end
3　1 f　2 j　3 a　4 h　5 c　6 i
　　7 g　8 d　9 e　10 b

Listening p125

1　1 C　2 B　3 C　4 A　5 B　6 B

Grammar p126

1　(Possible answers): a is as good as; b (much) faster than; c less exciting than; d just as tasty as; e far more interesting than; f not as friendly as; g doesn't suit you as much as; h more attractive than; i is much easier to do/use than; j a lot less expensive than

2　1　She works a lot harder at school than she used to.
　　　 She works much harder at school than she used to.
　　2　This book isn't nearly as good as the last one he wrote.
　　　 The last book he wrote was considerably better than this one.
　　3　Dale is fitter by far than his brother, Simon.
　　　 Dale is a lot fitter than his brother, Simon.
　　4　They are much happier now that they've moved to the country.
　　　 They are happier by far now that they've moved to the country.
　　5　He's considerably more irritable than he used to be.
　　　 He's much more irritable than he used to be.
　　6　I've never tasted such an awful curry!
　　　 This is by far the worst curry I've ever tasted!

3　a much; b a lot; c by far; d not nearly as; e far

Use of English p127

1　1 C　2 A　3 D　4 A　5 B　6 C
　　7 B　8 D　9 C　10 B　11 A　12 C

Writing p128

1　Underline: reference for a friend of yours who has applied for a job as a tourist guide for your local town; will speak English well, be good at dealing with different people and will display knowledge of the local area; include information about your friend's character and personal qualities and skills, their previous relevant experience and reasons why they should be considered for this job.

2　Opening paragraph: my relationship with the person, and how long I have known them.
　　Second paragraph: The person's qualities that make her suitable, and her fluency in English.
　　Third paragraph: knowledge of and interest in local history, and her reasons for wanting this job.
　　Conclusion: Summary of why she is suitable for the position.

Practice Test

PAPER 1: READING

Part 1

　　1 C　2 B　3 C　4 A　5 C　6 A

Part 2

　　7 G　8 F　9 B　10 E　11 C　12 A

Part 3

　　13 C　14 A　15 B　16 B　17 D　18 C　19 B

Part 4

　　20 D　21 B　22 A　23 B　24 E　25 C
　　26 D　27 E　28 C　29 B　30 E　31 A
　　32 C　33 D　34 A

PAPER 3: USE OF ENGLISH

Part 1

　　1 A　2 C　3 B　4 D　5 B　6 C
　　7 B　8 D　9 C　10 B　11 A　12 A

Part 2

　　13　it　　　　　　21　which
　　14　all　　　　　 22　could
　　15　until　　　　 23　not
　　16　however　　　24　whose
　　17　according　　25　being
　　18　with　　　　 26　through
　　19　what　　　　 27　were
　　20　despite

Part 3

　　28　profitable　　　33　regeneration
　　29　consumption　　34　sleeplessness
　　30　invaluable　　　35　irritability
　　31　nutritional　　　36　increasingly
　　32　numerous　　　 37　outlive

Part 4

　　38　direct　　　　41　held
　　39　contact　　　42　drive
　　40　rich

Part 5

　　43　had no (hadn't any) hesitation in accepting
　　44　Jane would not (wouldn't) lose her
　　45　without doubt the group's best performance
　　46　on the point of leaving
　　47　from being the terrifying
　　48　has been made in regard to
　　49　us to give up
　　50　we took umbrellas in case it

PAPER 4: LISTENING

Part 1

　　1 B　2 B　3 A　4 A　5 C　6 A

Part 2

　　7　Exotic Earth　　　11　soil
　　8　creativity　　　　12　climate
　　9　drawing skills　　13　practical purpose
　　10　urban gardens　　14　headaches

Part 3

　　15 A　16 B　17 D　18 D　19 C　20 B

Part 4

　　21 C　22 H　23 A　24 F　25 D　26 A
　　27 C　28 E　29 H　30 B

NOTES

NOTES

NOTES

NOTES

NOTES

Credits

The publishers would like to thank the following sources for permission to reproduce their copyright protected texts:

Page 2: 'The clock strikes twelve' from 'Yesterday's Britain' Copyright © Reader's Digest Association, London, 1998. Page 2: 'The Beginning of an idea' from 'This Thing of Darkness' by Harry Thompson (page 352) Copyright © Headline Review, 2005 Page 3: 'Assistant hydrologist required' Copyright © New Scientist magazine issue 2631 Pages 18–19: Cycle toddling: an adventure in parenting by Stuart Wickes and Kirstie Pelling © Wickes and Pelling at http://www.familyonabike.org/stories Pages 26–27: 'The Science of Persuasion' from 'How to get exactly what you want' by Dan Jones and Alison Motluk Copyright © New Scientist magazine issue 2655 Page 31: 'Dirt is good for you!' from 'Filthy Healthy' by Jessica Marshall Copyright © New Scientist magazine issue 2638 Pages 34–35: 'Behind bars: Bragg to bring sound of music to prisons' by Nick Duerden Copyright © The Independent Page 43 'Quantum Healing' by Deepak Chopra, back cover blurb, Copyright © Random House; 'Maggots a good thing?' from 'Maggots and leeches make a comeback' by Aisha El-Awady Copyright © IslamOnline.net http://www.islamonline.net/servlet/Satellite?c=Article_C&pagename=Zone-English-HealthScience%2FHSELayout&cid=1158321476138 Page 55: 'Catch me a Colobus' by Gerald Durrell Copyright © Curtis Brown Ltd Page 59: 'Uffington White Horse: ancient hillside chalk art' by Joe Kissell Copyright © Kissell http://itotd.com/articles/259/uffington-white-horse/ Page 66: 'A Map with a purpose' from 'Beck's London Underground Map' Copyright © Bill Richmond, Design & Technology on the wed, http://www.design-technology.info/alevelsubsite/Page5.htm Page 67: 'Now Showing: Exhibition of film posters' Copyright © Now Showing (Barcelona) http://designtaxi.com/features.jsp?id=100433; 'Power of the Image' from 'The image-soaked future' by Bryan Appleyard Copyright © The Times Online http://entertainment.timesonline.co.uk Pages 74–75: 'Negotiating Animal Rights' by Dr Kate Rawls Copyright © Dr Kate Rawls http://www.animalliberationfront.com/ALFront/Premise_History/NegotiatingHumanRights.htm Page 91: Text B Copyright (C) Bruce Sterling, INNOVATION online, http://blog.wired.com/sterling/2005/02/whats_a_science.html; Text C Copyright (C) Ivana Primorace; The Times Online http://entertainment.timesonline.co.uk/tol/arts_and_entertainment/film/article3370452.ece Page 92: 'Quantum of Solace' review by Peter Bradshaw Copyright (C) The Guardian http://www.guardian.co.uk/film/2008/oct/18/jamesbond1 Page 95: 'Snow White and the Seven Dwarfs A Film Review' (C) Christopher Null, Filmcritic.com Pages 98–99: 'English as she will be spoke' from 'How global success is changing English forever' by Michael Erard Copyright (C) New Scientist magazine issue 2649 Page 107: 'Lost in the Cosmos' from 'A Short History of Nearly Everything' by Bill Bryson Copyright (C) Random House Page 114: Extract 1, 'Chapter 1' from 'Notes from a Small Island' by Bill Bryson Copyright (C) Random House 1995; Extract 2, 'Lessons about Boys' from 'The No.1 Ladies' Detective Agency' by Alexander McCall Smith Copyright © Birlinn Ltd; Extract 3, 'Burying bones of contention' Copyright © New Scientist magazine issue 2672 Page 123: Text A from 'Saying Goodbye to Polaroid Instant Film' by Amy Tiemann Copyright © CNET News, Amy Tiemann http://news.cnet.com/8301-13507_3-9892800-18.html; Text B from 'Probing question: are print newspapers dying?' by Sue Marquette Poremba Copyright © Penn State, Sue Marquette Poremba, http://www.rps.psu.edu/probing/printnewspapers.html; Text C from 'Saying goodbye to air travel' by Richard Heinberg Copyright © Post Carbon Institute http://www.globalpublicmedia.com/saying_goodbye_to_air_travel; Text D from 'Goodbye Video Tape, Hello Flash memory' by Paul Hochman Copyright © 2009 MSNBC Interactive http://www.msnbc.msn.com/id/3303539/; Page 127: 'Breakfast: the end of an era?' Copyright © 2008/2009 Decision News Media SAS http://www.foodnavigator.com/Financial-Industry/Breakfast-the-end-of-an-era.

Photo Credits

The publishers would like to thanks the following sources for permission to reproduce their copyright protected photographs:

11bg (123rf), 13 (matka_Wariatka/Shutterstock), 14tl (Pavel Losevsky/Dreamstime), 14bl (shutterstock), 14r (istockphoto), 15 (Jonathan Hordle/Rex Features), 16 (Yuri Arcurs/Shutterstock), 17bg (Maxim Tupikov/Dreamstime), 18bl (emin kuliyev/Shutterstock), 18bg (Anthony Harris/Shutterstock), 19bg(Anthony Harris/Shutterstock), 21 (Shutterstock), 23 (Eloy Alonso/REUTERS), 24 (Steve Estvanik/Dreamstime), 25l (Vaclav Volrab/Shutterstock), 25bl (Marek Szumlas/Shutterstock), 25br(Shutterstock), 27 (Jon Feingersh/Photolibrary), 32 (Franck Boston/Shutterstock), 33 (Kirill Smirnov/Shutterstock), 33tr (Dave Bartruff/CORBIS), 33tl (Heide Benser/zefa/Corbis), 34 (David Reed/CORBIS), 35 (Scott Houston/Corbis), 37 (XinHua/Xinhua Press/Corbis), 38etl (shutterstock), 38tl (123rf), 38br (Thomas Perkins/Bigstockphoto), 39 (Yuri Arcurs/Shutterstock), 40 (Kevin Dodge/Corbis), 41bg (Denis Pepin/Shutterstock), 41l (Alfred Wekelo/Shutterstock) 41el (Alfred Wekelo/Shutterstock), 41 (iStockphoto), 42 (Al Wekelo/Dreamstime), 43 (Shutterstock), 44 (Andi Berger/Shutterstock), 45 (Robert Byron/Dreamstime), 46bl (Patrick Durand/CORBIS), 46br (Vladimir Prusakov/Shutterstock), 46t (123rf), 47t (Yanik Chauvin/Shutterstock), 47b (Daniel Hixon/Shutterstock), 48 (Cathy Yeulet/123rf), 50t (Elena Elisseeva/Fotolia), 50b (Avid Creative, Inc/iStockphoto), 51tl (Jean-Jacques/Fotolia), 51tr (iStockphoto), 51bl (Shutterstock), 51br (Louise Cukrov/Shutterstock), 53 (Shutterstock), 54bg(123rf), 55 (iStockphoto), 57tr (Dmitry Terentjev/Shutterstock), 57tl (Shutterstock), 58 (Skyscan/CORBIS), 59b (Duncan McNicol/Gettyimages), 59t (David Hughes/Shutterstock), 59mt (June Marie Sobrito/Shutterstock), 59mb (Martin Trajkovski/Shutterstock), 61t (Shutterstock), 61b (Bigstock), 62bl (Stephen Inglis/Dreamstime), 62r (Dreamstime), 62tl (Shutterstock), 63l (iStockphoto), 63m (iStockphoto), 63br (Joseph Calev/Shutterstock), 63tl (iStockphoto), 63tr (Martin Horsky/Shutterstock), 63c (iStockphoto), 64 (Shutterstock), 65mr (Mike Walter/Bigstockphoto), 65bl (Dreamstime), 65tr (Shutterstock), 65tm (Rex features), 65bl (Shutterstock), 66l (Dave Willding/Bigstockphoto), 66r (Mary Evans Picture Library/Photolibrary), 67l (Rex features), 69 (Despotovic Dusko/CORBIS), 72 (Shutterstock), 73l (Yuri Arcurs/Shutterstock), 73r (Shutterstock), 73t (Shutterstock), 73b (Paco Ayala/Fotolia), 75 (Fotolia), 76 (Canstockphoto), 78 (Hemera Technologies/Jupiterimages), 79l (Hans-Peter Merten/Photolibrary), 79r (Shutterstock), 81bg (Shutterstock), 82 (Trae Patton/NBCU Photo Ban/AP Images), 83 (Alex Oliveria/Associated press), 84 (Teresa Azevedo/Shutterstock), 85l (Shutterstock), 85tr (iStockphoto), 85bl (Paulus Rusyanto/123rf), 85br (iStockphoto), 87 (Nasser Nuri/Reuters), 89l (Terry Chan/Shutterstock), 89ml (Shutterstock), 89mr (Ray Tang/Rex features) 89r (Norbert Kesten/Rex features), 90 (Shutterstock),

91tr (Clark Samuels/Rex features), 91tl (Res Features), 91bl (Capital Picture), 91br (Capital Picture), 92 (Entertainment Press/Shutterstock), 94 (iStockphoto), 95 (Entertainment Press/Shutterstock), 96 (Time & Life Pictures/Getty Images), 97m (Lisa F. Young/Dreamstime), 97t (Glenda M. Powers/Shutterstock), 97b (Digital Vision/Gettyimages), 101tl (Monika Adamczyk/Fotolia), 101tr (Josef Muellek/Dreamstime), 101ml (Scott Rothstein/Dreamstime), 101mr (Mirela Schenk), 101b (Pavel Losevsky/Fotolia), 101bl (Losevsky Pavel/Shutterstock), 102l (iStockphoto), 102r (Shutterstock), 103r (Jaimie Duplass/Shutterstock), 103c (Shutterstock), 103l (Losevsky Pavel/Shutterstock), 104 (123rf), 105 (Shutterstock), 106tl (Christian Anthony/iStockphoto), 106tr (Jurgen Ziewe/Shutterstock), 107rn (123rf), 107bl (Shutterstock), 109bg (Fotolia), 110 (Shutterstock), 110bg (iStockphoto), 111 (iStockphoto), 113l (Sandra Cunningham/Shutterstock), 113m (Gideon Mendel/CORBIS), 113r (Victorian Traditions/Shutterstock), 113mt (Victor Burnside/Dreamstime), 113bg (Shutterstock), 114 (Mark William Richardson/Shutterstock), 115 (Paul Miller/Associated Press), 115bg (Joan Kerrigan/Shutterstock), 117bgt (Dreamstime), 117bgb (Shutterstock), 119br (Jose Gil/Dreamstime), 119l (Jose Gil/Dreamstime), 119tr (Shutterstock), 120m (Magdalena Bujak/Shutterstock), 120t (Palis Michael/Shutterstock), 120b (emin kuliyev/Dreamstime), 121t (Shutterstock), 121etl (Anton Bryksin/Shutterstock), 121tl (Shutterstock), 121m (JJ. Lim), 121bl (Balázs Justin/Shutterstock), 121ebl (Morgan Lane Photography/Shutterstock) 121bg (Alex Kalmbach/Shutterstock), 122r (Diego Cervo/Shutterstock), 122l (Shutterstock), 123br (Terry Chan/Shutterstock), 123tr (Shutterstock), 123l (Shutterstock), 125 (Shutterstock), 150tl (Elena Elisseeva/Shutterstock), 150ml (Shutterstock), 150r (Anna Jurkovska/Shutterstock), 150bl (James Horning/Shutterstock), 150mr (Tonis Valing/Shutterstock), 150br (Aga & Miko/Shutterstock), 152tl (Dainis Derics/Shutterstock), 152ml (Markus Gann/Shutterstock), 152bl (Christian Wheatley/Shutterstock), 152tr (Pot of Grass Productions/Shutterstock), 152mr (Shutterstock), 152br (Elena Yakusheva/Shutterstock), 152b (123rf)

Every effort has been made to trace all the copyright holders but if any have been inadvertently overlooked, the publisher will be pleased to make the necessary arrangements at the first opportunity. Please contact the publisher directly.

Spotlight on CAE Exam Booster
Audio Track Listings

DISC 1

Track	Unit	Page	Listening #	Duration
1	Copyright notice			
2	1	6	1.1 – Extract 1	01:14
3	1	6	1.1 – Extract 2	01:11
4	1	6	1.1 – Extract 3	01:10
5	2	14	2.1	03:00
6	3	22	3.1	00:32
7	3	22	3.2 – Extract 1	01:05
8	3	22	3.2 – Extract 2	01:05
9	3	22	3.2 – Extract 3	01:15
10	4	30	4.1 – Speaker 1	00:53
11	4	30	4.1 – Speaker 2	00:52
12	4	30	4.1 – Speaker 3	01:02
13	4	30	4.1 – Speaker 4	00:43
14	4	30	4.1 – Speaker 5	00:45
15	5	38	5.1	03:21
16	5	39	5.2	01:08
17	6	41	6.1 – Speaker 1	00:42
18	6	41	6.1 – Speaker 2	00:45
19	6	41	6.1 – Speaker 3	00:41
20	6	45	6.2	04:15
21	6	46	6.3	01:17
22	7	54	7.1 – Speaker 1	00:53
23	7	54	7.1 – Speaker 2	00:45
24	7	54	7.1 – Speaker 3	00:43
25	7	54	7.1 – Speaker 4	00:43
26	7	54	7.1 – Speaker 5	00:44
27	7	55	7.2	01:38
28	8	61	8.1	00:42
29	8	61	8.2 – Extract 1	01:05
30	8	61	8.2 – Extract 2	01:12
31	8	61	8.2 – Extract 3	01:15
32	9	69	9.1	03:51
33	9	71	9.2	04:17
34	10	76	10.1 – Speaker 1	00:50
35	10	76	10.1 – Speaker 2	00:48
36	10	76	10.1 – Speaker 3	00:45
37	10	76	10.1 – Speaker 4	00:43
38	10	76	10.1 – Speaker 5	00:44
39	10	78	10.2	04:40
40	11	85	11.1	03:10
41	11	87	11.2	00:48

Track Duration CD1 – 57 minutes 47 seconds

DISC 2

Track	Unit	Page	Listening #	Duration
1	Copyright Notice			
2	12	93	12.1 – Extract 1	01:13
3	12	93	12.1 – Extract 2	00:59
4	12	93	12.1 – Extract 3	01:05
5	12	93	12.2	01:59
6	13	101	13.1 – Speaker 1	00:46
7	13	101	13.1 – Speaker 2	00:44
8	13	101	13.1 – Speaker 3	00:43
9	13	101	13.1 – Speaker 4	00:33
10	13	101	13.1 – Speaker 5	00:49
11	13	103	13.2	03:59
12	14	110	14.1	02:59
13	15	113	15.1 – Speaker 1	00:50
14	15	113	15.1 – Speaker 2	00:39
15	15	113	15.1 – Speaker 3	00:36
16	15	113	15.1 – Speaker 4	00:38
17	15	113	15.1 – Speaker 5	00:45
18	15	117	15.2	03:55
19	15	117	15.3	02:55
20	16	125	16.1 – Extract 1	01:16
21	16	125	16.1 – Extract 2	01:13
22	16	125	16.1 – Extract 3	01:14
23	Practice Test	145	Part 1	09:57
24	Practice Test	146	Part 2 – Intro	01:03
25	Practice Test	146	Part 2	03:01
26	Practice Test	147	Part 3 – Intro	01:30
27	Practice Test	147	Part 3	05:59
28	Practice Test	148	Part 4 – Intro	01:41
29	Practice Test	148	Part 4	04:04

Track Duration CD2 – 57 minutes 35 seconds